Sue & Tai-chan

2

Konami Kanata

Contents

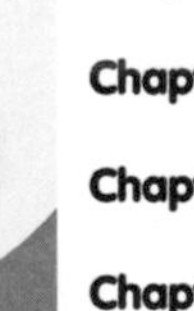

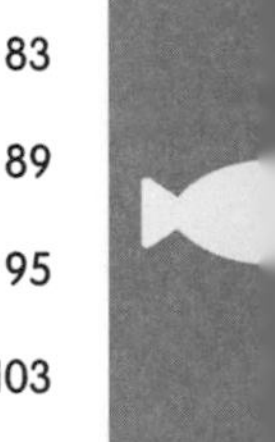

CHAPTER 17 Cat-isthenics

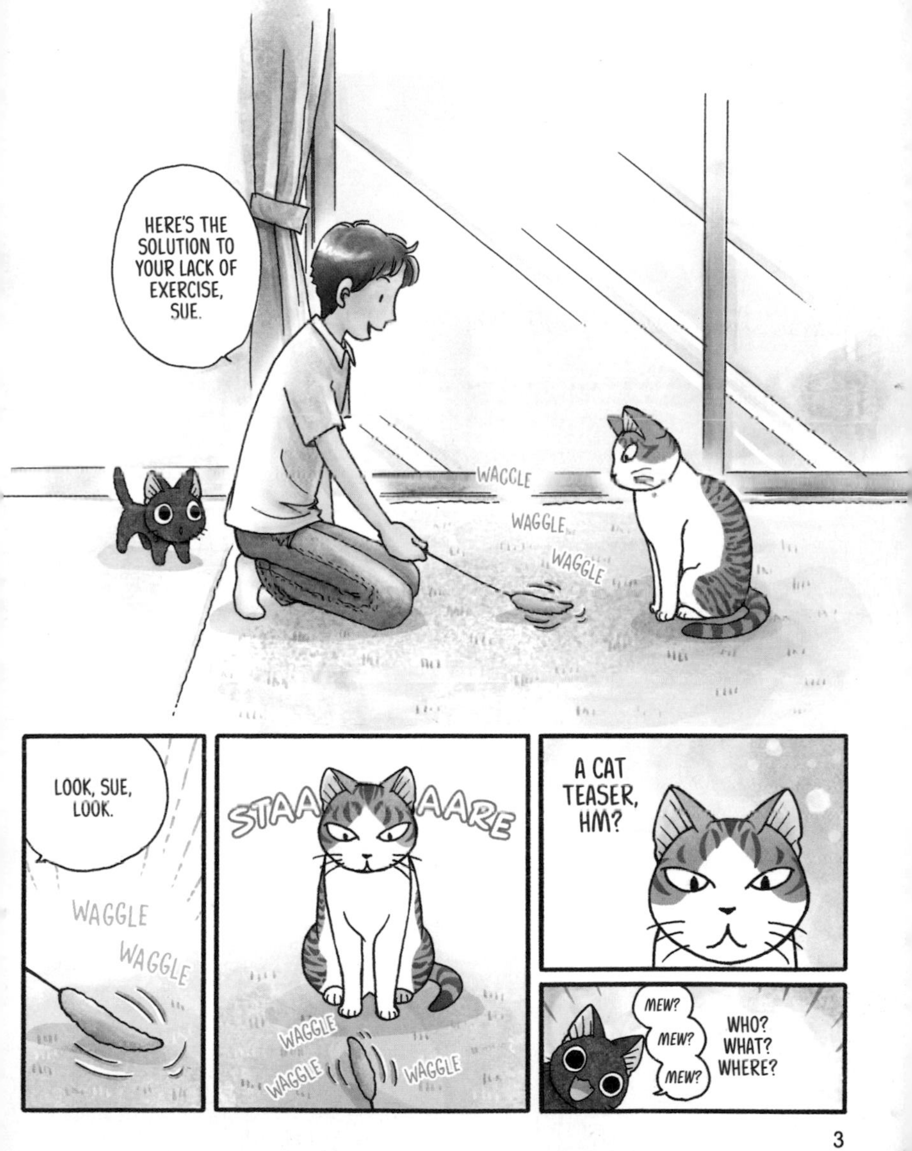
HERE'S THE SOLUTION TO YOUR LACK OF EXERCISE, SUE.
WAGGLE
WAGGLE
WAGGLE
LOOK, SUE, LOOK.
WAGGLE
WAGGLE
STAAAARE
WAGGLE
WAGGLE
WAGGLE
A CAT TEASER, HM?
MEW?
MEW?
MEW?
WHO? WHAT? WHERE?

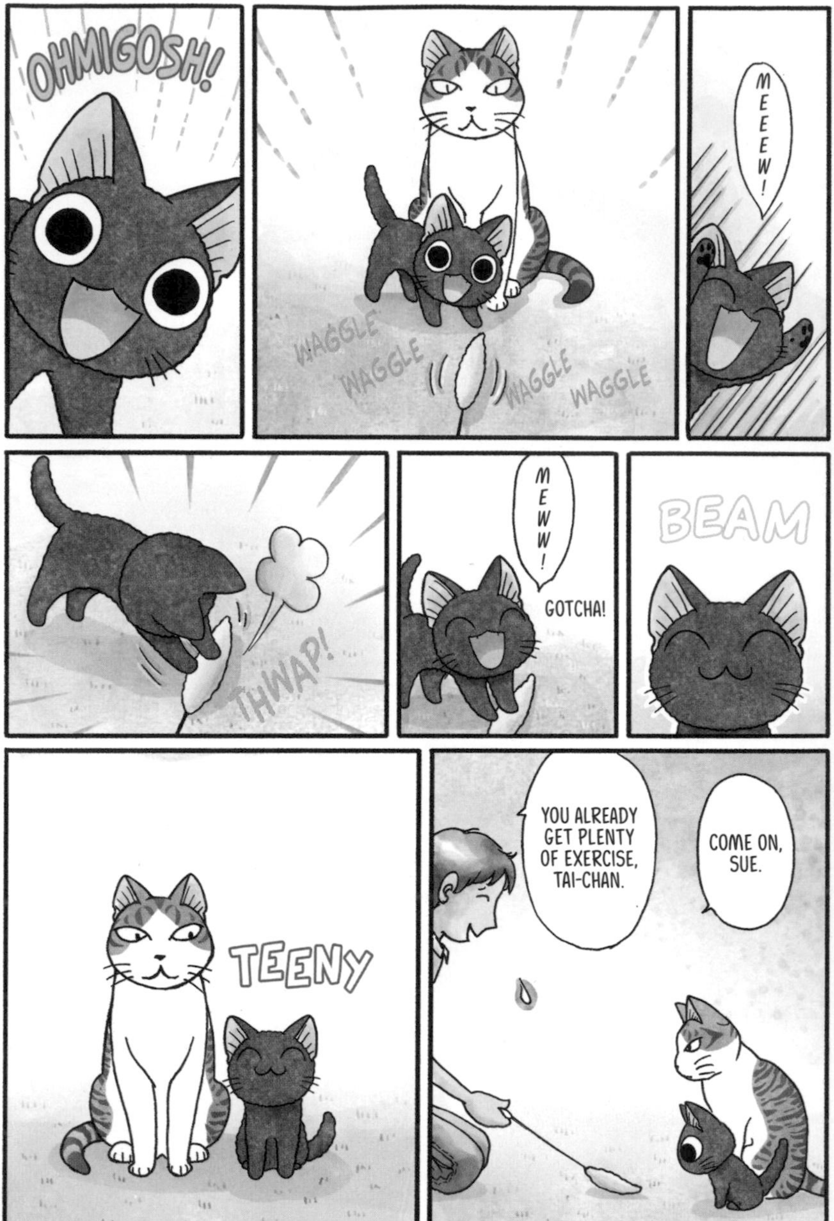
OHMIGOSH!
WAGGLE
WAGGLE
WAGGLE
WAGGLE
MEEEEW!
THWAP!
MEWW!
GOTCHA!
BEAM
TEENY
YOU ALREADY GET PLENTY OF EXERCISE, TAI-CHAN.
COME ON, SUE.

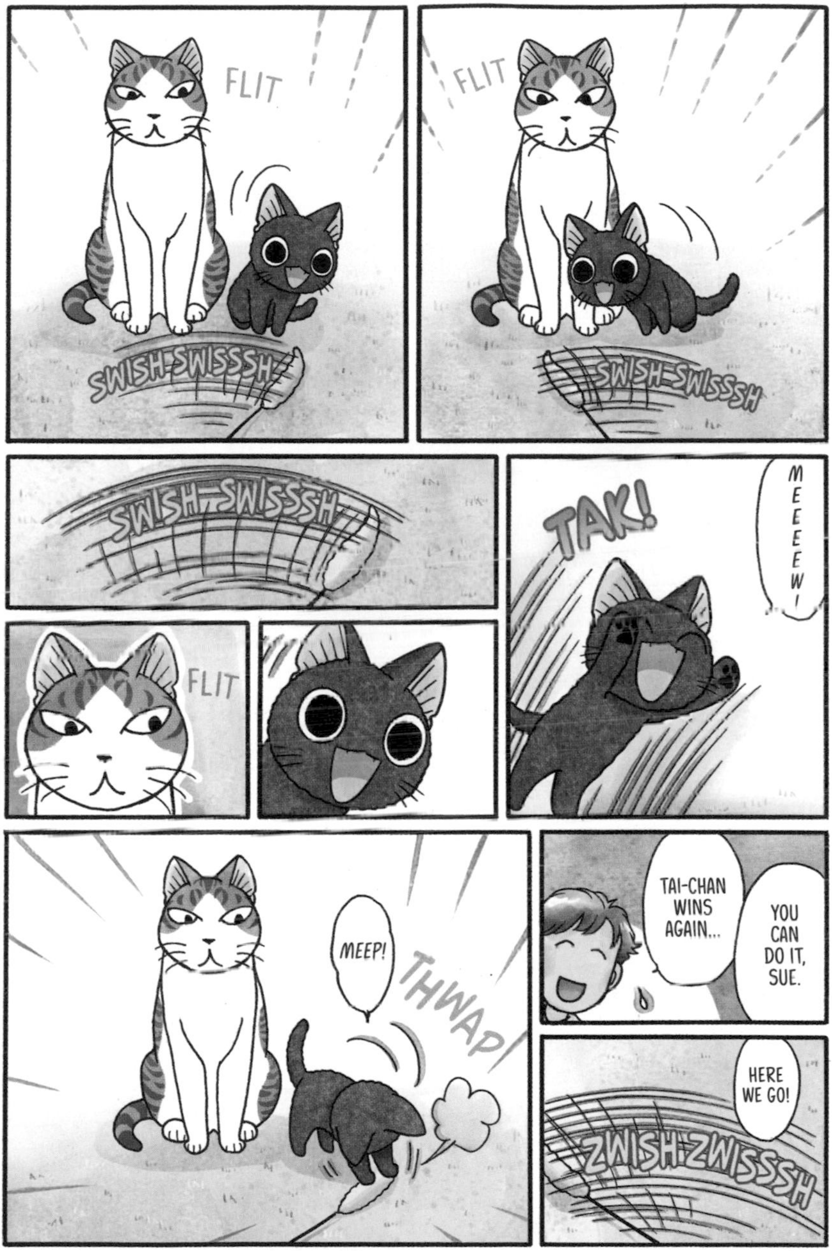
FLIT
SWISH SWISSSH
FLIT
SWISH SWISSSH
SWISH SWISSSH
FLIT
TAK!
MEEEEEW!
MEEP!
THWAP
TAI-CHAN WINS AGAIN...
YOU CAN DO IT, SUE.
HERE WE GO!
ZWISH ZWISSSH

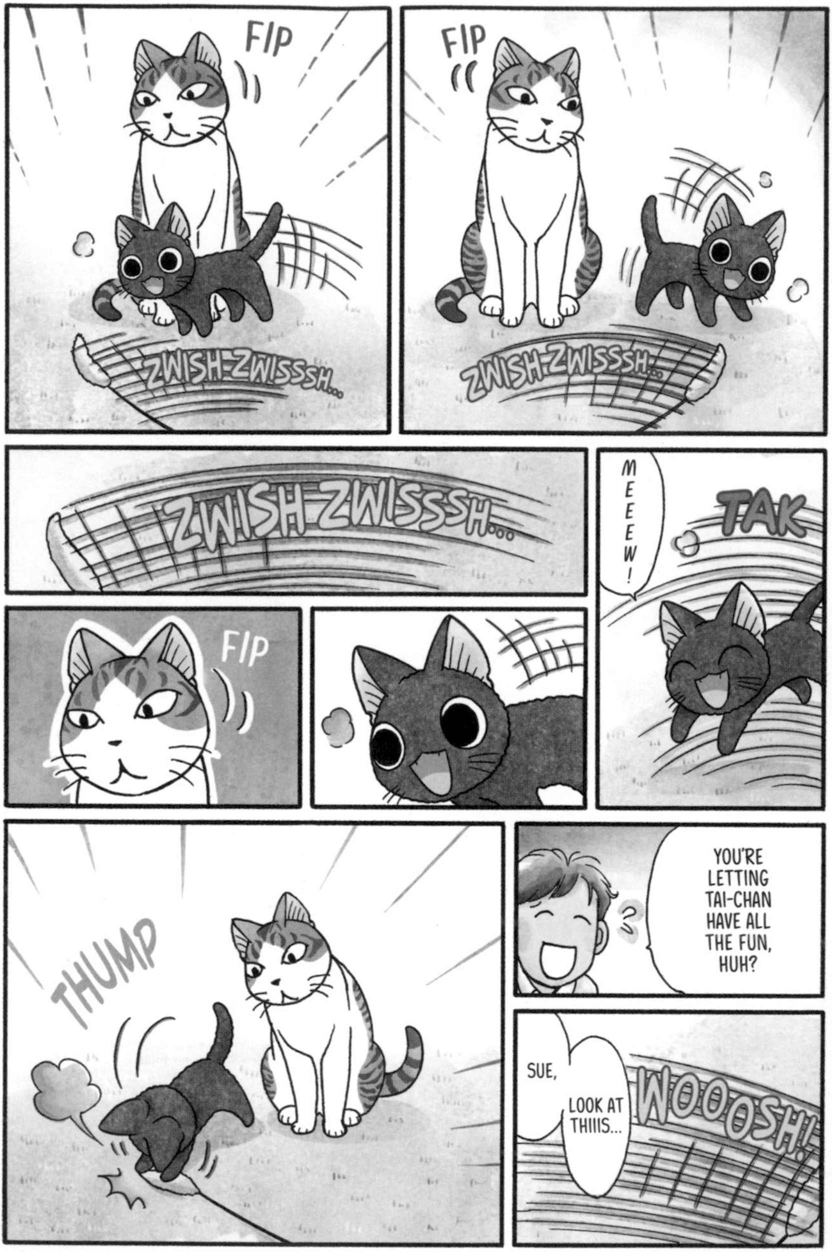
FIP
ZWISH ZWISSSH...
FIP
ZWISH ZWISSSH...
ZWISH ZWISSSH...
MEEEEW!
TAK
FIP
THUMP
YOU'RE LETTING TAI-CHAN HAVE ALL THE FUN, HUH?
SUE,
LOOK AT THIIIS...
WOOOSH!

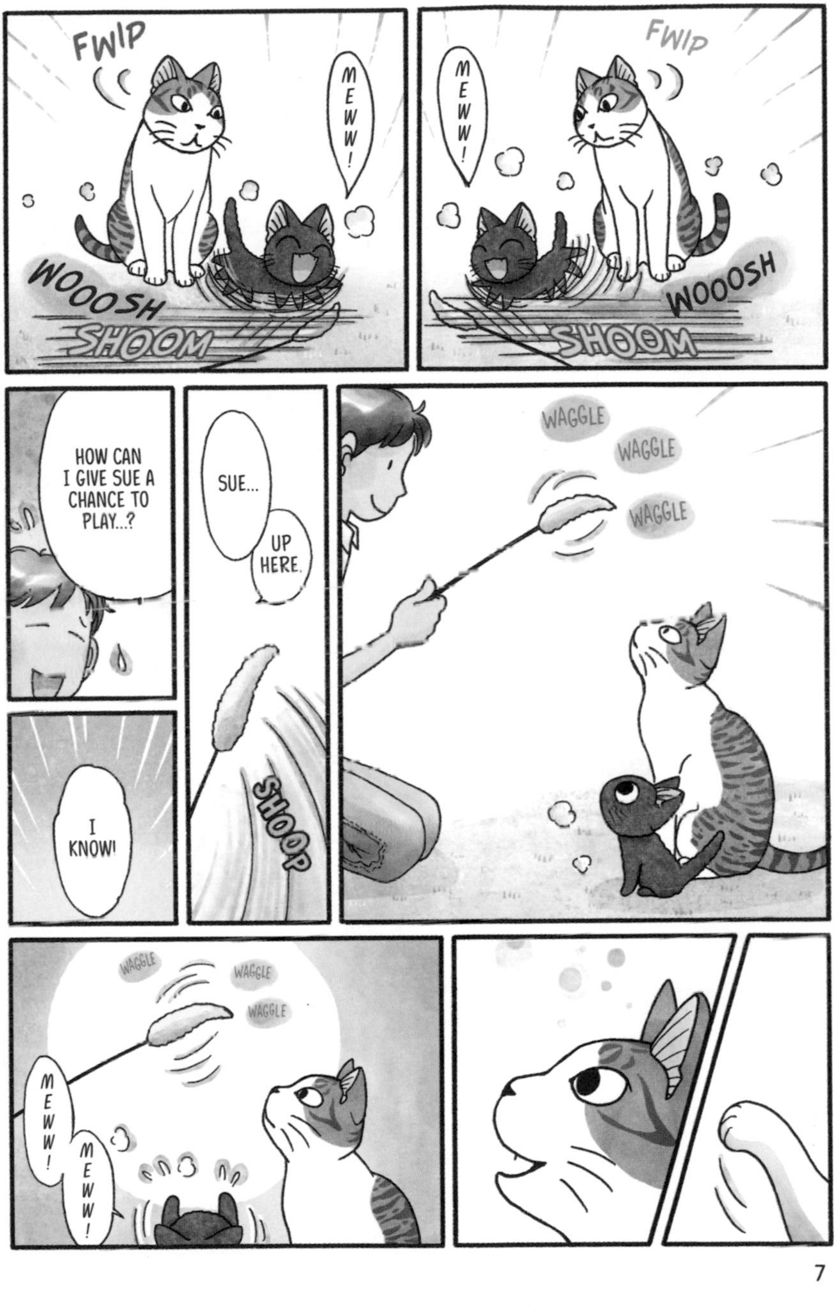
FWIP
MEWW!
WOOOSH
SHOOM
MEWW!
FWIP
WOOOSH
SHOOM
HOW CAN I GIVE SUE A CHANCE TO PLAY...?
I KNOW!
SUE...
UP HERE.
SHOOP
WAGGLE
WAGGLE
WAGGLE
WAGGLE
WAGGLE
WAGGLE
MEWW!
MEWW!

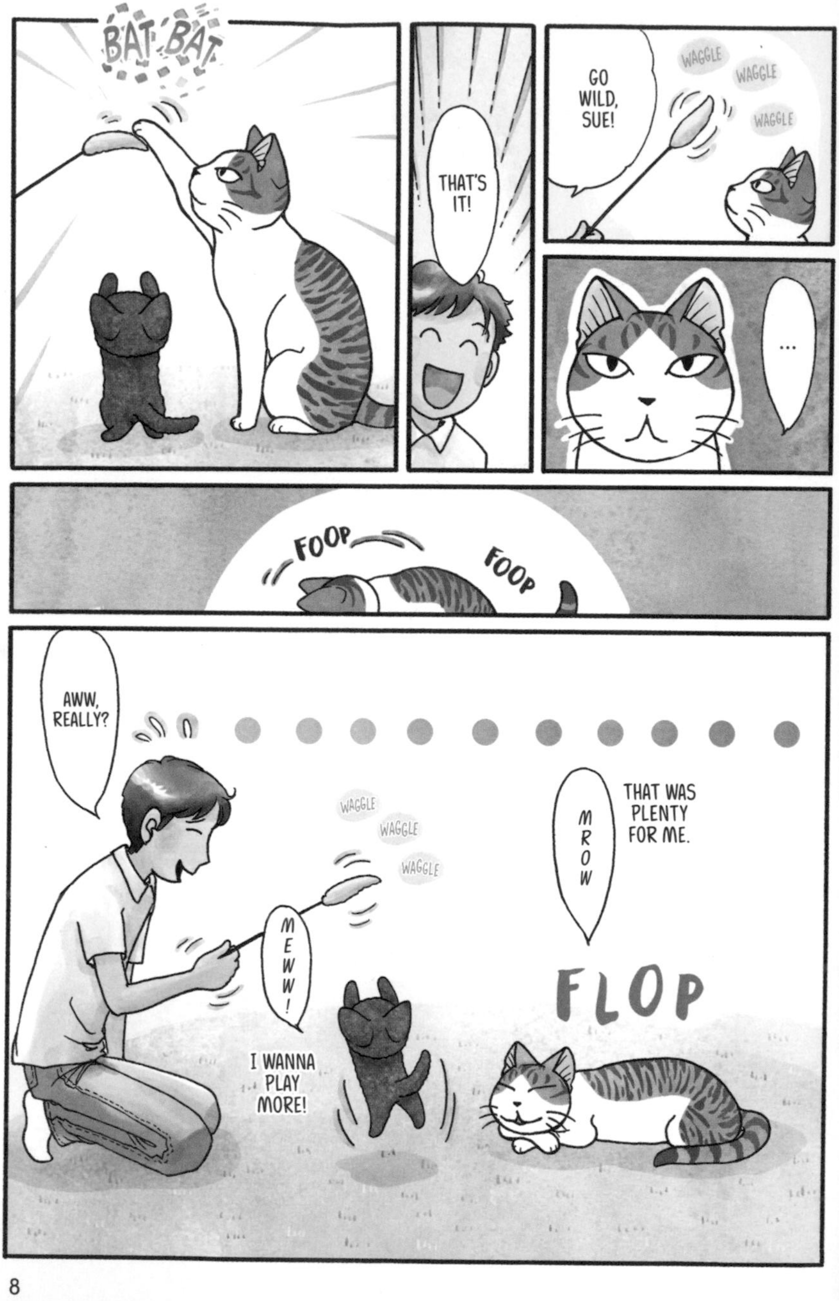
BAT BAT
THAT'S IT!
GO WILD, SUE!
WAGGLE
WAGGLE
WAGGLE
...
FOOP
FOOP
AWW, REALLY?
WAGGLE
WAGGLE
WAGGLE
MEWW!
I WANNA PLAY MORE!
MROW
THAT WAS PLENTY FOR ME.
FLOP

CHAPTER 18 It's for Grown-Ups?!

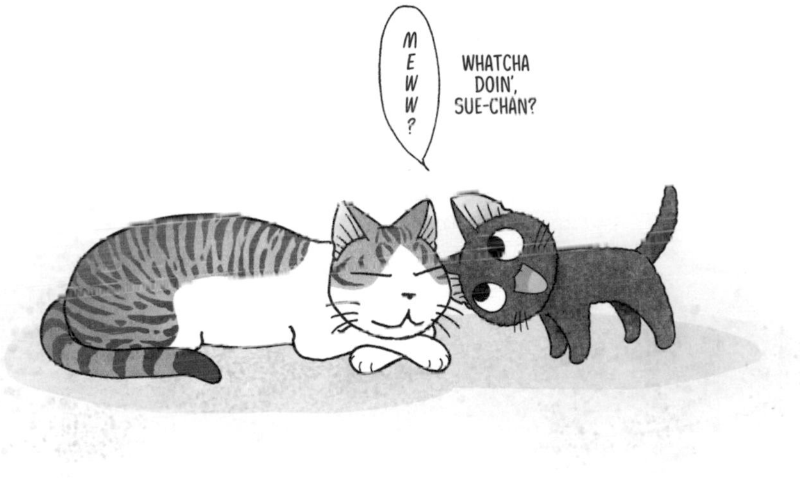
MEWW?
WHATCHA DOIN', SUE-CHAN?

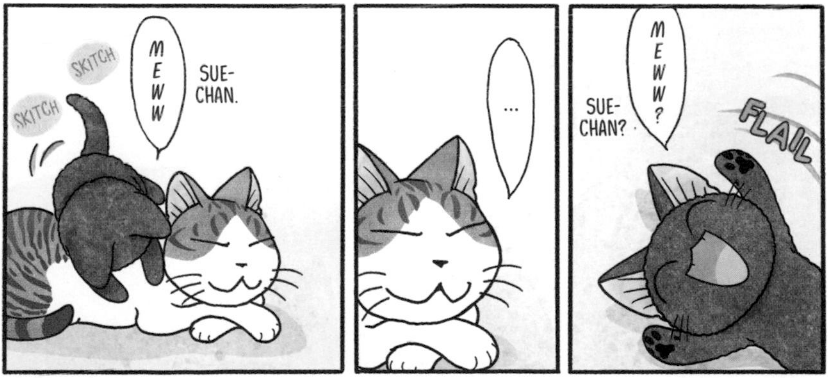
SKITCH
SKITCH
MEWW
SUE-CHAN.
...
MEWW?
SUE-CHAN?
FLAIL

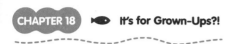

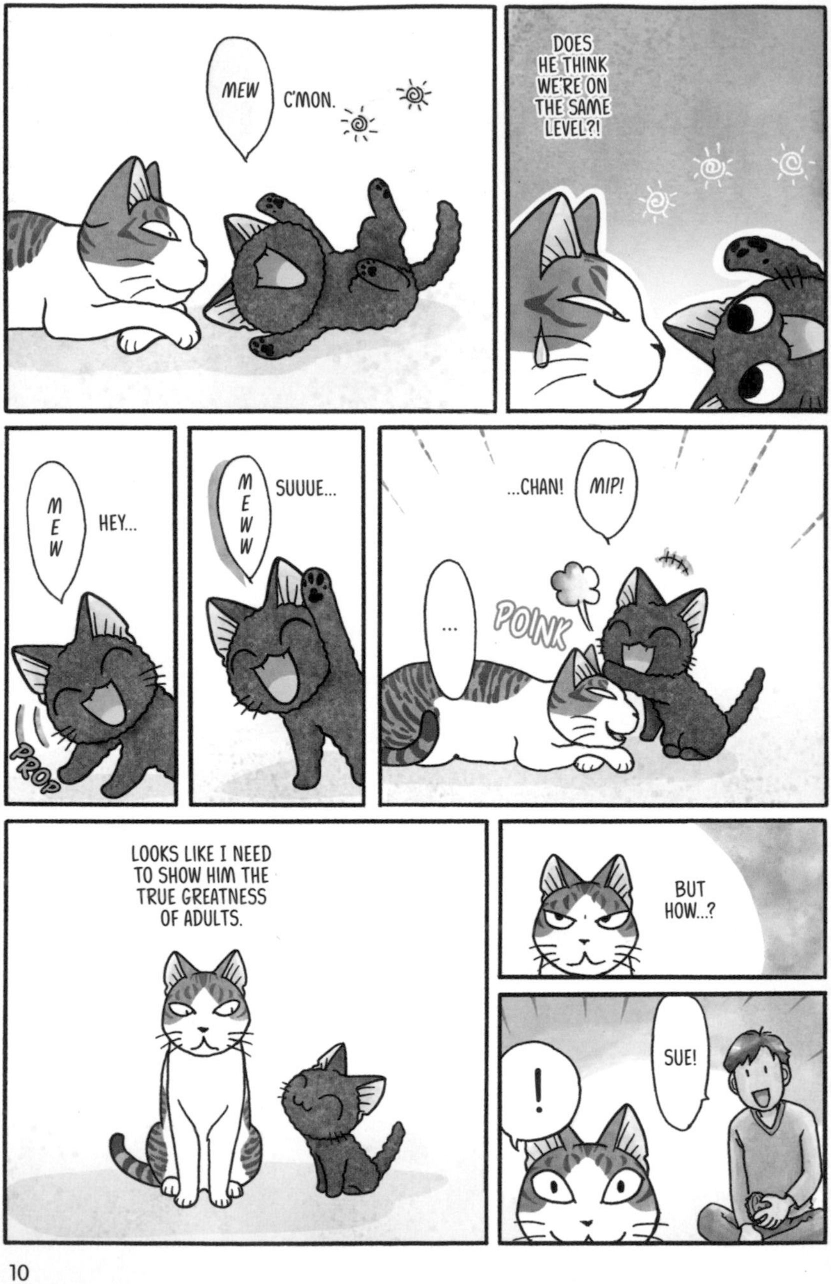
MEW
C'MON.
DOES HE THINK WE'RE ON THE SAME LEVEL?!
MEW
HEY...
MEWW
SUUUE...
...CHAN!
MIP!
PROP
...
POINK
LOOKS LIKE I NEED TO SHOW HIM THE TRUE GREATNESS OF ADULTS.
BUT HOW...?
!
SUE!

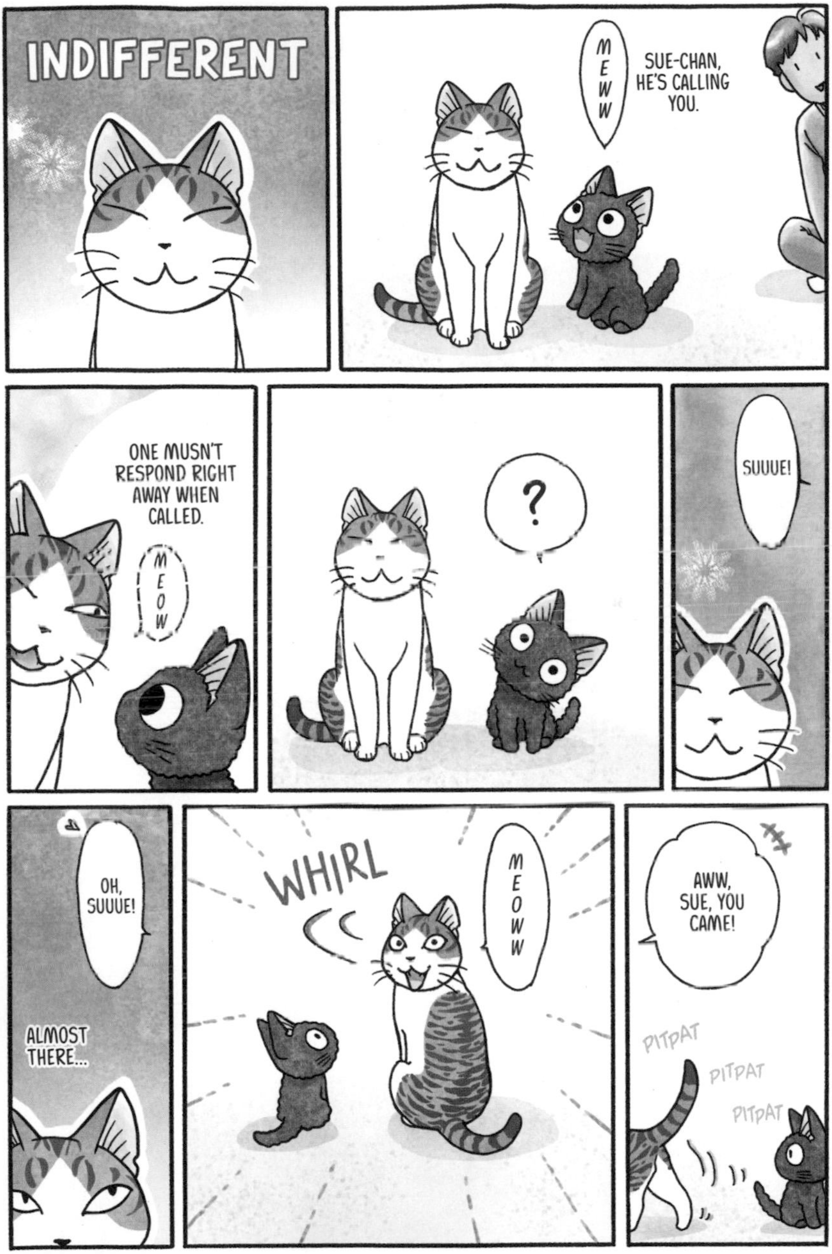
INDIFFERENT
MEWW
SUE-CHAN, HE'S CALLING YOU.
ONE MUSN'T RESPOND RIGHT AWAY WHEN CALLED.
MEOW
?
SUUUE!
OH, SUUUE!
ALMOST THERE...
WHIRL
MEOWW
AWW, SUE, YOU CAME!
PITPAT
PITPAT
PITPAT

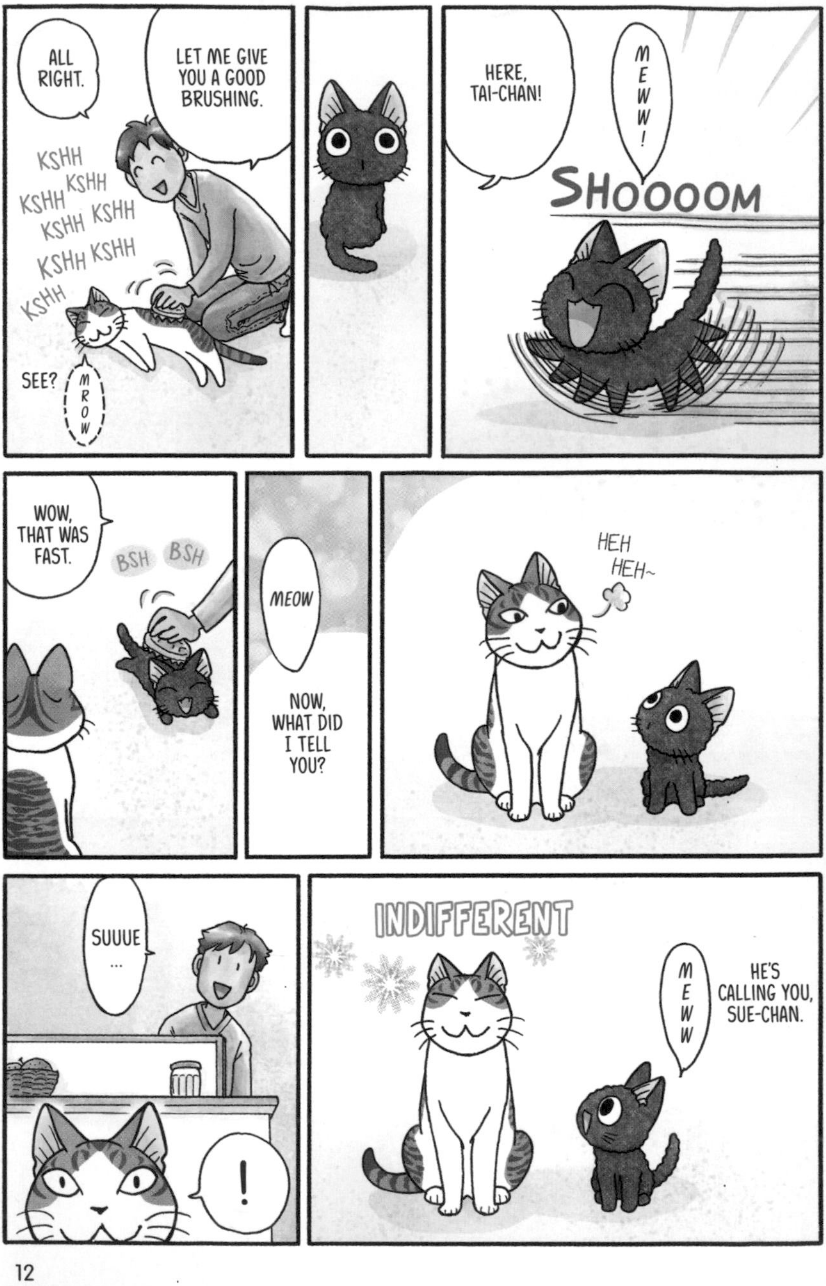
ALL RIGHT.
LET ME GIVE YOU A GOOD BRUSHING.
KSHH KSHH KSHH KSHH KSHH KSHH KSHH KSHH
SEE?
MROW
HERE, TAI-CHAN!
MEWW!
SHOOOOM
WOW, THAT WAS FAST.
BSH BSH
MEOW
NOW, WHAT DID I TELL YOU?
HEH HEH~
SUUUE ...
!
INDIFFERENT
MEWW
HE'S CALLING YOU, SUE-CHAN.

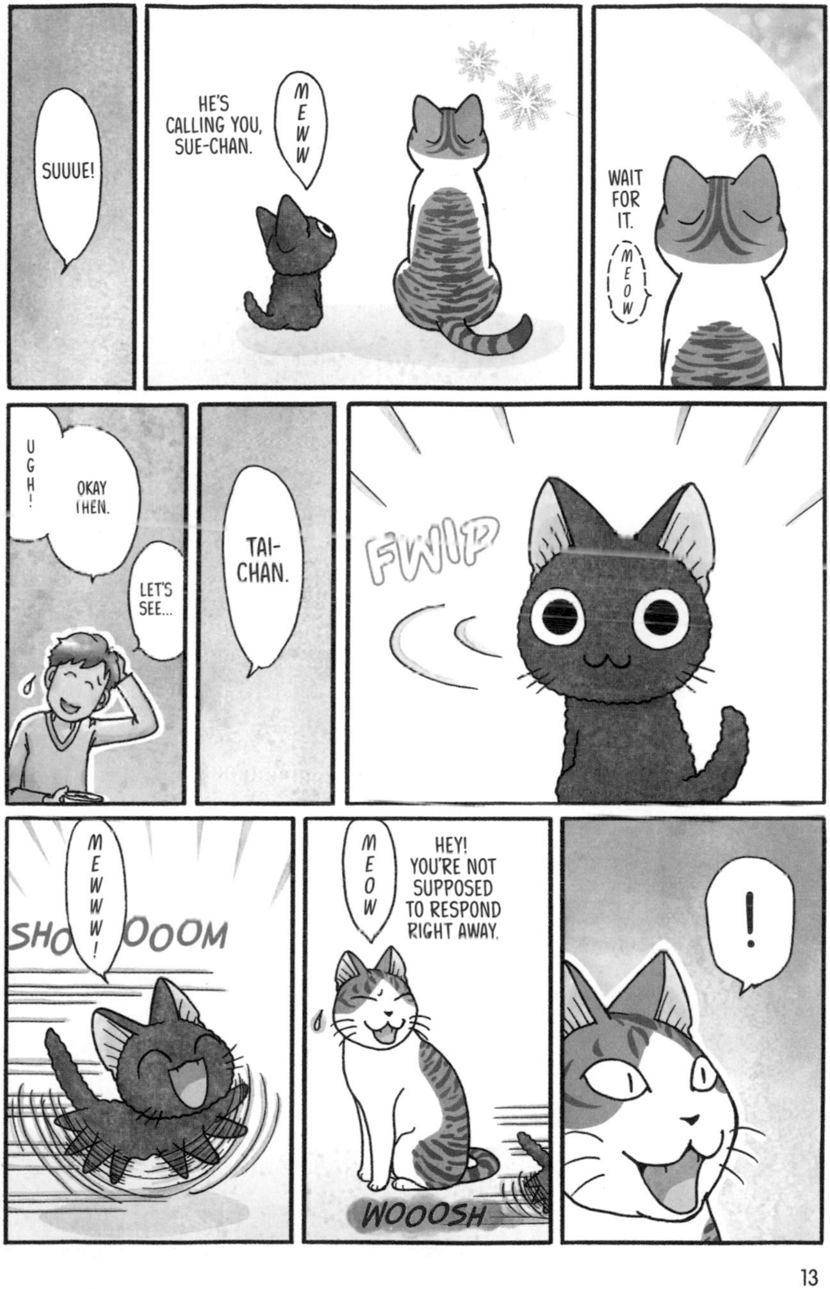
SUUUE!
HE'S CALLING YOU, SUE-CHAN.
MEWW
WAIT FOR IT.
MEOW
UGH!
OKAY THEN.
LET'S SEE...
TAI-CHAN.
FWIP
MEWWW!
SHOOOOM
MEOW
HEY! YOU'RE NOT SUPPOSED TO RESPOND RIGHT AWAY.
WOOOSH
!

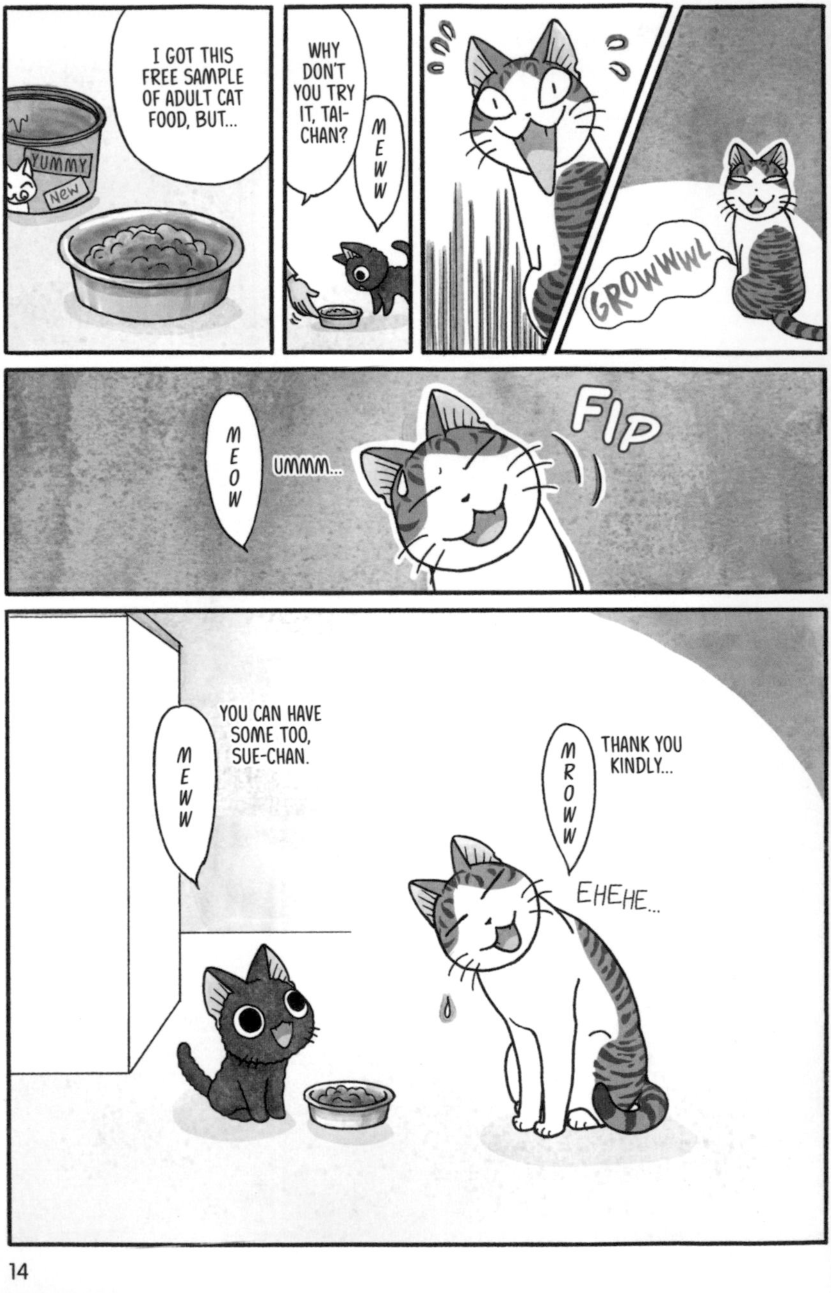

I GOT THIS FREE SAMPLE OF ADULT CAT FOOD, BUT...
YUMMY
New
WHY DON'T YOU TRY IT, TAI-CHAN?
MEWW
GROWWWL
MEOW
UMMM...
FIP
MEWW
YOU CAN HAVE SOME TOO, SUE-CHAN.
MROWW
THANK YOU KINDLY...
EHEHE...

CHAPTER 19 Coming Through!

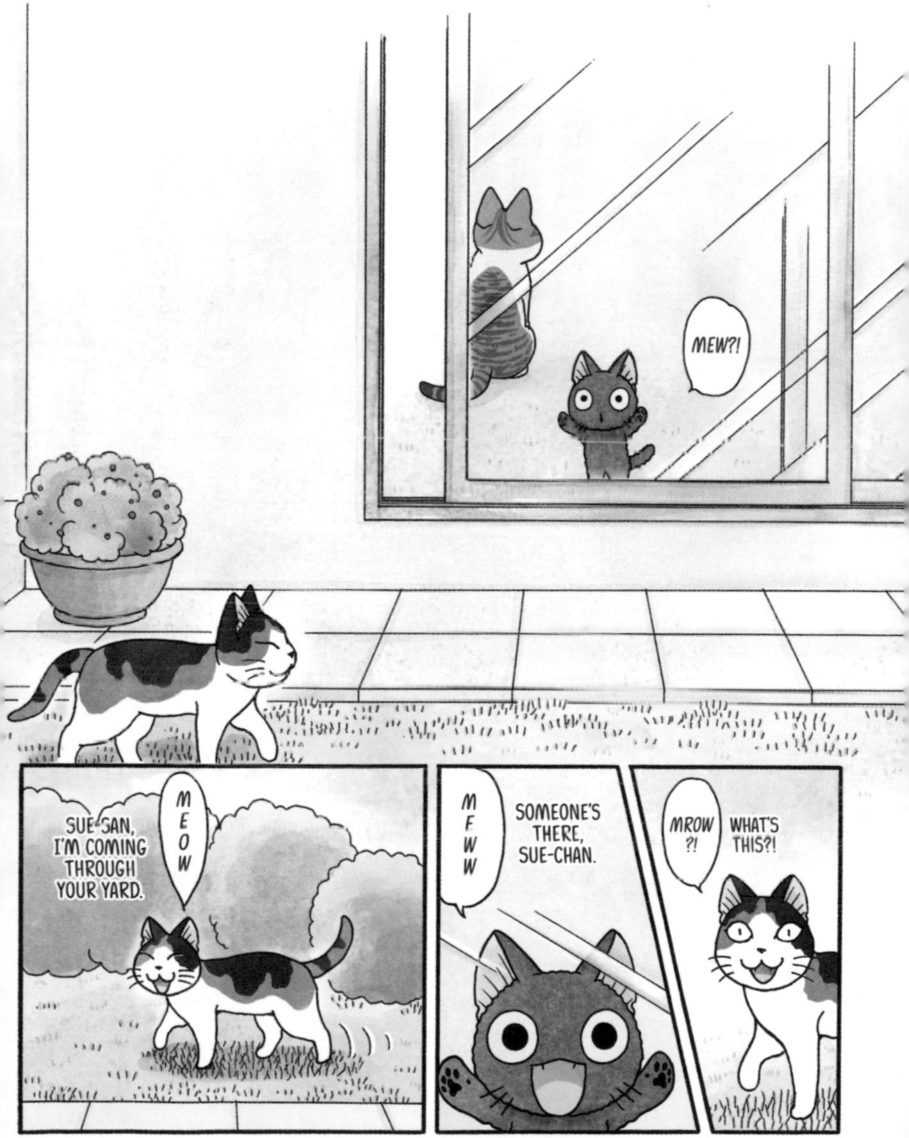
MEW?!
SUE-SAN, I'M COMING THROUGH YOUR YARD.
MEOW
MFWW
SOMEONE'S THERE, SUE-CHAN.
MROW ?!
WHAT'S THIS?!

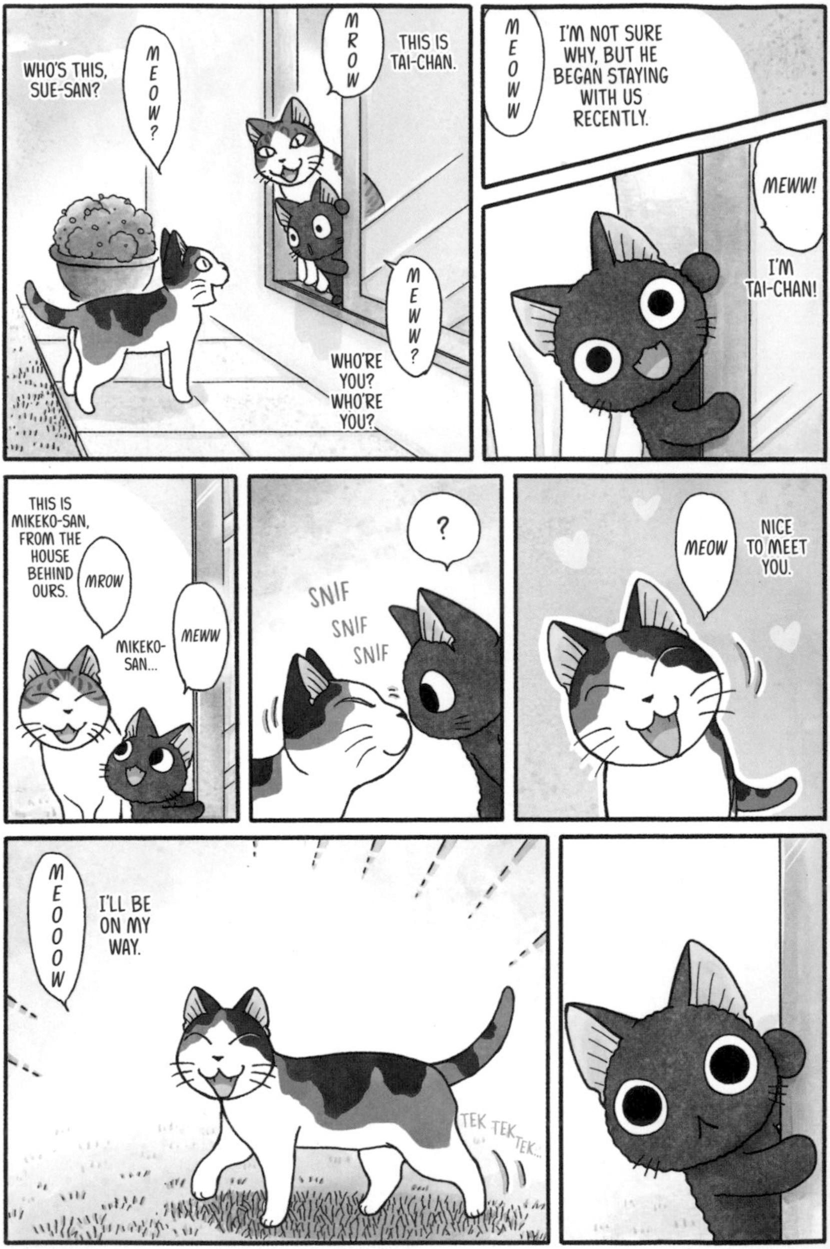
WHO'S THIS, SUE-SAN?
MEOW?
MROW
THIS IS TAI-CHAN.
MEWW?
WHO'RE YOU? WHO'RE YOU?
MEOWW
I'M NOT SURE WHY, BUT HE BEGAN STAYING WITH US RECENTLY.
MEWW!
I'M TAI-CHAN!
THIS IS MIKEKO-SAN, FROM THE HOUSE BEHIND OURS.
MROW
MEWW
MIKEKO-SAN...
?
SNIF SNIF SNIF
MEOW
NICE TO MEET YOU.
MEOOOOW
I'LL BE ON MY WAY.
TEK TEK TEK...

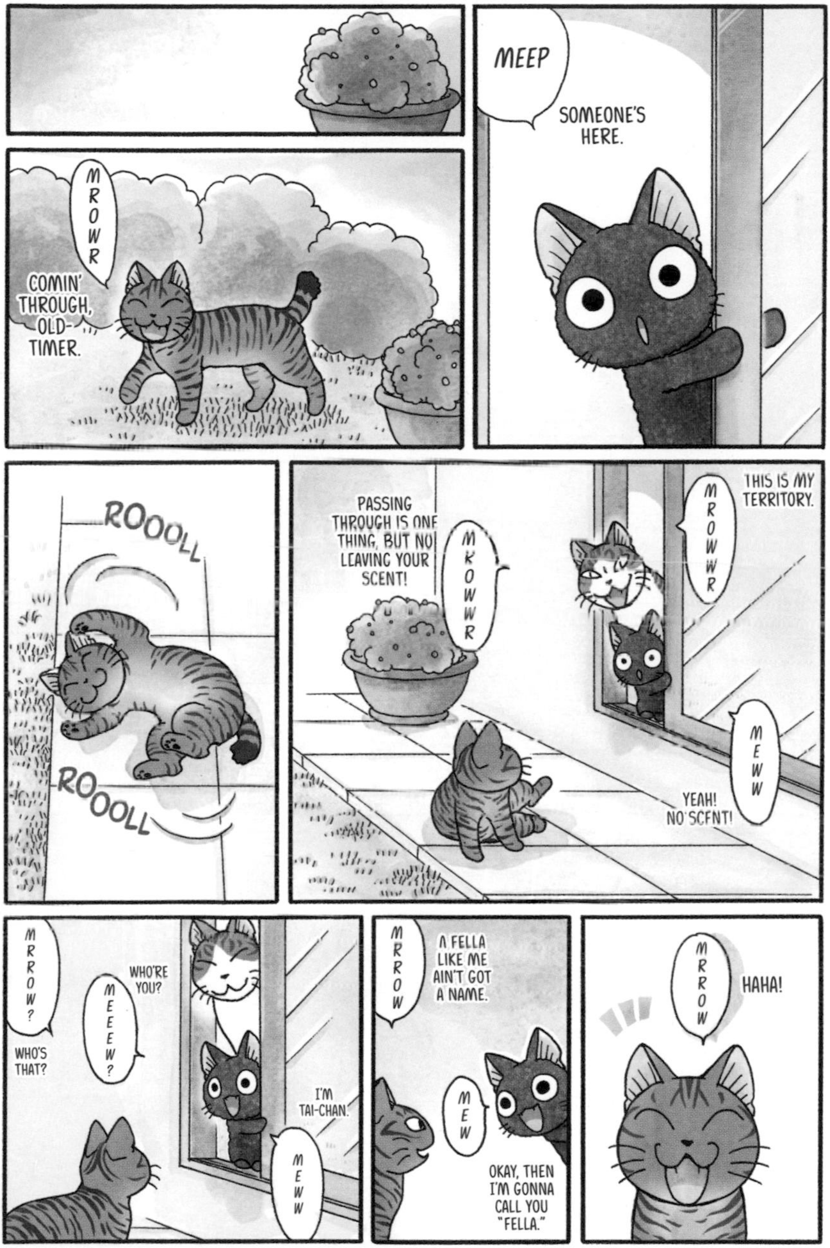

MEEP
SOMEONE'S HERE.
MROWR
COMIN' THROUGH, OLD-TIMER.
ROOOLL
ROOOLL
PASSING THROUGH IS ONE THING, BUT NO LEAVING YOUR SCENT!
MROWWR
THIS IS MY TERRITORY.
MROWWR
MEWW
YEAH! NO SCENT!
MRROW?
WHO'S THAT?
MEEEW?
WHO'RE YOU?
I'M TAI-CHAN.
MEWW
MRROW
A FELLA LIKE ME AIN'T GOT A NAME.
MEW
OKAY, THEN I'M GONNA CALL YOU "FELLA."
MRROW
HAHA!

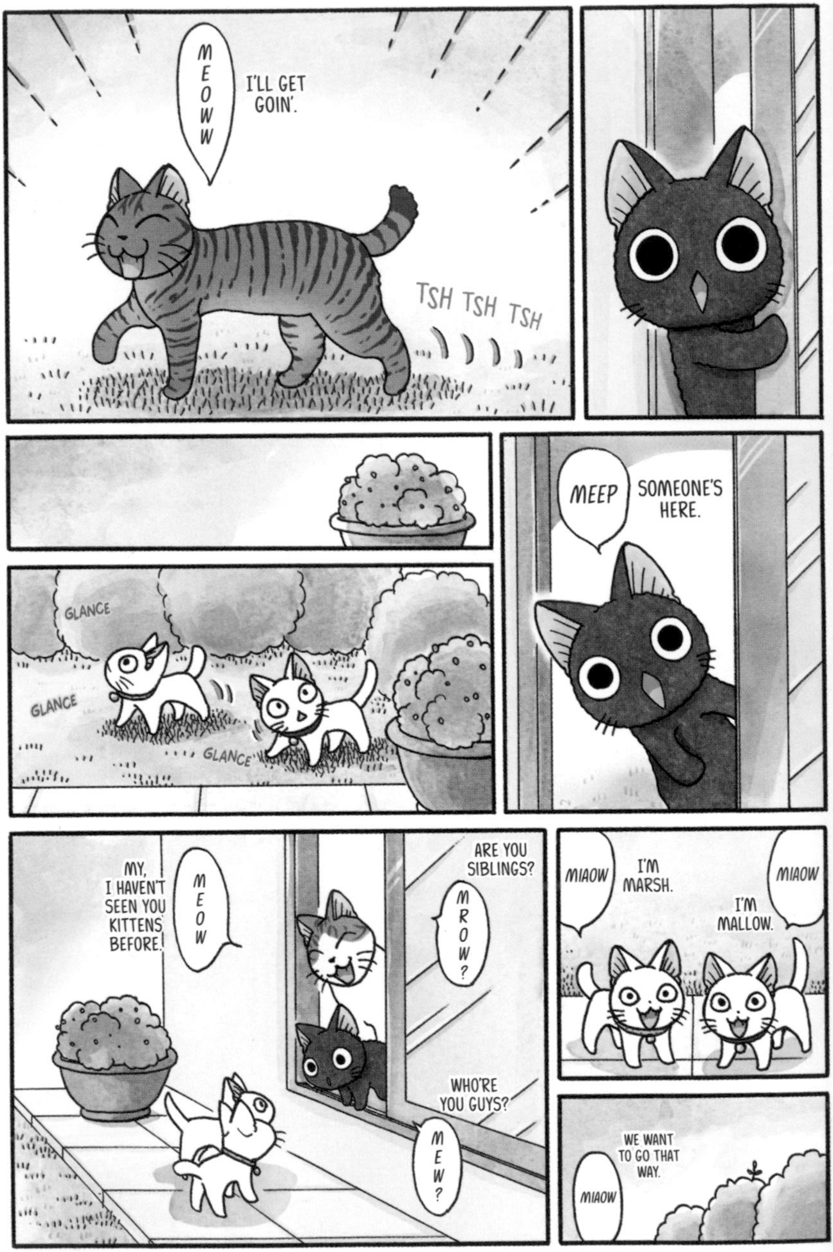
MEOWW
I'LL GET GOIN'.
TSH TSH TSH
MEEP
SOMEONE'S HERE.
GLANCE
GLANCE
GLANCE
MY, I HAVEN'T SEEN YOU KITTENS BEFORE!
MEOW
ARE YOU SIBLINGS?
MROW?
WHO'RE YOU GUYS?
MEW?
MIAOW
I'M MARSH.
MIAOW
I'M MALLOW.
WE WANT TO GO THAT WAY.
MIAOW

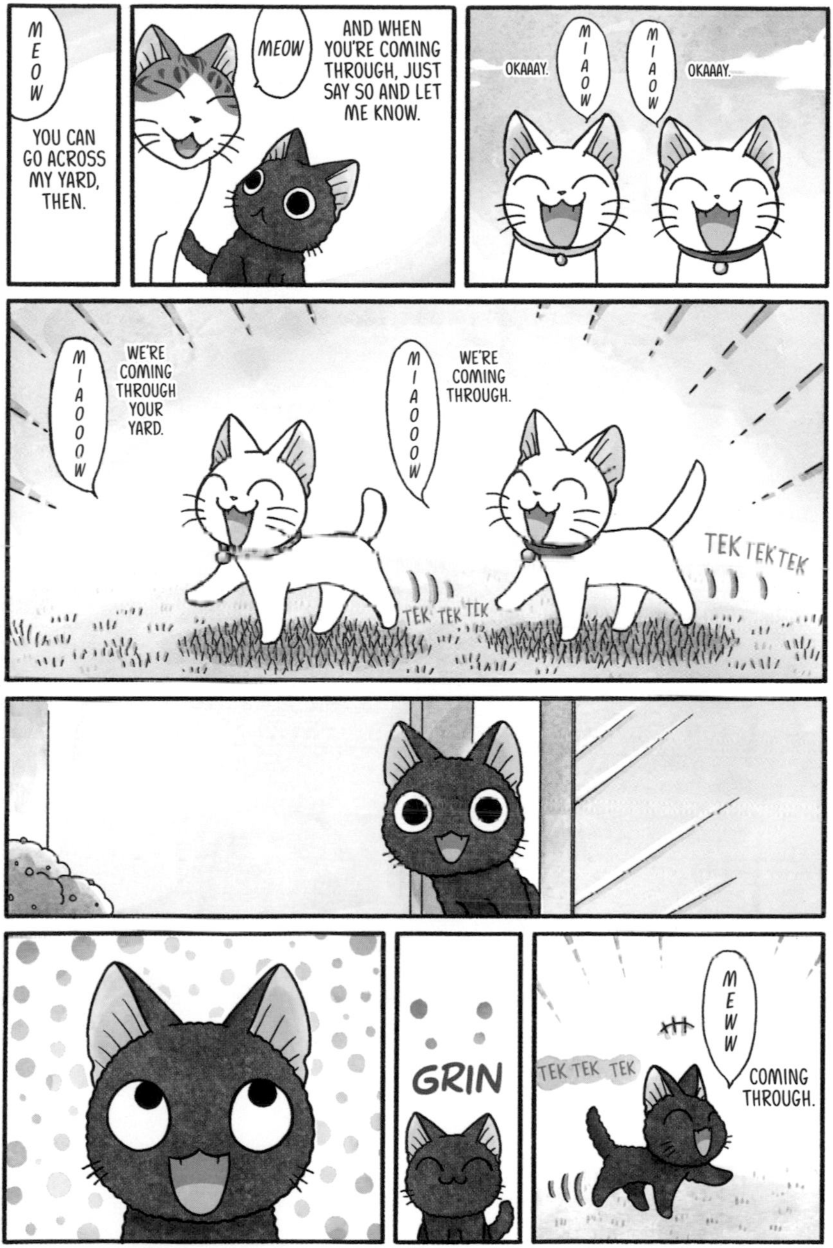
MEOW
YOU CAN GO ACROSS MY YARD, THEN.
MEOW
AND WHEN YOU'RE COMING THROUGH, JUST SAY SO AND LET ME KNOW.
OKAAAY.
MIAOW
MIAOW
OKAAAY.
MIAOOOOW
WE'RE COMING THROUGH YOUR YARD.
MIAOOOOW
WE'RE COMING THROUGH.
TEK TEK TIK
TEK TEK TEK
GRIN
TEK TEK TEK
MEWW
COMING THROUGH.

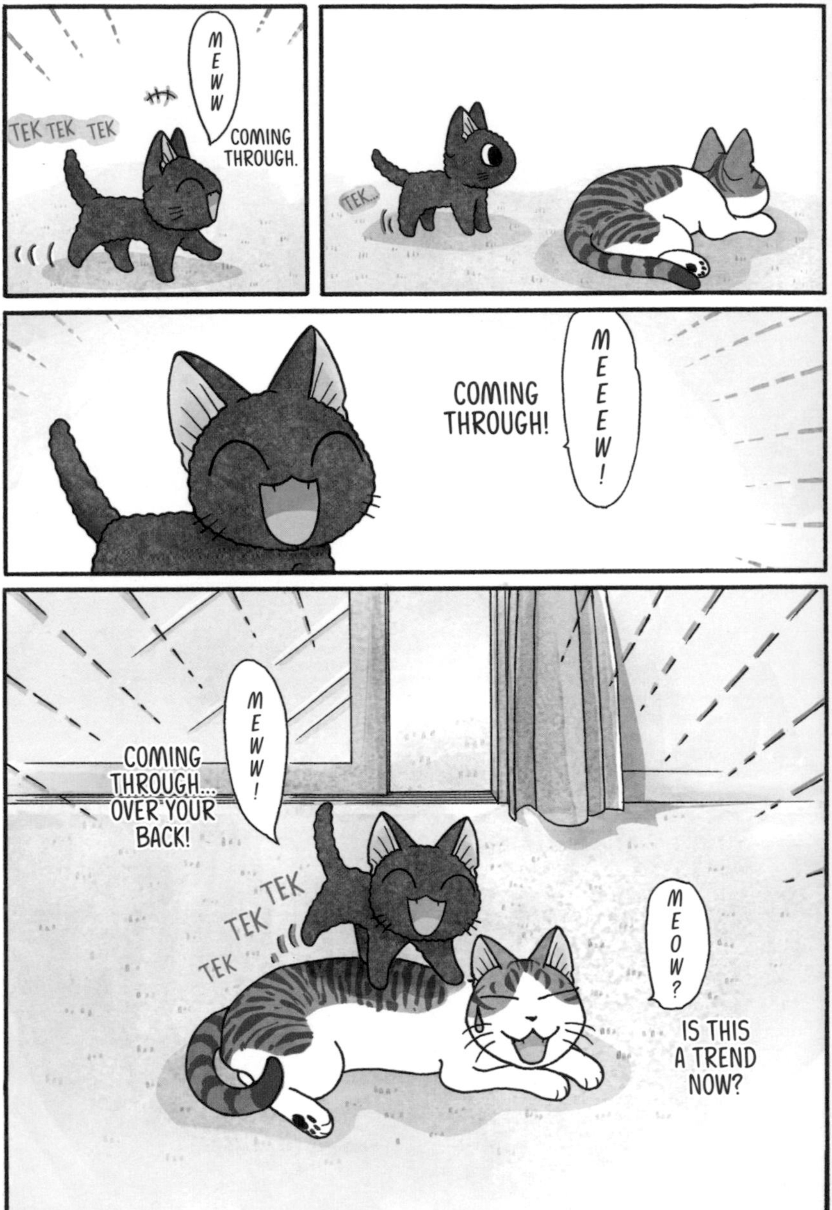
MEWW
COMING THROUGH.
TEK TEK TEK
TEK...
COMING THROUGH!
MEEEW!
COMING THROUGH... OVER YOUR BACK!
MEWW!
TEK TEK TEK
MEOW?
IS THIS A TREND NOW?

CHAPTER 20 Coming Through! Part II

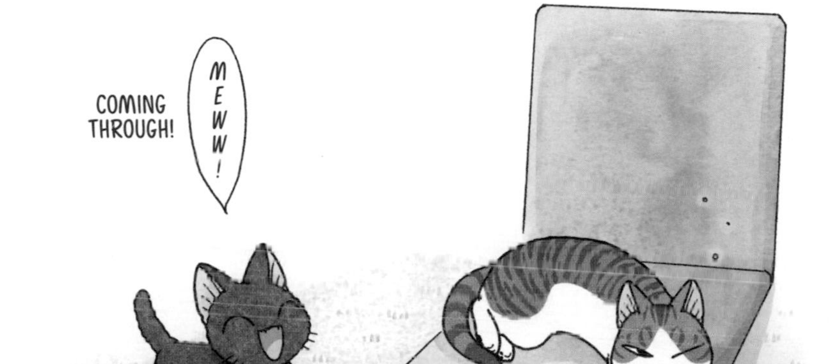
COMING THROUGH!
MEWW!
TEK TEK TEK TEK

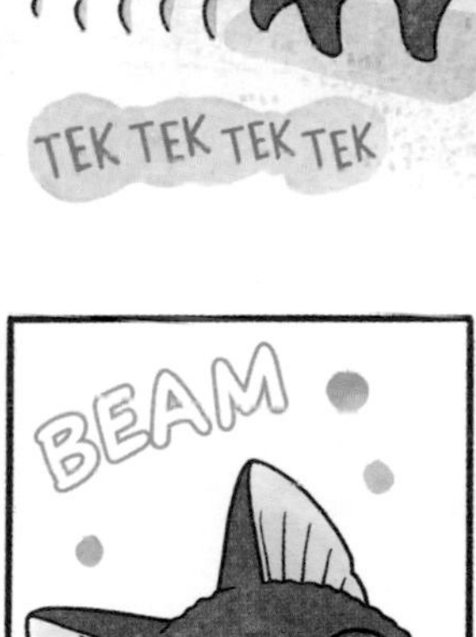
BEAM

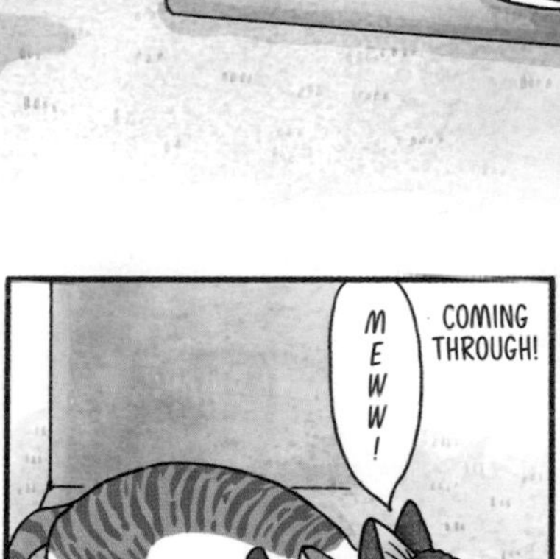
MEWW!
COMING THROUGH!
TEK TEK TEK TEK

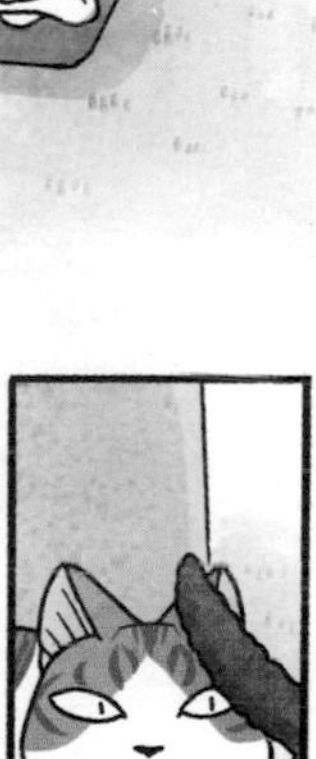
TEK TEK

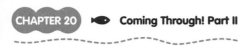

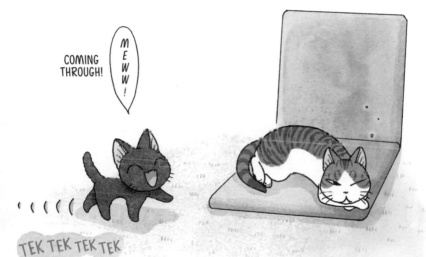

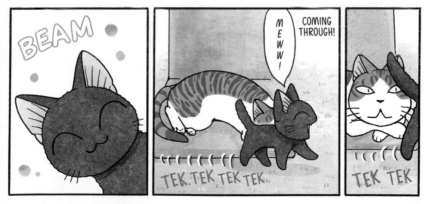

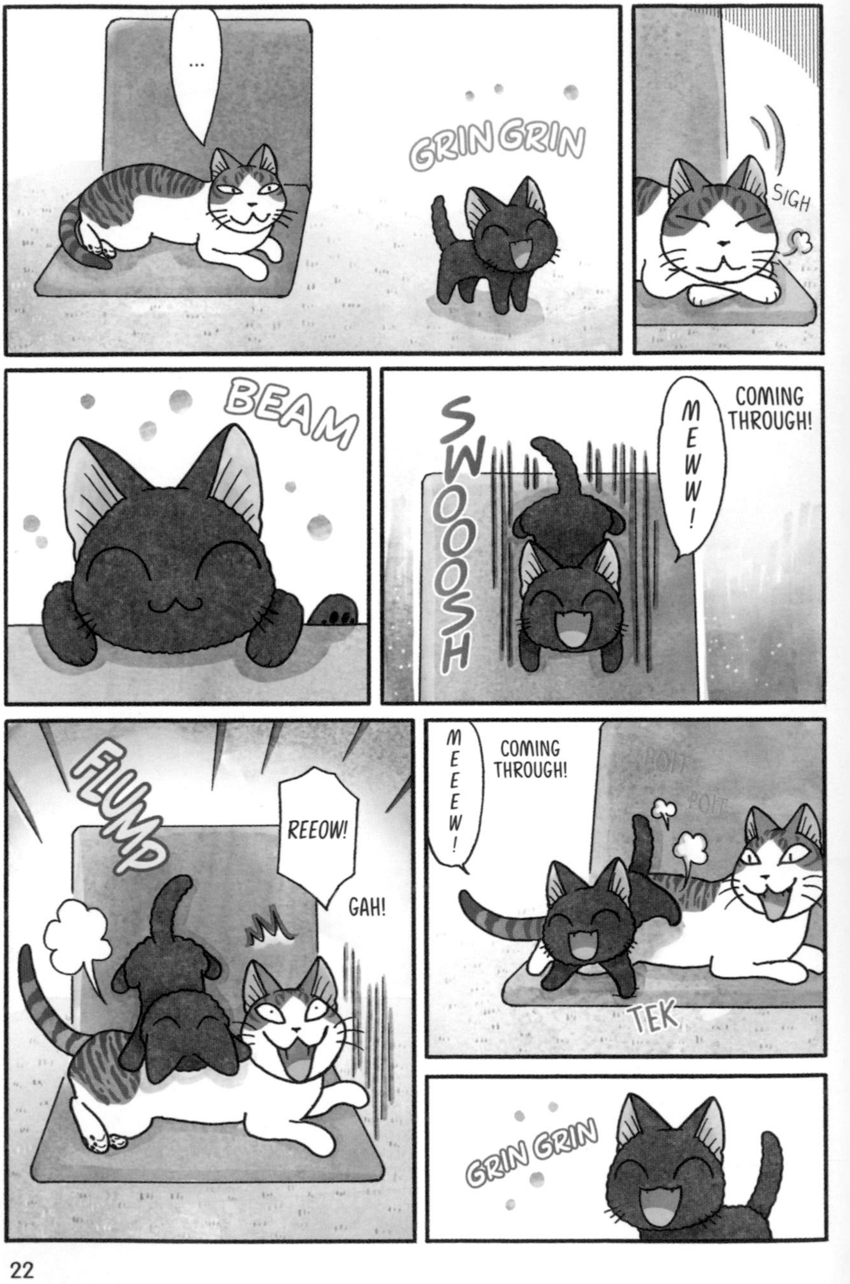
...
GRIN GRIN
SIGH
BEAM
SWOOOSH
MEWW!
COMING THROUGH!
FLUMP
REEOW!
GAH!
MEEEEW!
COMING THROUGH!
POIT
POIT
TEK
GRIN GRIN

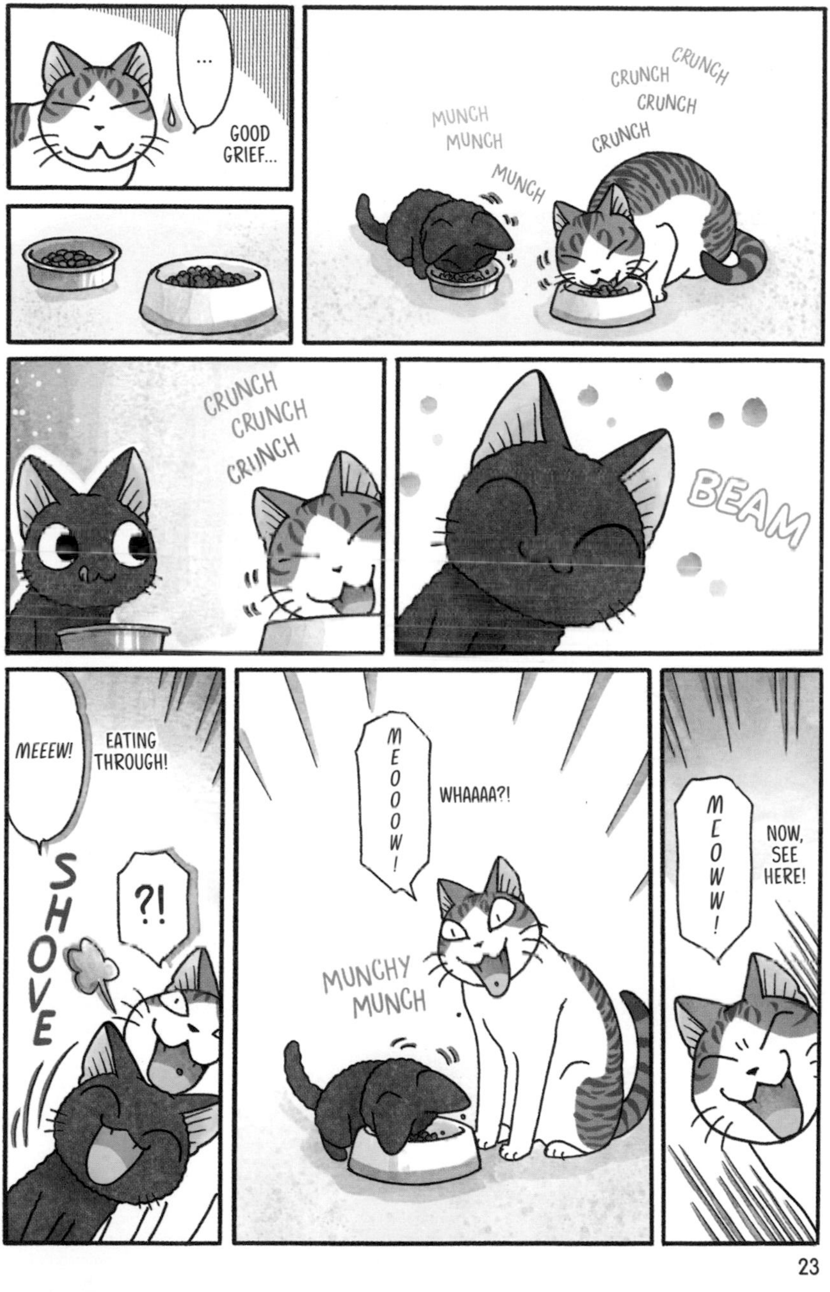

...
GOOD GRIEF...
MUNCH MUNCH
MUNCH
CRUNCH CRUNCH
CRUNCH
CRUNCH
CRUNCH CRUNCH CRUNCH
BEAM
MEEEW!
EATING THROUGH!
SHOVE
?!
MEOOOOW!
WHAAAA?!
MUNCHY MUNCH
MEOWW!
NOW, SEE HERE!

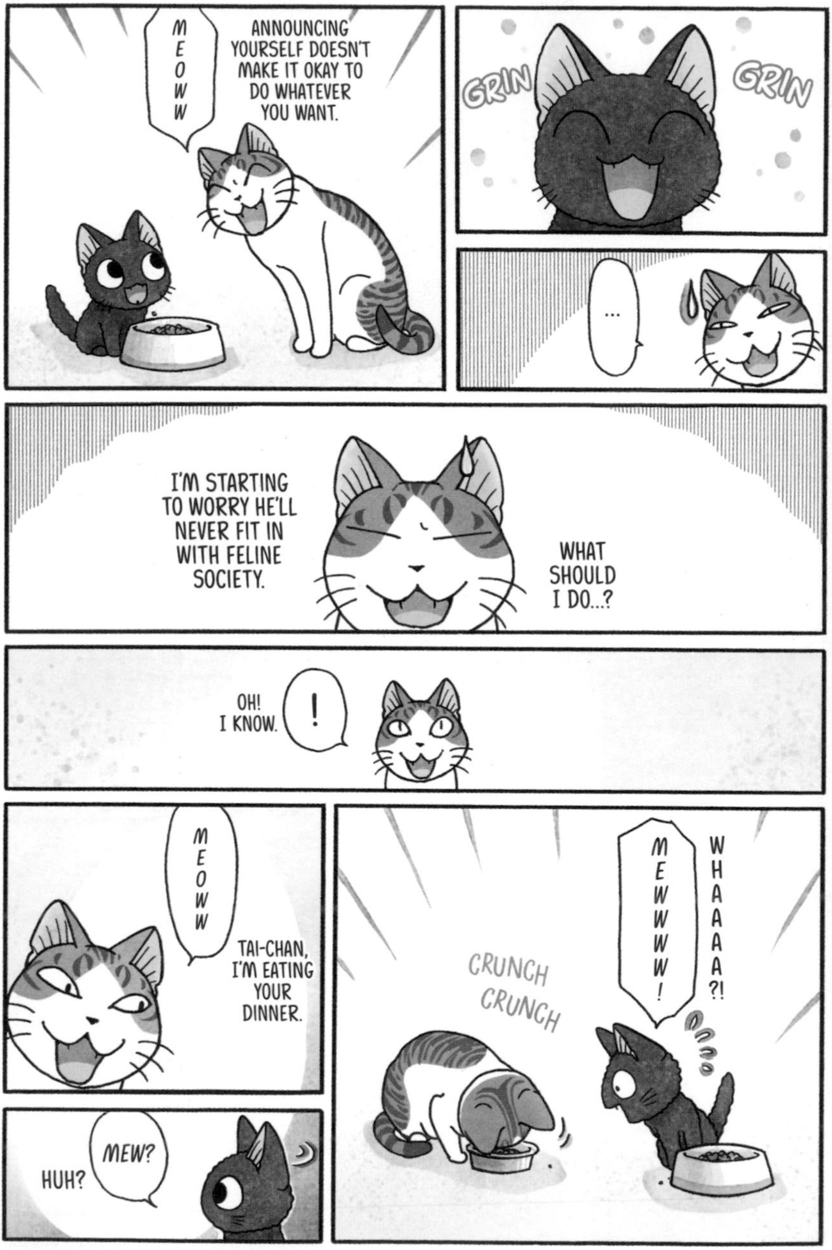
MEOWW
ANNOUNCING YOURSELF DOESN'T MAKE IT OKAY TO DO WHATEVER YOU WANT.
GRIN
GRIN
...
I'M STARTING TO WORRY HE'LL NEVER FIT IN WITH FELINE SOCIETY.
WHAT SHOULD I DO...?
OH! I KNOW.
!
MEOWW
TAI-CHAN, I'M EATING YOUR DINNER.
MEW?
HUH?
MEWWWWW!
WHAAAAA?!
CRUNCH
CRUNCH

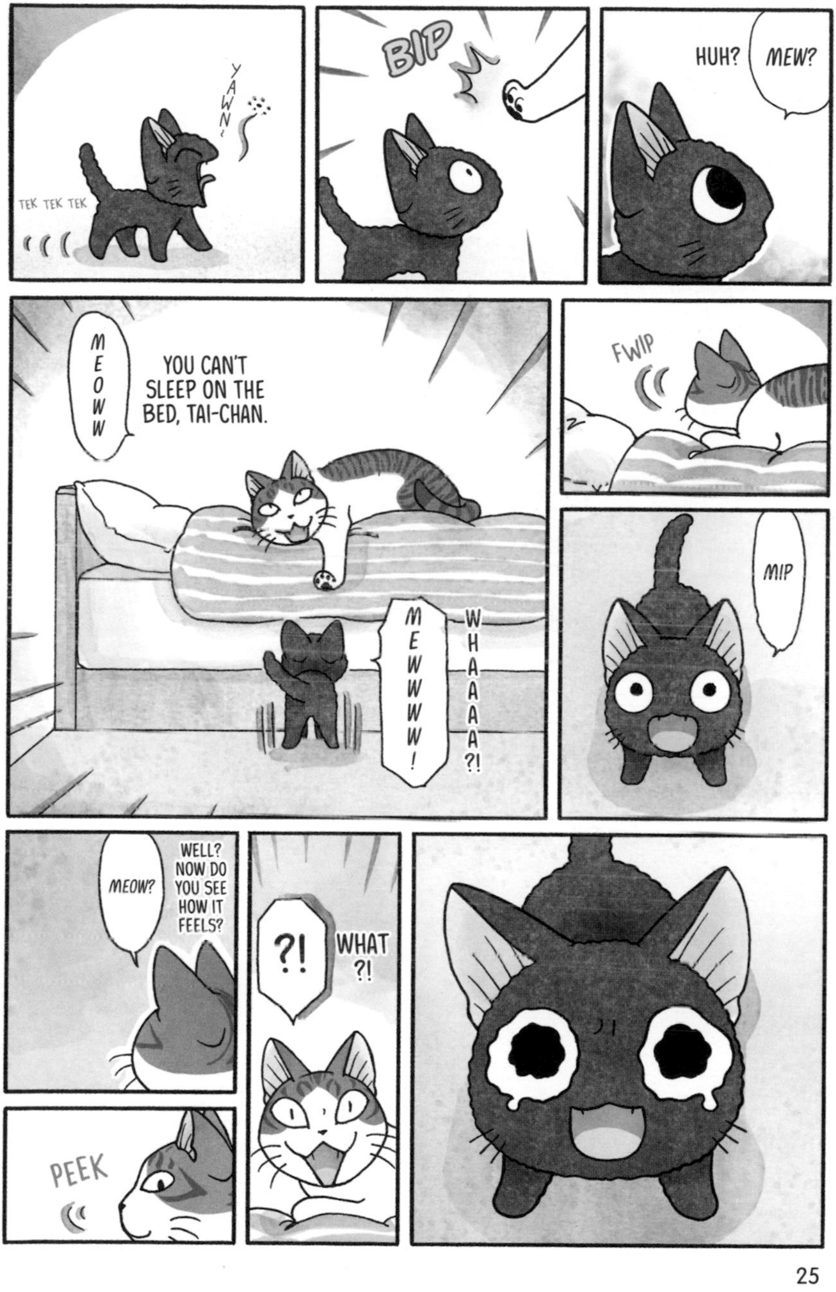
YAWN~
TEK TEK TEK
BIP
HUH?
MEW?
MEOWW
YOU CAN'T SLEEP ON THE BED, TAI-CHAN.
MEWWWWW!
WHAAAAA?!
FWIP
MIP
MEOW?
WELL? NOW DO YOU SEE HOW IT FEELS?
PEEK
?!
WHAT?!

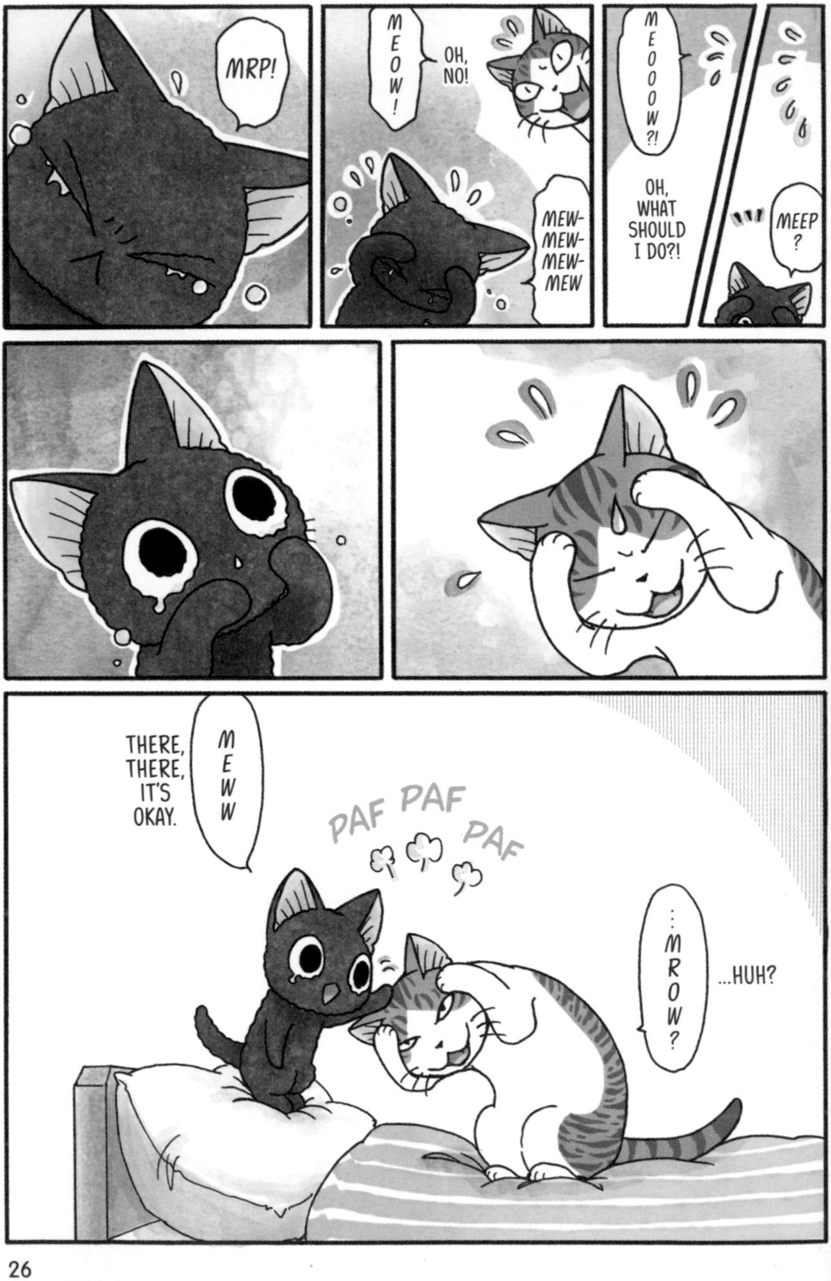
MRP!
MEOW!
OH, NO!
MEW-MEW-MEW-MEW
MEOOOW?!
OH, WHAT SHOULD I DO?!
MEEP?
MEWW
THERE, THERE, IT'S OKAY.
PAF PAF PAF
...MROW?
...HUH?

GRIN GRIN

Sue & Tai-chan

CHAPTER 21 A Funny Face?!

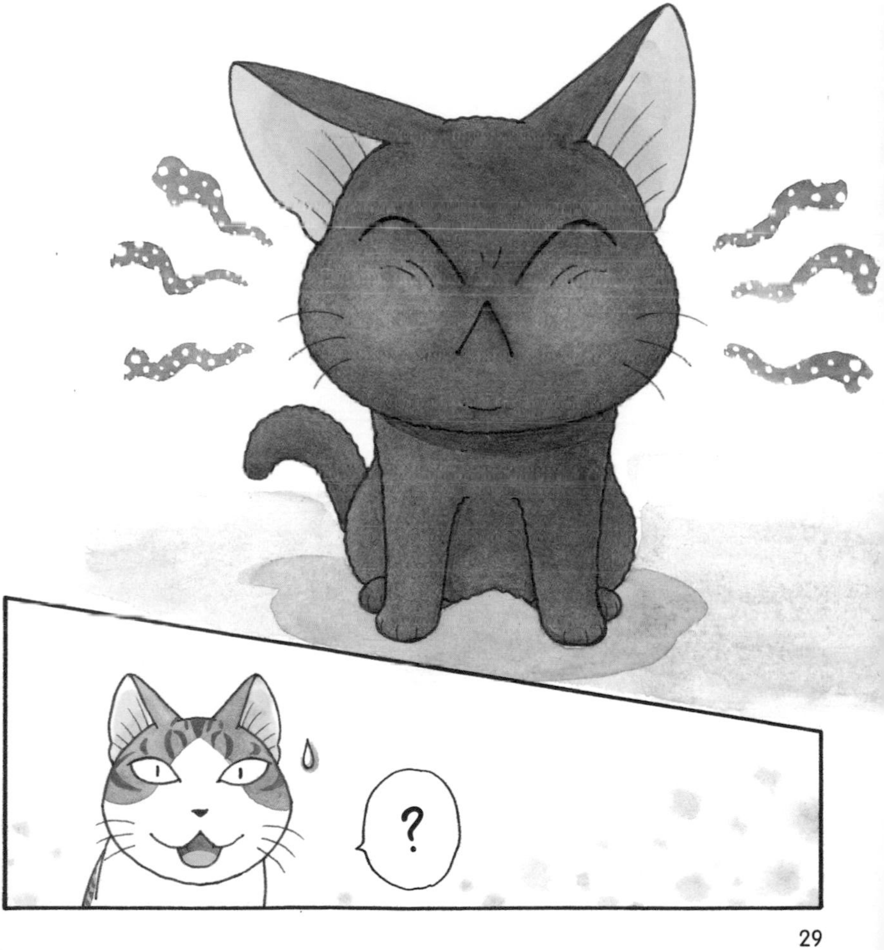
?

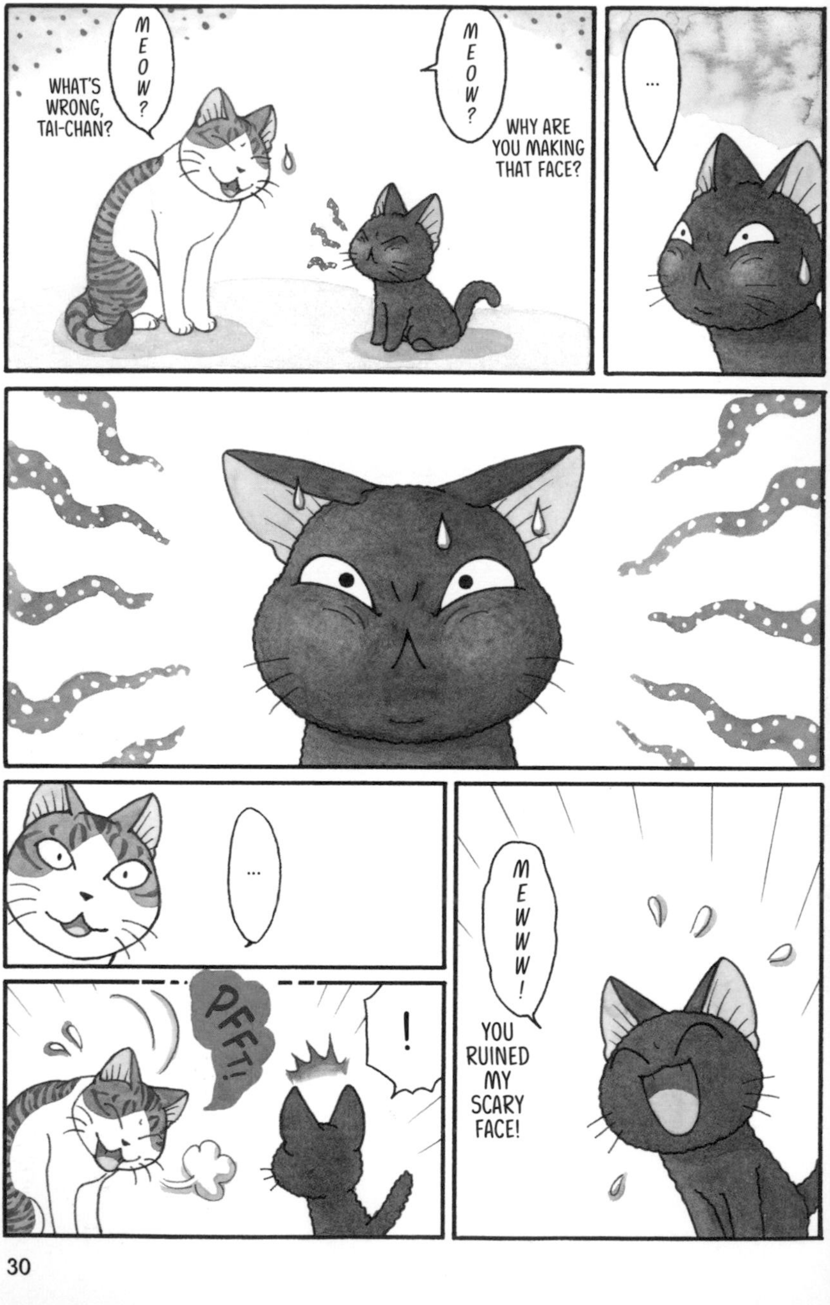
MEOW?
WHAT'S WRONG, TAI-CHAN?
MEOW?
WHY ARE YOU MAKING THAT FACE?
...
...
PFFT!
!
MEWWW!
YOU RUINED MY SCARY FACE!

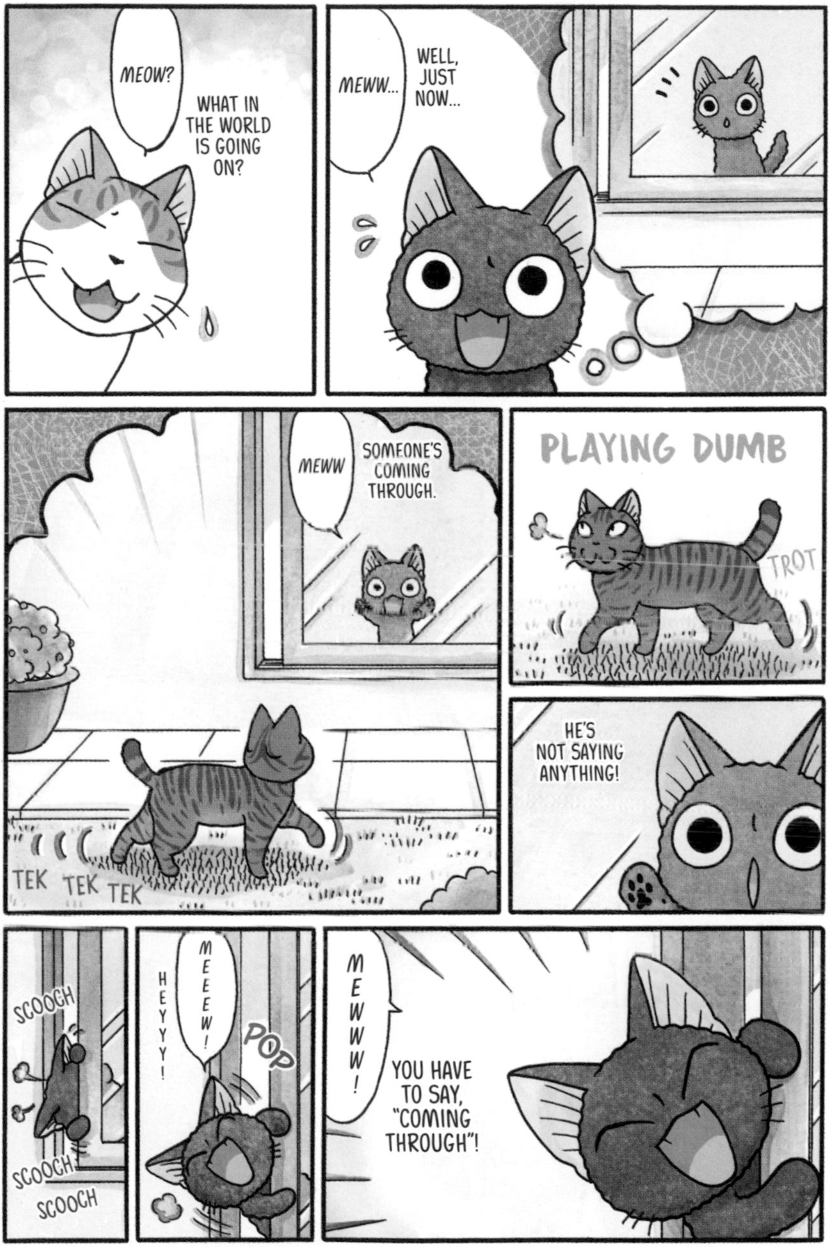
MEOW?
WHAT IN THE WORLD IS GOING ON?
MEWW...
WELL, JUST NOW...
MEWW
SOMEONE'S COMING THROUGH.
TEK TEK TEK
PLAYING DUMB
TROT
HE'S NOT SAYING ANYTHING!
SCOOCH
SCOOCH
SCOOCH
MEEEEW!
HEYYY!
POP
MEWWW!
YOU HAVE TO SAY, "COMING THROUGH"!

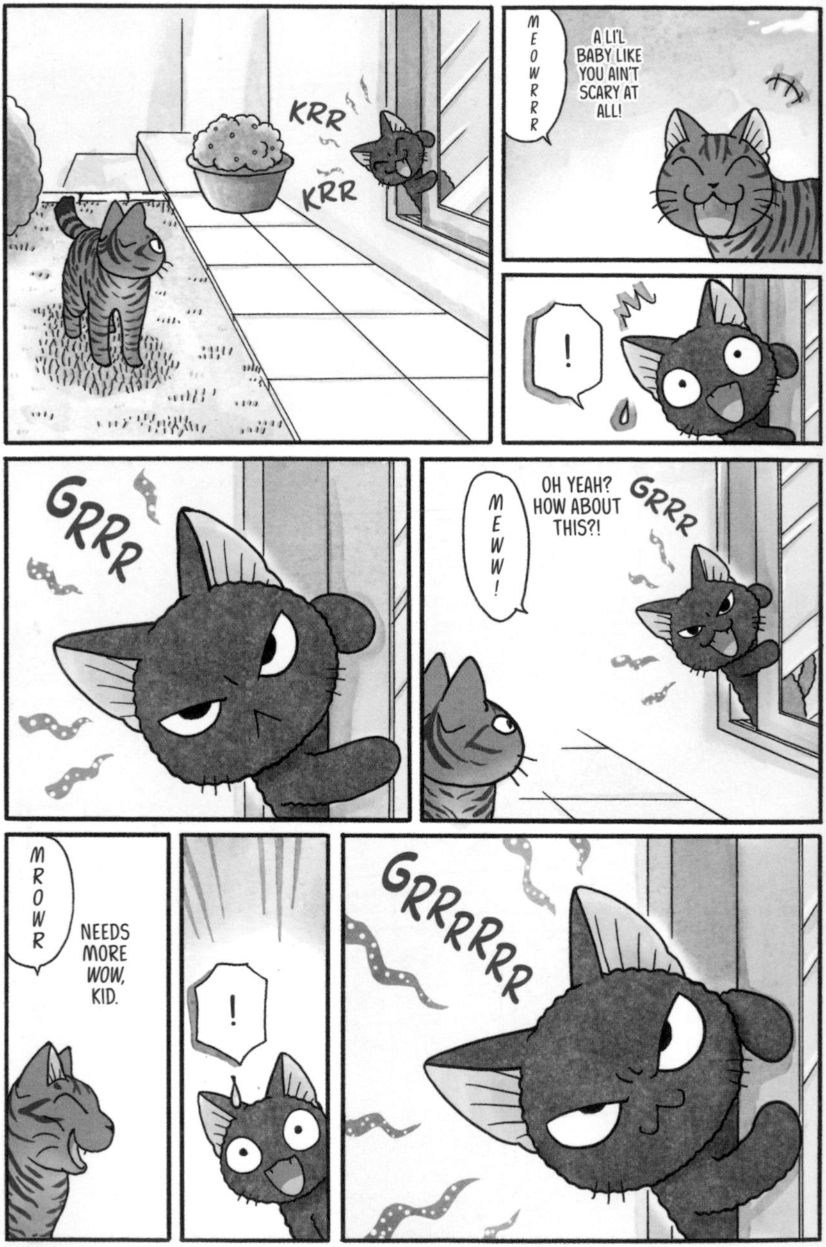
KRR
KRR
MEOWRRR
A LI'L BABY LIKE YOU AIN'T SCARY AT ALL!
!
GRRR
MEWW!
OH YEAH? HOW ABOUT THIS?!
GRRR
MROWR
NEEDS MORE WOW, KID.
!
GRRRRRRR

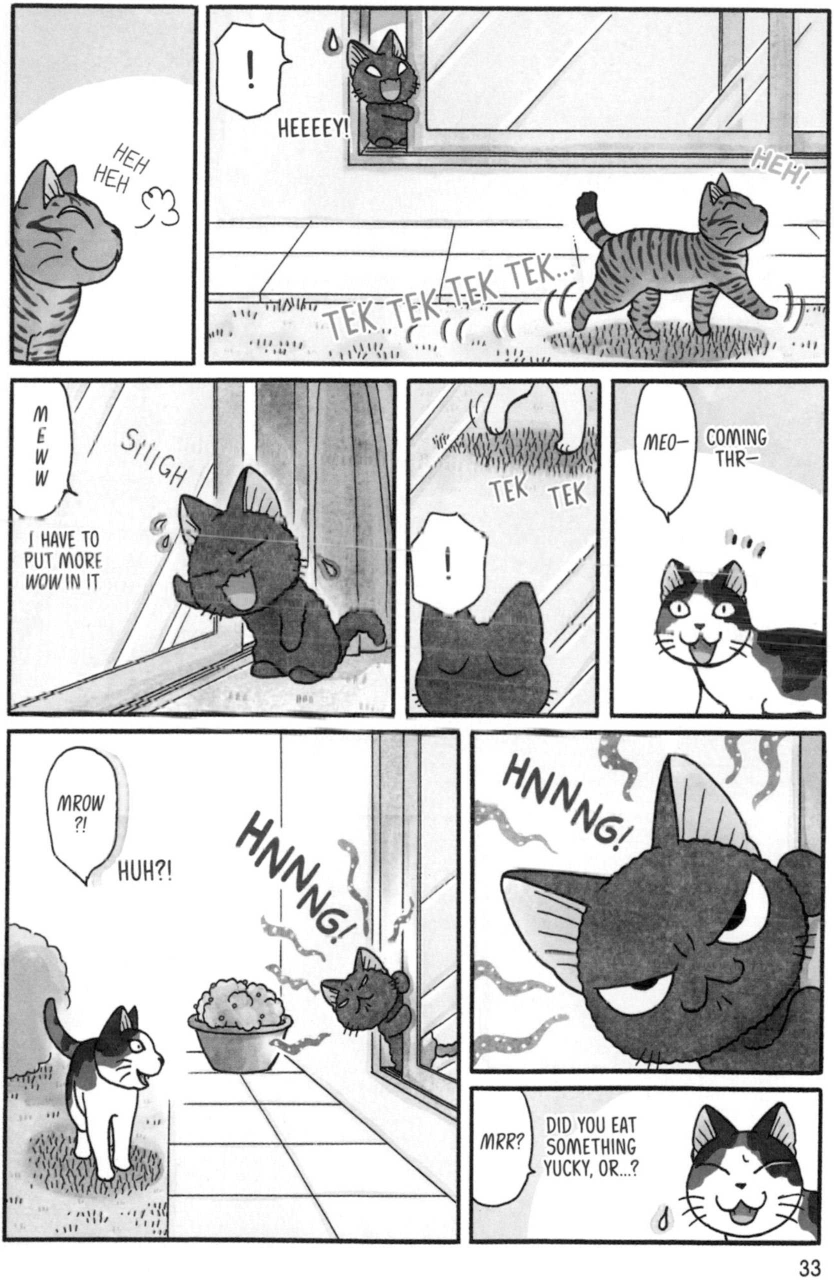
HEH HEH
!
HEEEEY!
HEH!
TEK TEK TEK TEK...!
MEWW
SIIIGH
I HAVE TO PUT MORE WOW IN IT
TEK TEK
!
MEO—
COMING THR—
MROW ?!
HUH?!
HNNNG!
HNNNG!
MRR?
DID YOU EAT SOMETHING YUCKY, OR...?

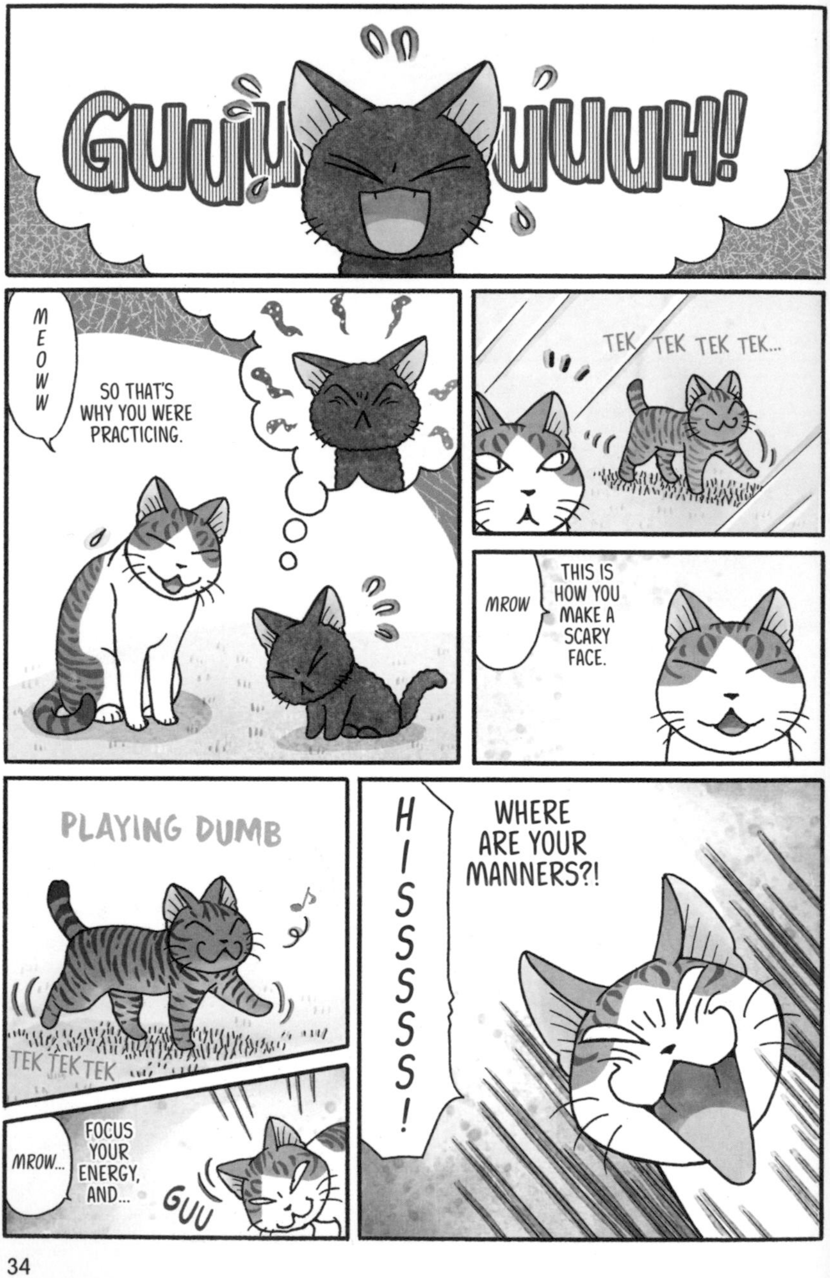
GUUUUUUUUH!
MEOWW
SO THAT'S WHY YOU WERE PRACTICING.
TEK TEK TEK TEK...
MROW
THIS IS HOW YOU MAKE A SCARY FACE.
PLAYING DUMB
TEK TEK TEK
MROW...
FOCUS YOUR ENERGY, AND...
GUU
HISSSSS!
WHERE ARE YOUR MANNERS?!

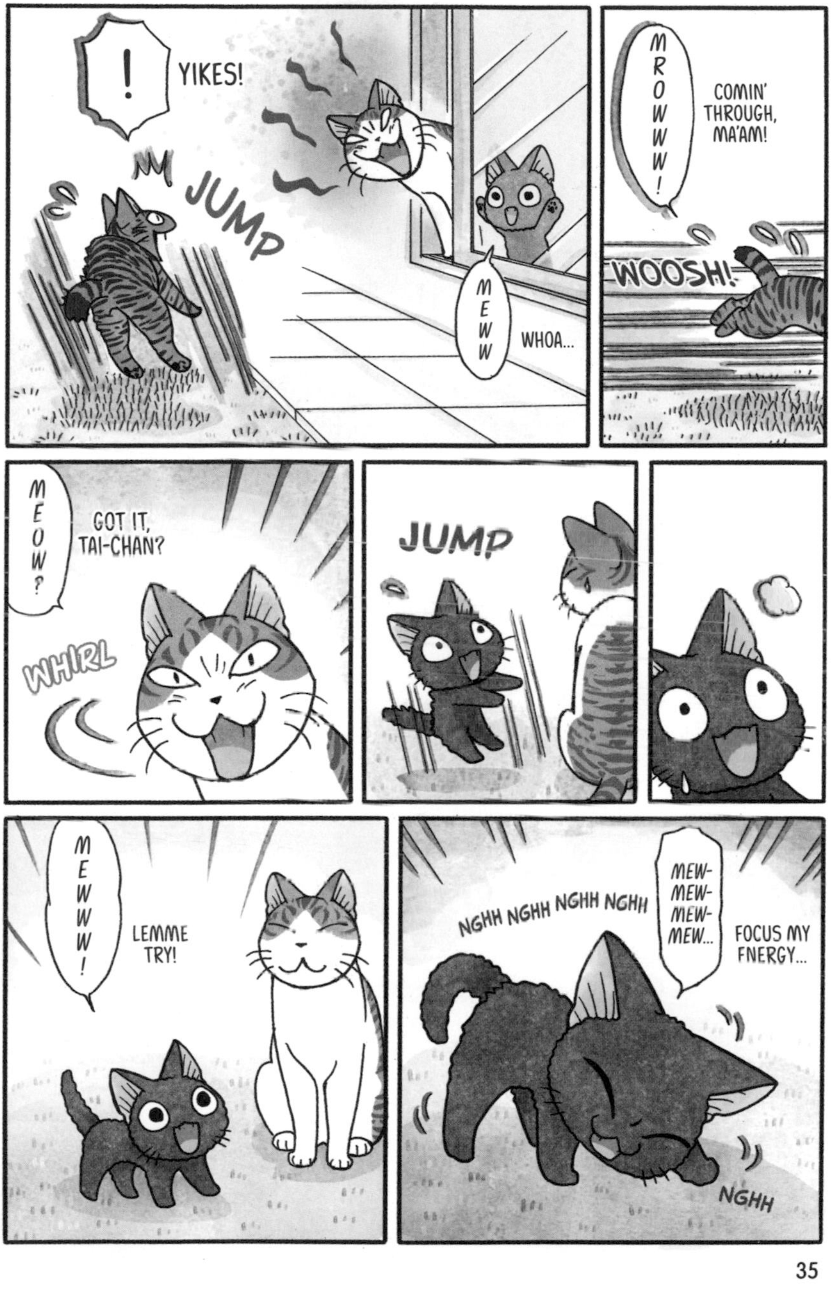
!
YIKES!
JUMP
MEWW
WHOA...
MROWWWW!
COMIN' THROUGH, MA'AM!
WOOSH!
MEOW?
GOT IT, TAI-CHAN?
WHIRL
JUMP
MEWWW!
LEMME TRY!
NGHH NGHH NGHH NGHH
MEW-MEW-MEW-MEW...
FOCUS MY ENERGY...
NGHH

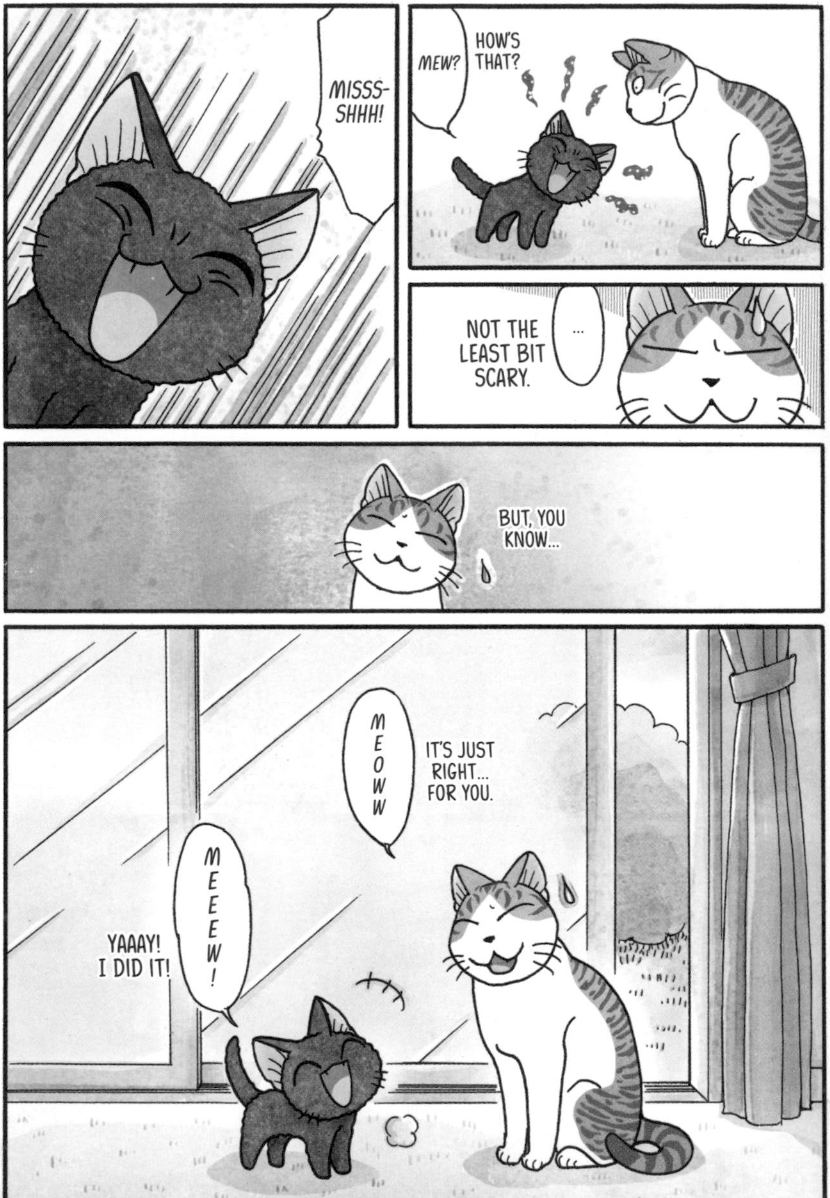
MISSS-SHHH!
MEW?
HOW'S THAT?
NOT THE LEAST BIT SCARY.
...
BUT, YOU KNOW...
MEOWW
IT'S JUST RIGHT... FOR YOU.
YAAAY! I DID IT!
MEEEEW!

CHAPTER 22 Heat-Stealing Kitty

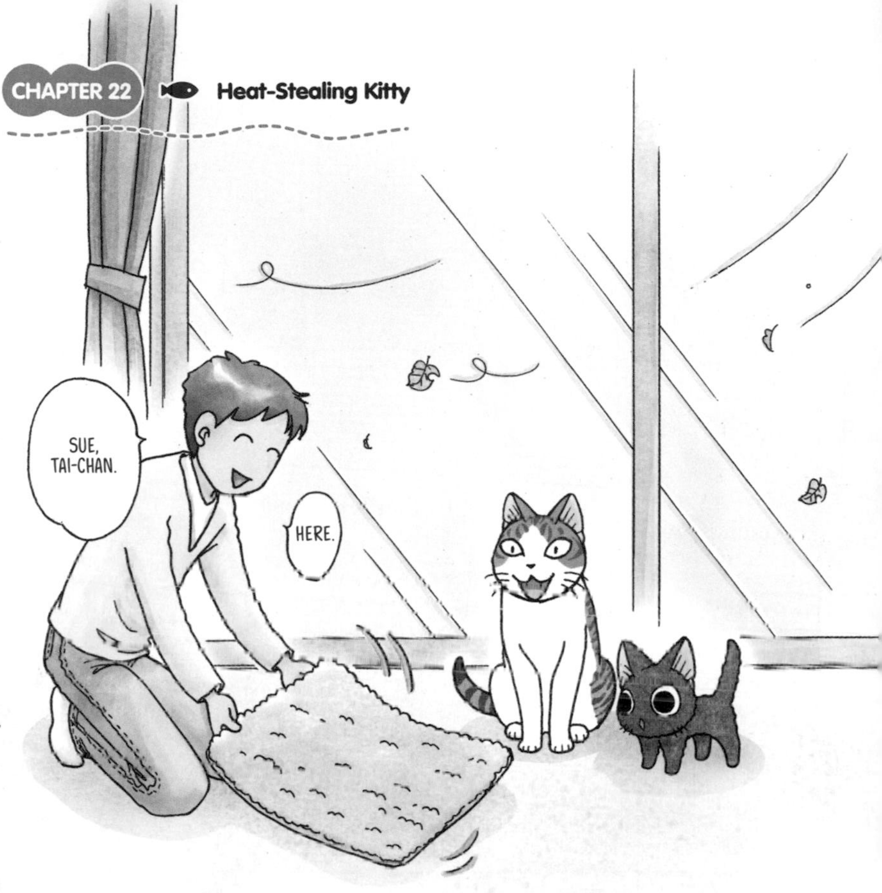
SUE, TAI-CHAN.
HERE.

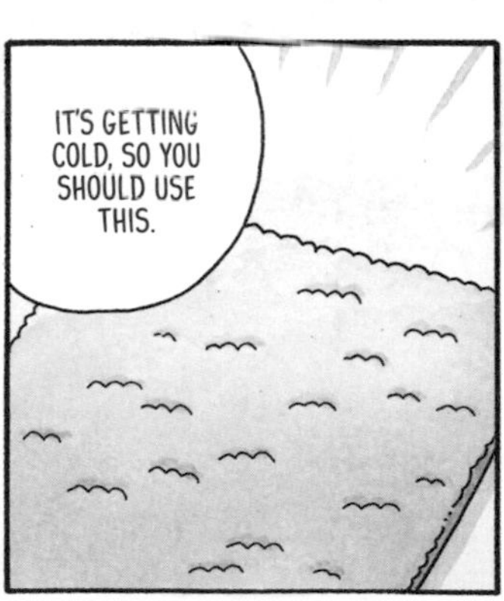
IT'S GETTING COLD, SO YOU SHOULD USE THIS.

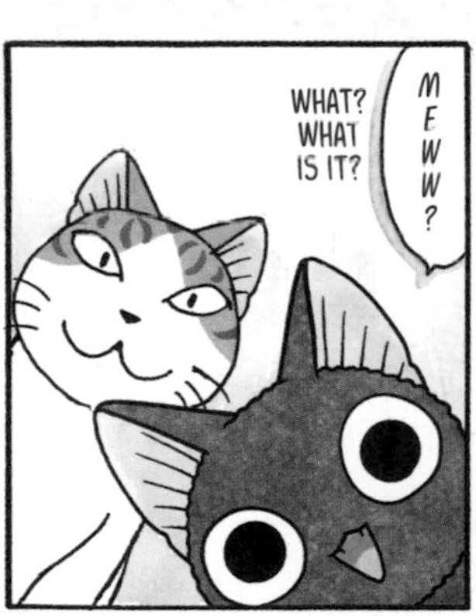
WHAT? WHAT IS IT?
MEWW?

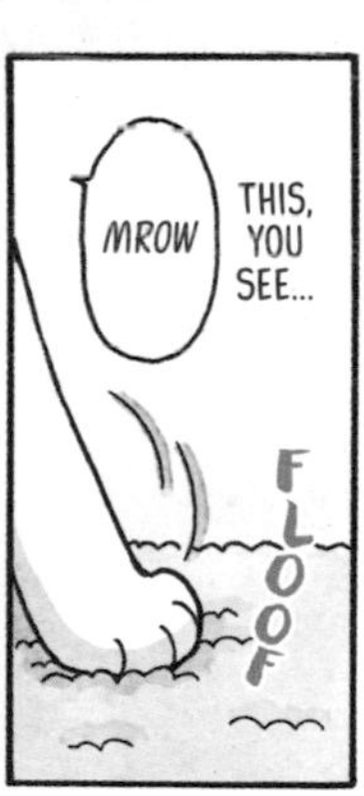
MROW
THIS, YOU SEE...
FLOOF

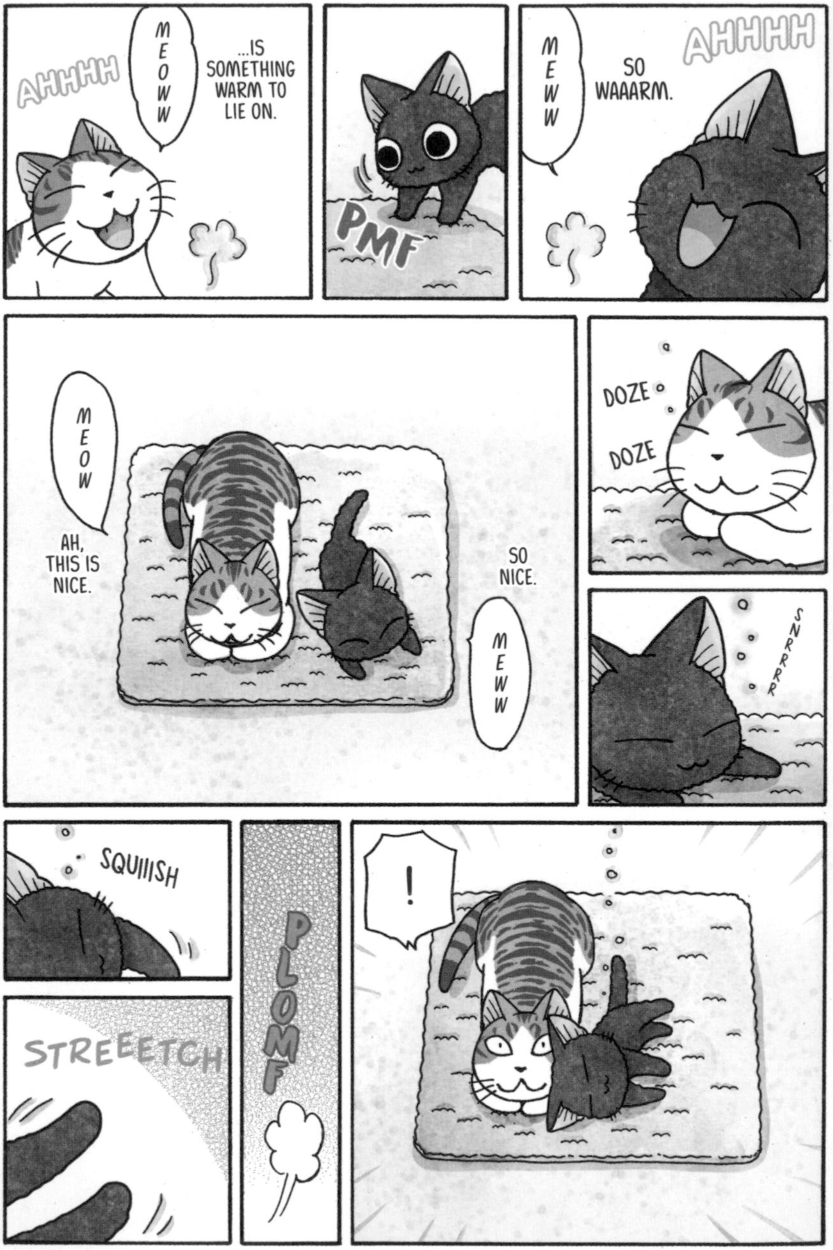
AHHHH
MEOWW
...IS SOMETHING WARM TO LIE ON.
PMF
MEWW
SO WAAARM.
AHHHH
MEOW
AH, THIS IS NICE.
SO NICE.
MEWW
DOZE
DOZE
SNRRRR
SQUIIISH
STREEETCH
PLOMF
!

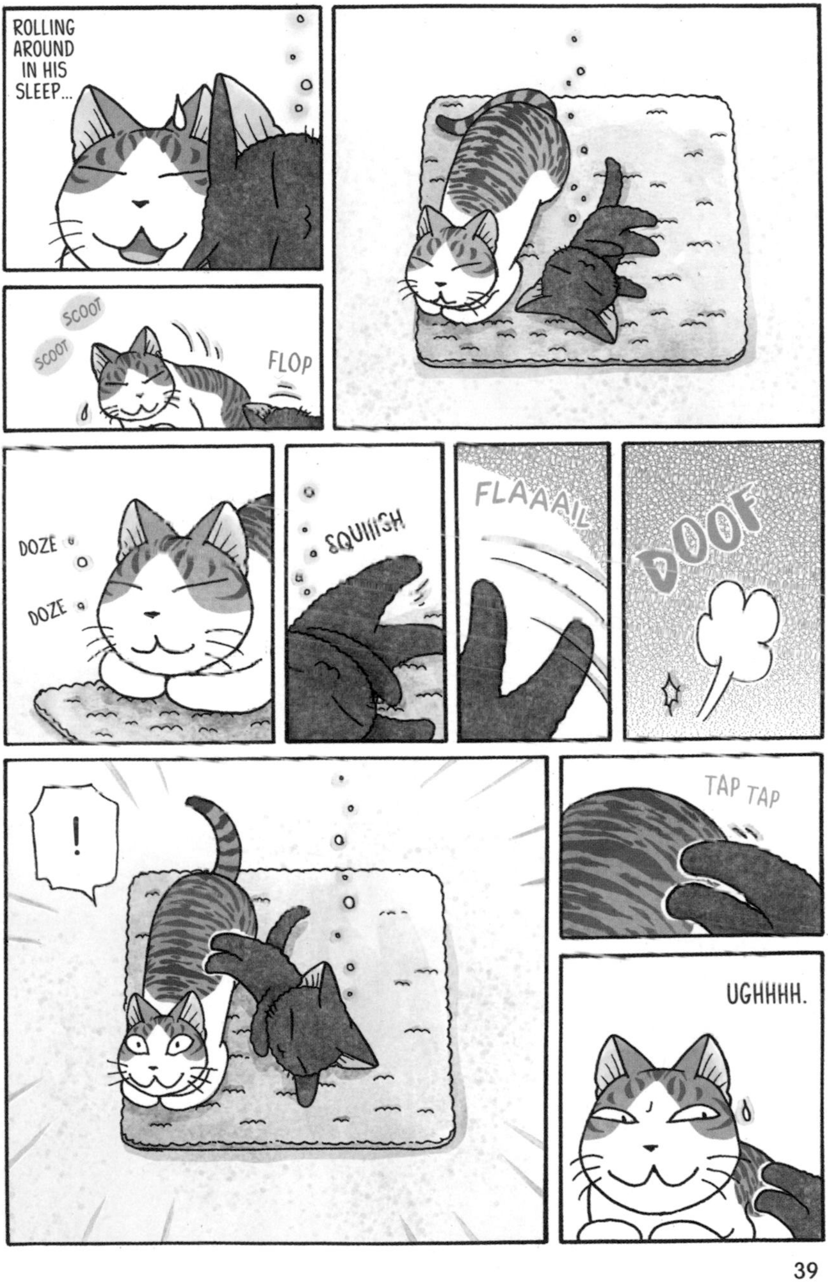
ROLLING AROUND IN HIS SLEEP...
SCOOT
SCOOT
FLOP
DOZE
DOZE
SQUIIISH
FLAAAIL
DOOF
!
TAP TAP
UGHHHH.

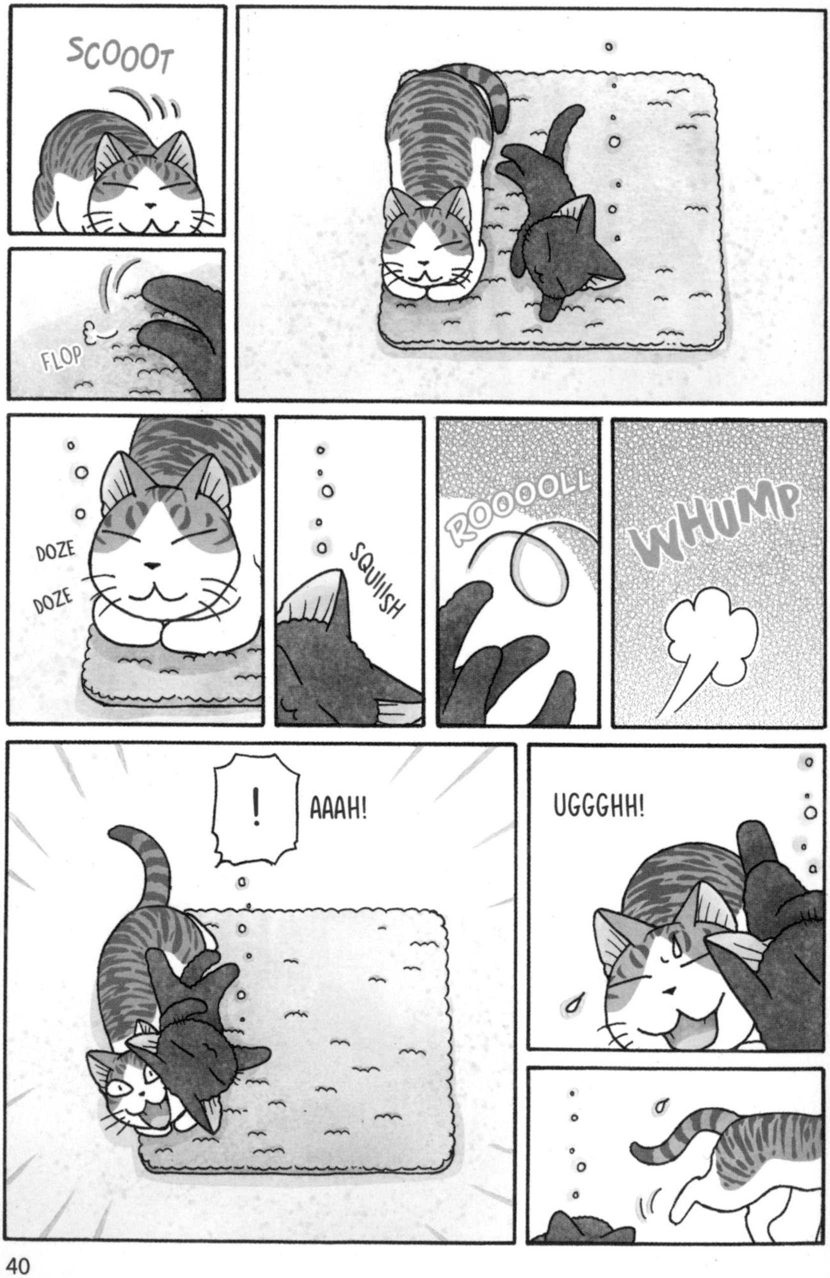
SCOOOT
FLOP
DOZE
DOZE
SQUIIISH
ROOOOLL
WHUMP
!
AAAH!
UGGGHH!

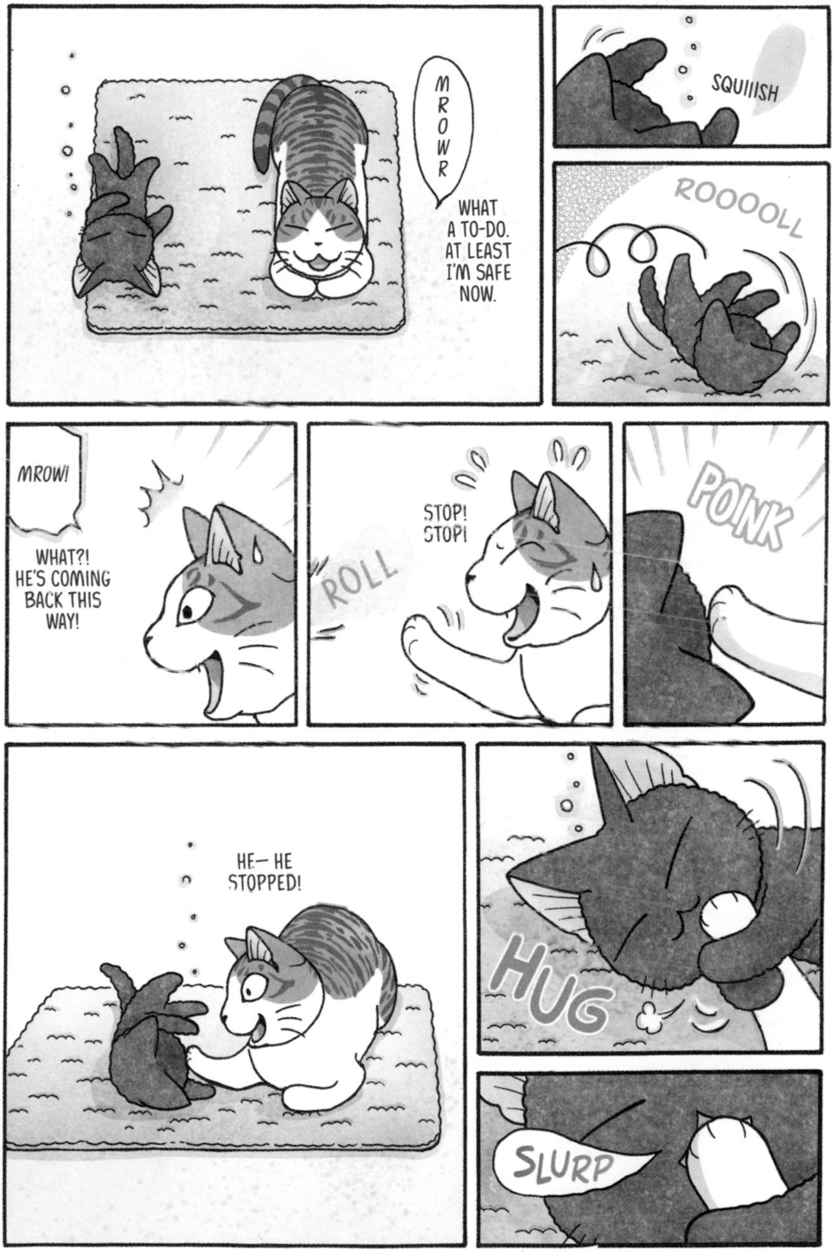
MROWR
WHAT A TO-DO. AT LEAST I'M SAFE NOW.
SQUIIISH
ROOOOLL
MROW!
WHAT?! HE'S COMING BACK THIS WAY!
ROLL
STOP! STOP!
POINK
HE— HE STOPPED!
HUG
SLURP

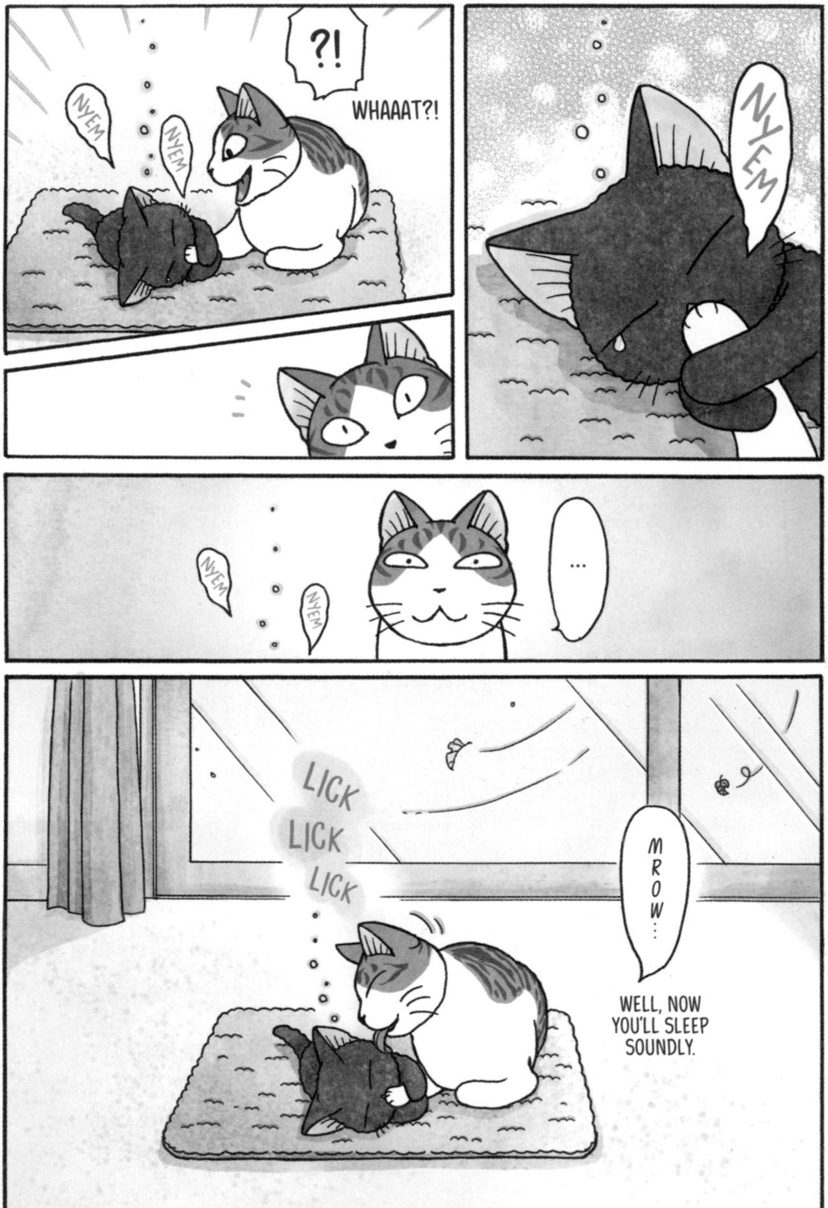
?!
WHAAAT?!
NYEM
NYEM
NYEM
NYEM
NYEM
...
LICK
LICK
LICK
MROW...
WELL, NOW YOU'LL SLEEP SOUNDLY.

CHAPTER 23 Growing-Up Strategies

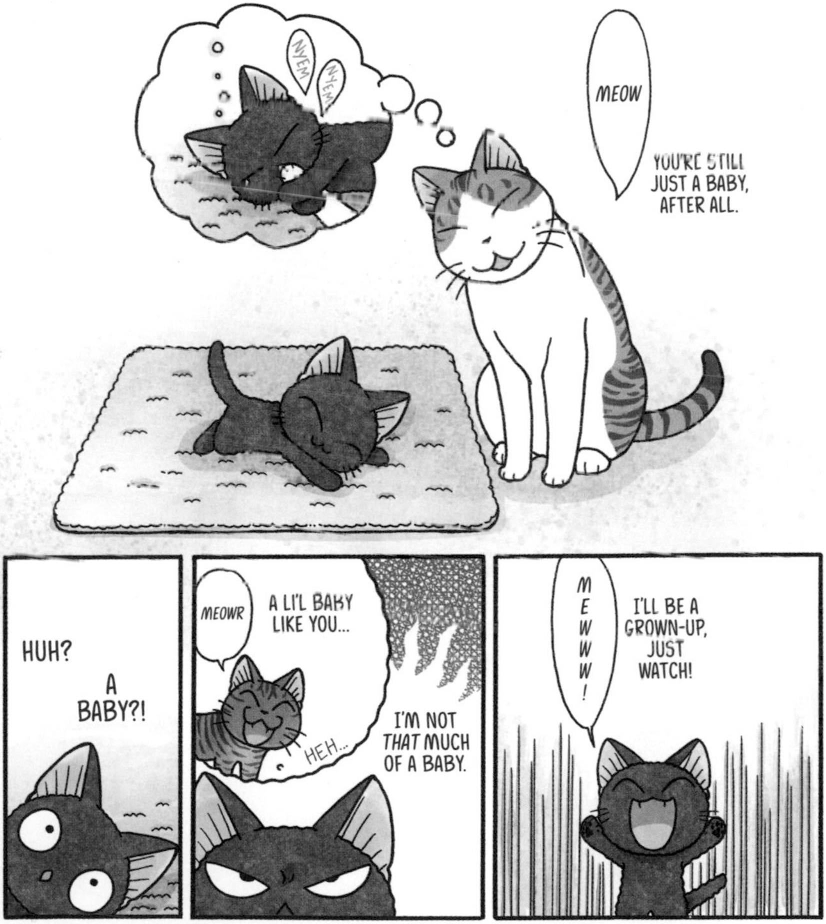

NYEM
NYEM
MEOW
YOU'RE STILL JUST A BABY, AFTER ALL.
HUH?
A BABY?!
MEOWR
A LI'L BABY LIKE YOU...
HEH...
I'M NOT *THAT* MUCH OF A BABY.
MEWWW!
I'LL BE A GROWN-UP, JUST WATCH!

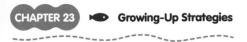

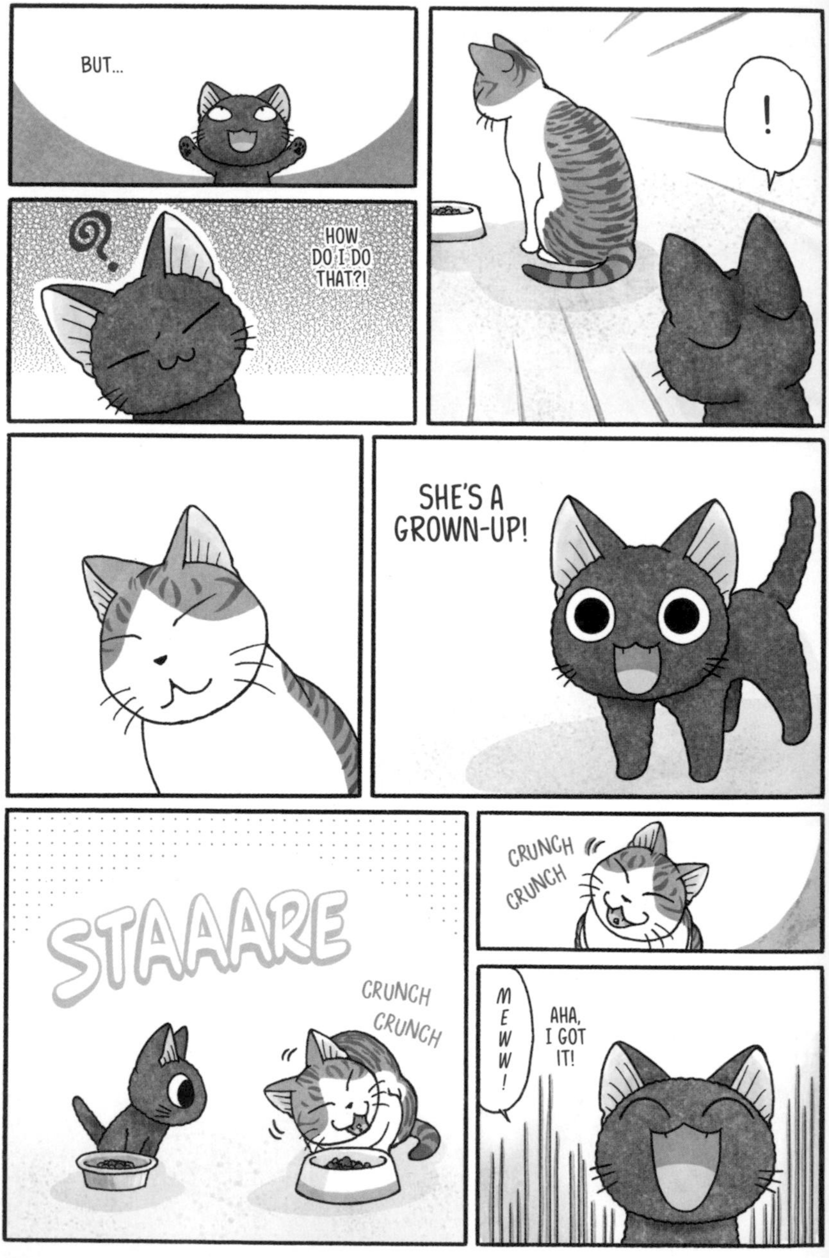
BUT...
HOW DO I DO THAT?!
!
SHE'S A GROWN-UP!
STAAARE
CRUNCH CRUNCH
CRUNCH CRUNCH
MEWW!
AHA, I GOT IT!

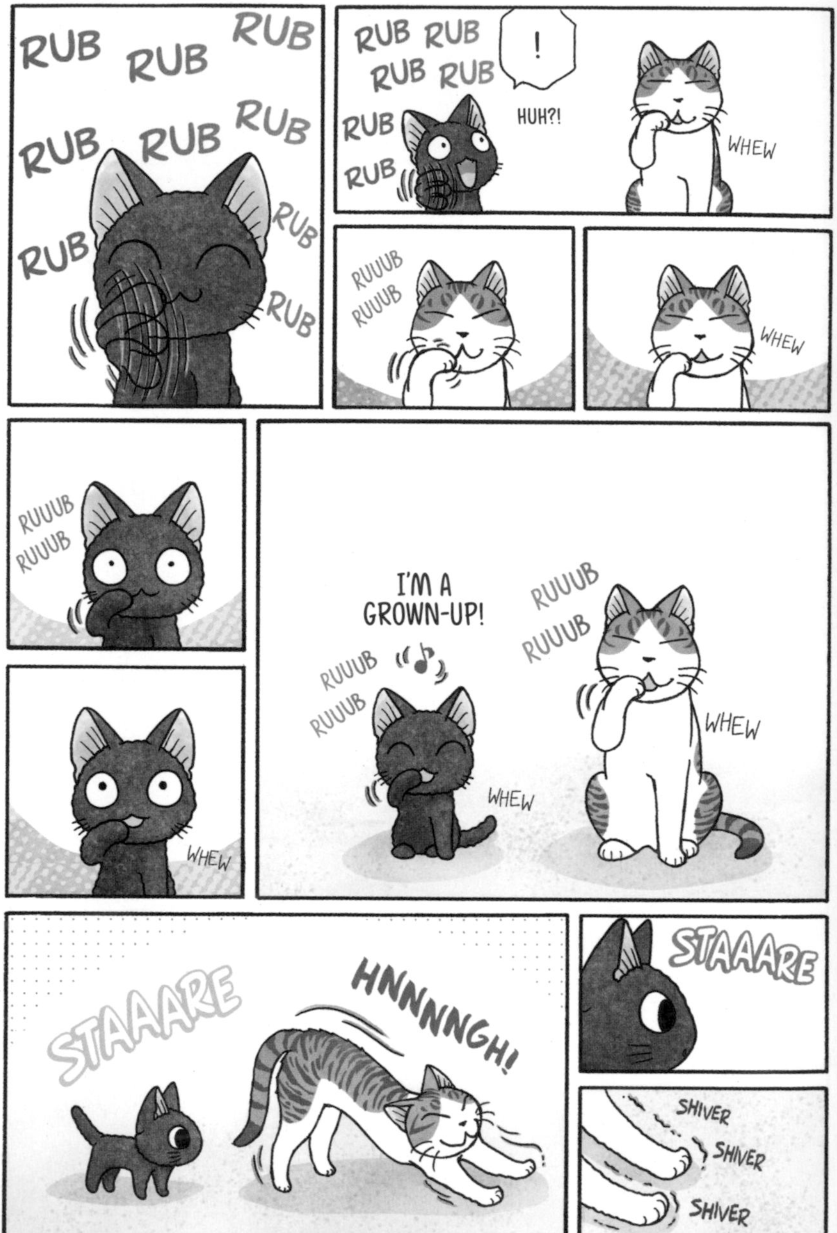
RUB RUB RUB
RUB RUB RUB
RUB RUB RUB
RUB RUB
RUB RUB
RUB RUB
!
HUH?!
WHEW
RUUUB RUUUB
WHEW
RUUUB RUUUB
WHEW
I'M A GROWN-UP!
RUUUB RUUUB
RUUUB RUUUB
WHEW
WHEW
STAAARE
HNNNNNGH!
STAAARE
SHIVER
SHIVER
SHIVER

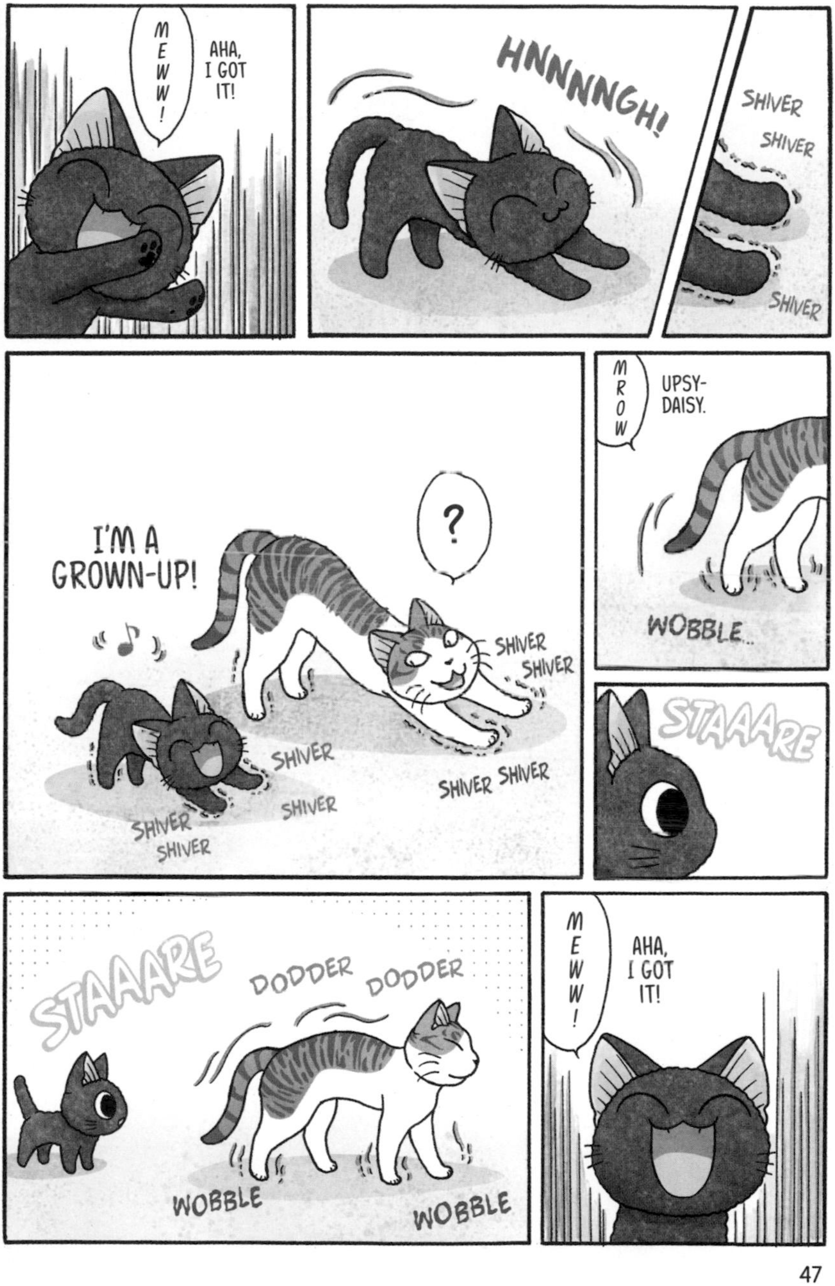
MEWW!
AHA, I GOT IT!
HNNNNGH!
SHIVER
SHIVER
SHIVER
I'M A GROWN-UP!
?
SHIVER SHIVER
SHIVER
SHIVER
SHIVER SHIVER
SHIVER SHIVER
MROW
UPSY-DAISY.
WOBBLE...
STAAARE
STAAARE
DODDER DODDER
WOBBLE
WOBBLE
MEWW!
AHA, I GOT IT!

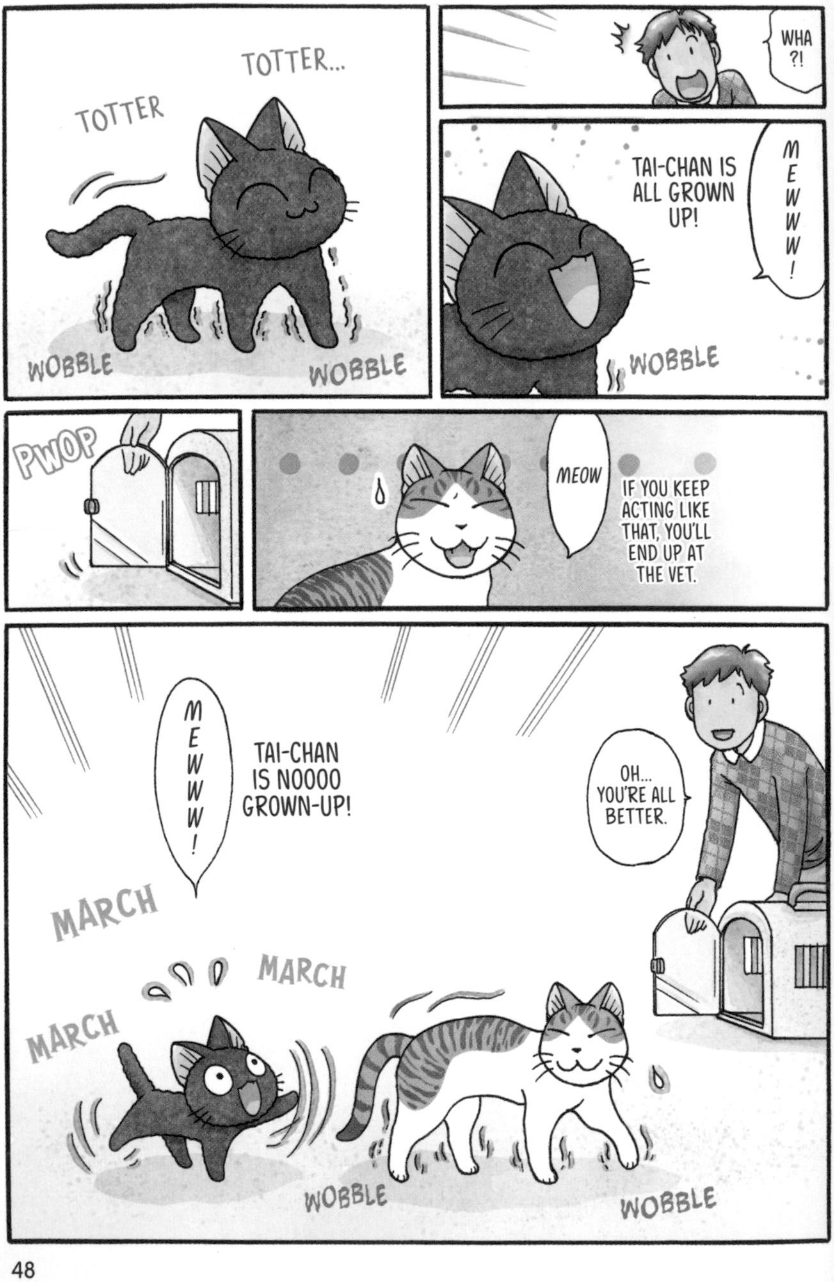
TOTTER
TOTTER...
WOBBLE
WOBBLE
WHA ?!
MEWWW!
TAI-CHAN IS ALL GROWN UP!
WOBBLE
PWOP
MEOW
IF YOU KEEP ACTING LIKE THAT, YOU'LL END UP AT THE VET.
MEWWW!
TAI-CHAN IS NOOOO GROWN-UP!
OH... YOU'RE ALL BETTER.
MARCH
MARCH
MARCH
WOBBLE
WOBBLE

CHAPTER 24 In Hot *Purrsuit*

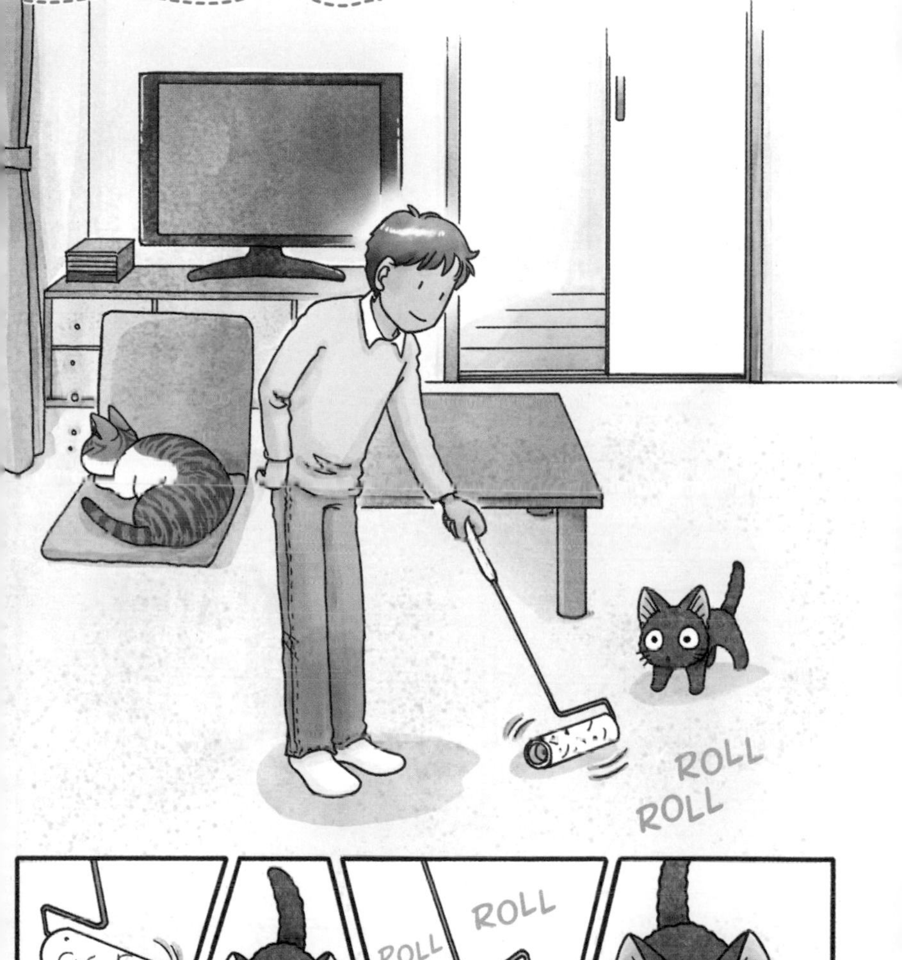
ROLL
ROLL

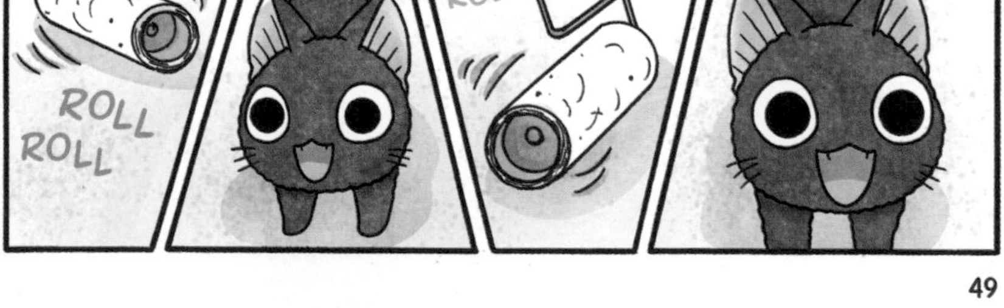
ROLL
ROLL
ROLL
ROLL

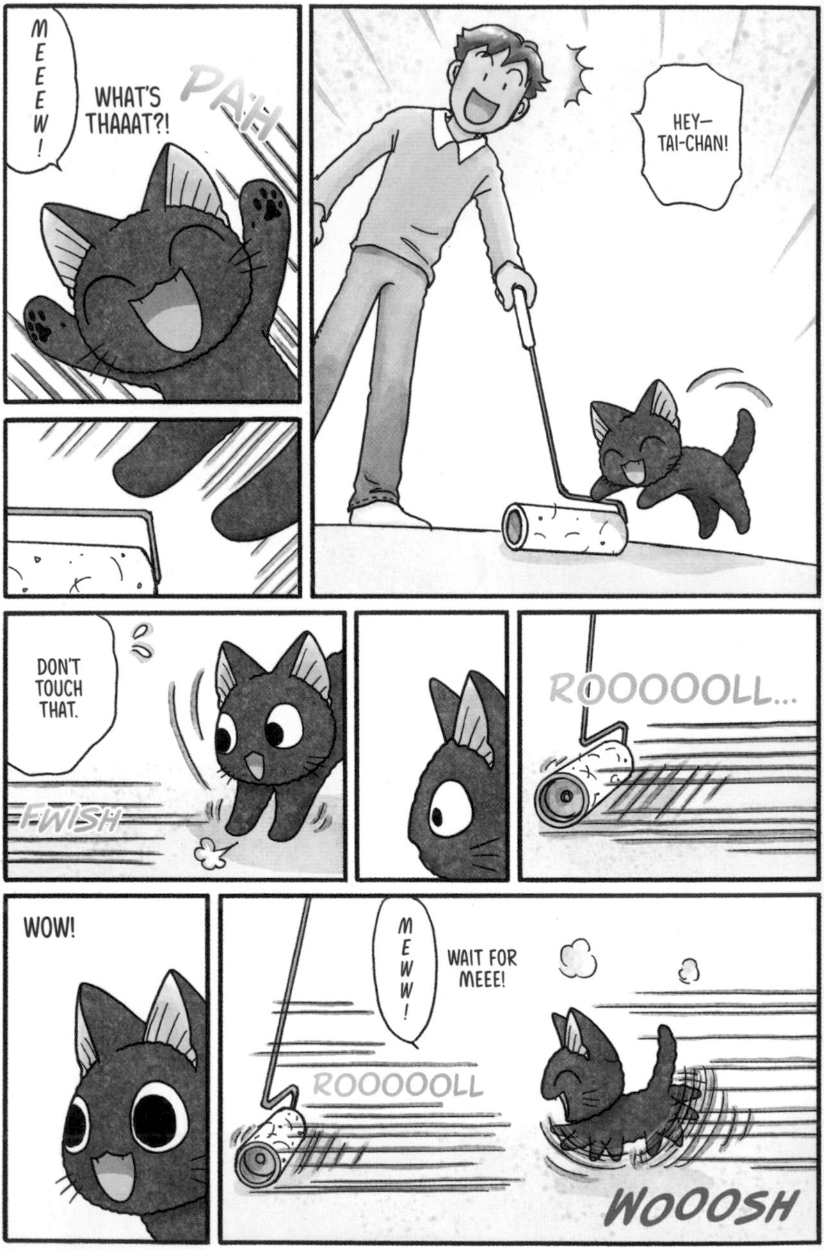
MEEEEW!
WHAT'S THAAAT?!
PAH
HEY— TAI-CHAN!
DON'T TOUCH THAT.
FWISH
ROOOOOLL...
WOW!
MEWW!
WAIT FOR MEEE!
ROOOOOLL
WOOOSH

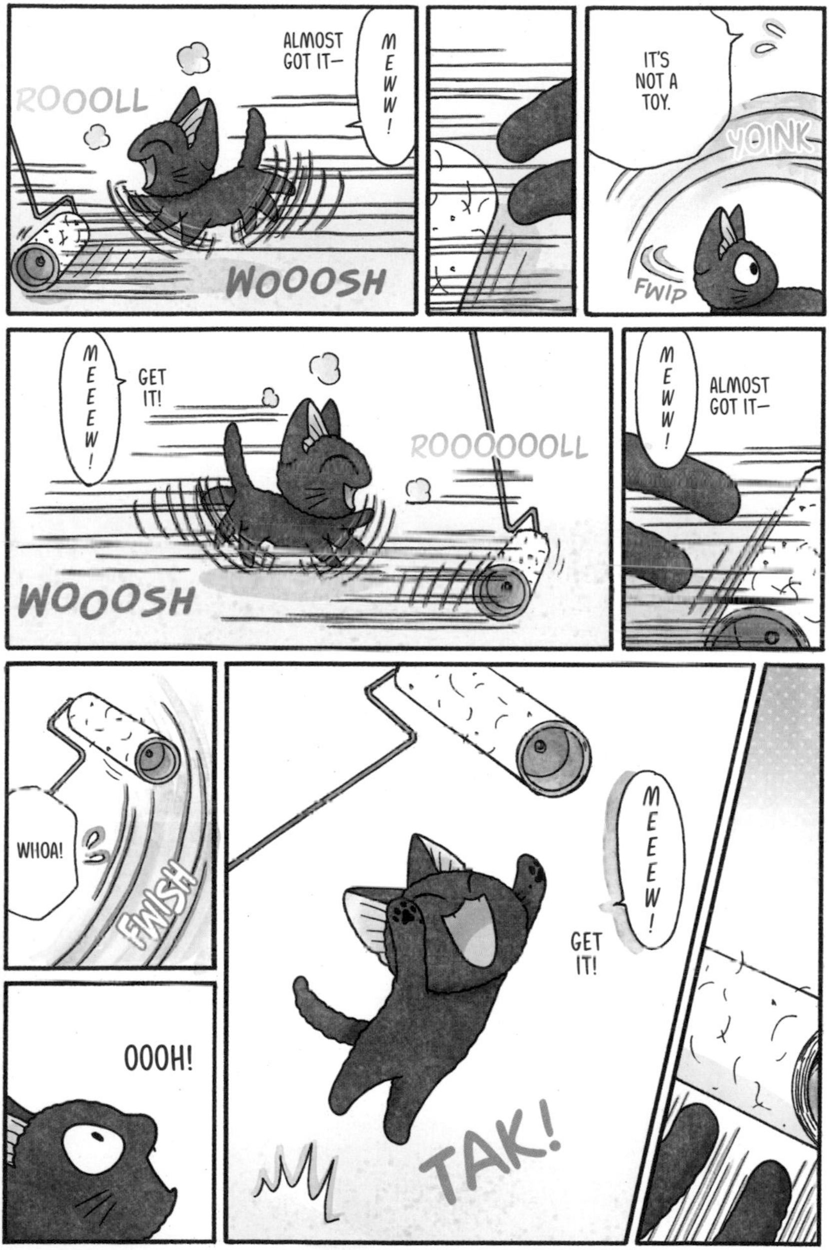
ROOOLL
ALMOST GOT IT—
MEWW!
WOOOSH
IT'S NOT A TOY.
YOINK
FWIP
MEEEEW!
GET IT!
ROOOOOOLL
WOOOSH
MEWW!
ALMOST GOT IT—
WHOA!
FWISH
MEEEEW!
GET IT!
TAK!
OOOH!

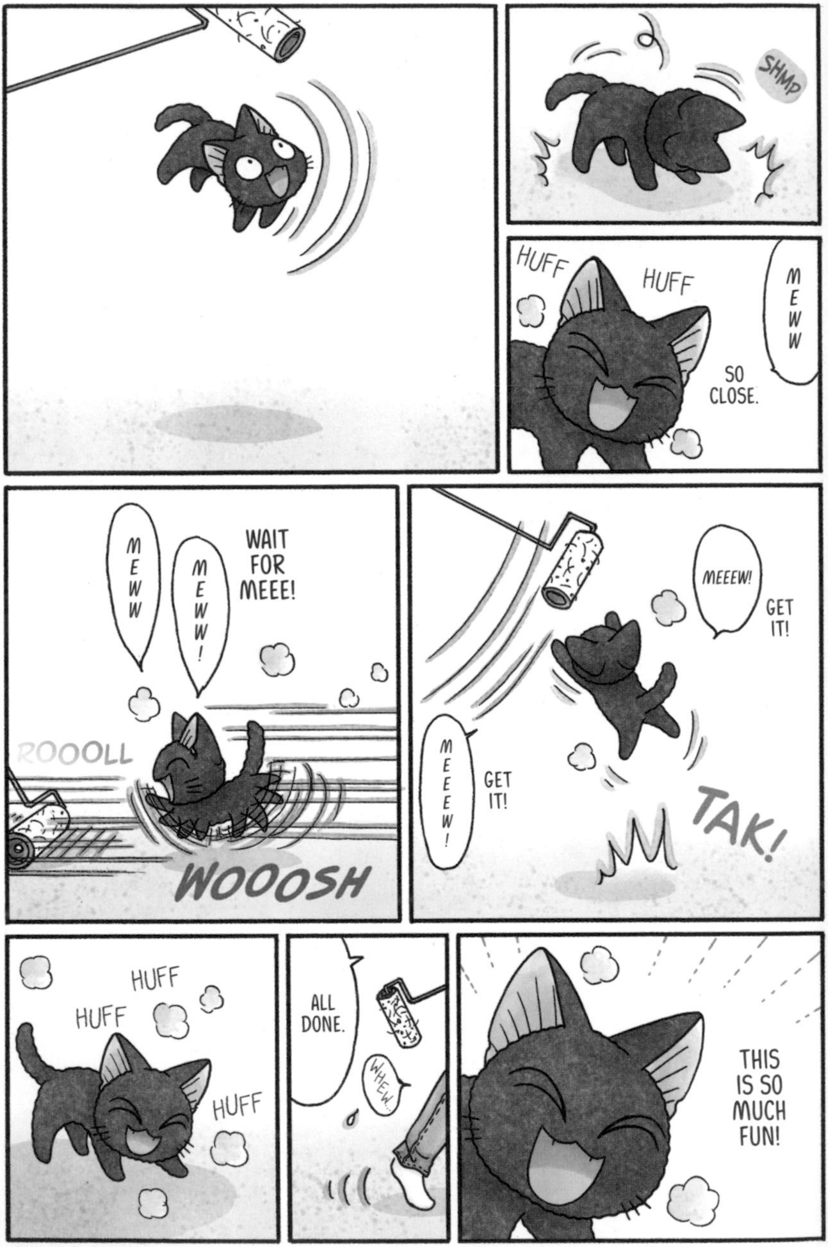
SHMP
HUFF
HUFF
MEWW
SO CLOSE.
MEWW
MEWW!
WAIT FOR MEEE!
ROOOLL
WOOOSH
MEEEW!
GET IT!
MEEEW!
GET IT!
TAK!
HUFF
HUFF
HUFF
ALL DONE.
WHEW...
THIS IS SO MUCH FUN!

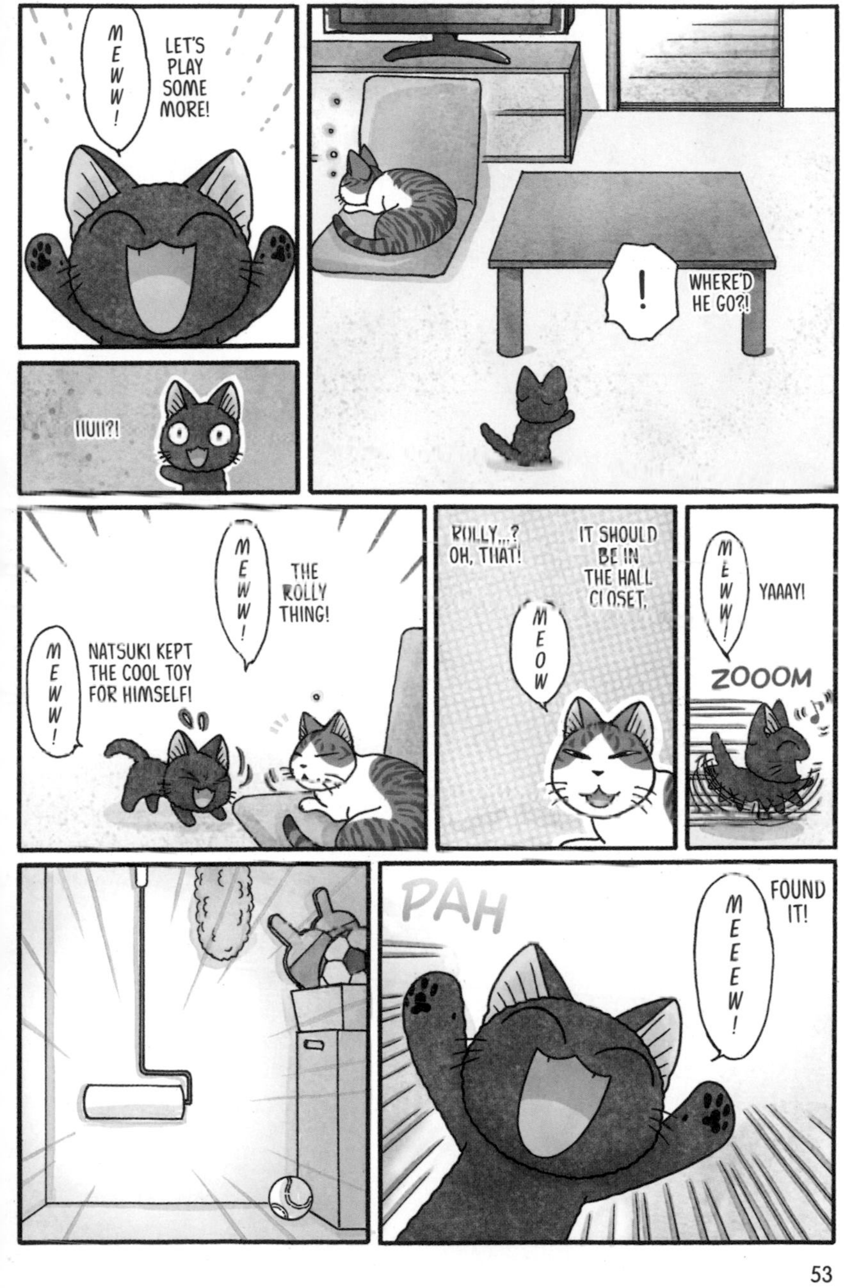

MEWW!
LET'S PLAY SOME MORE!
HUH?!
!
WHERE'D HE GO?!
MEWW!
THE ROLLY THING!
MEWW!
NATSUKI KEPT THE COOL TOY FOR HIMSELF!
ROLLY...? OH, THAT!
IT SHOULD BE IN THE HALL CLOSET.
MEOW
MEWW!
YAAAY!
ZOOOM
PAH
MEEEEW!
FOUND IT!

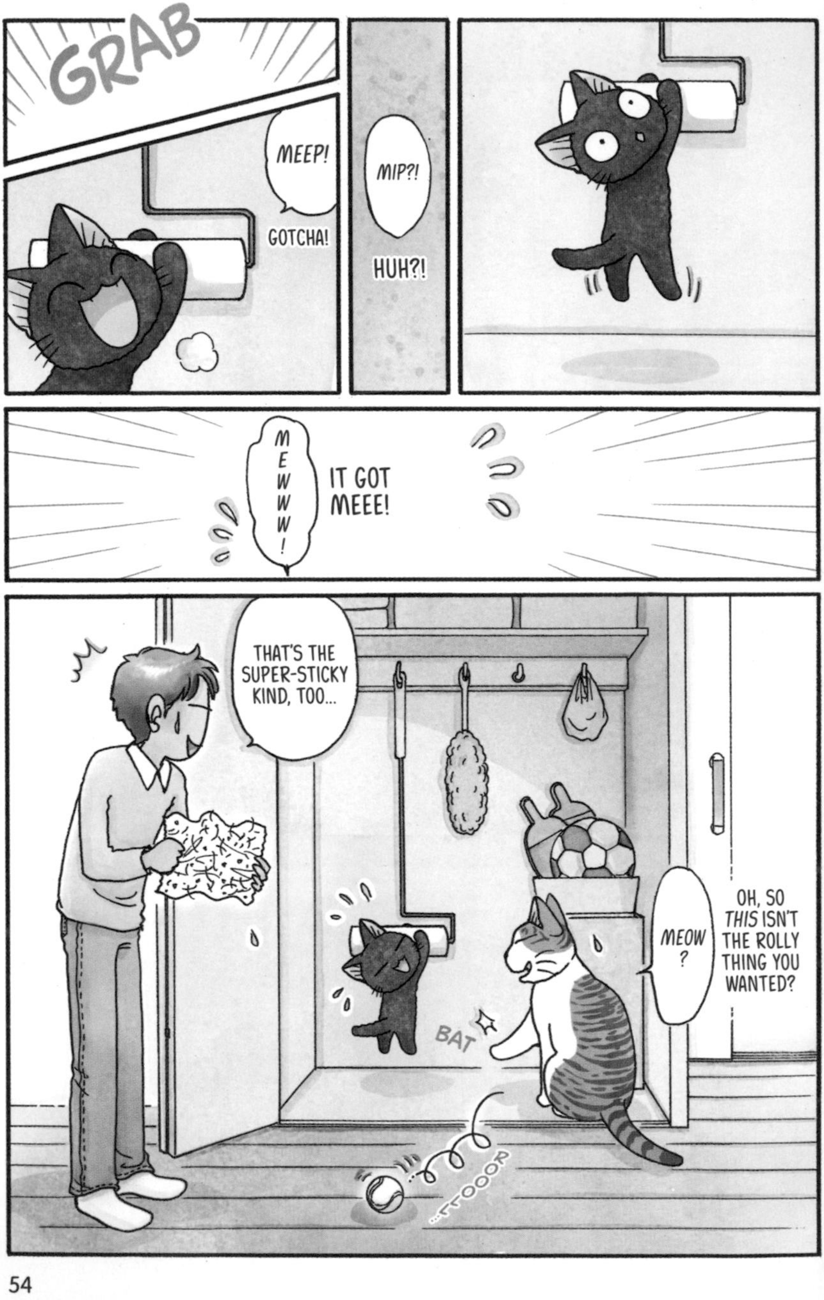
GRAB
MEEP!
GOTCHA!
MIP?!
HUH?!
MEWWWW!
IT GOT MEEE!
THAT'S THE SUPER-STICKY KIND, TOO...
BAT
...FLOOOR
MEOW?
OH, SO *THIS* ISN'T THE ROLLY THING YOU WANTED?

Sue & Tai-chan

CHAPTER 25 The Hiding Place

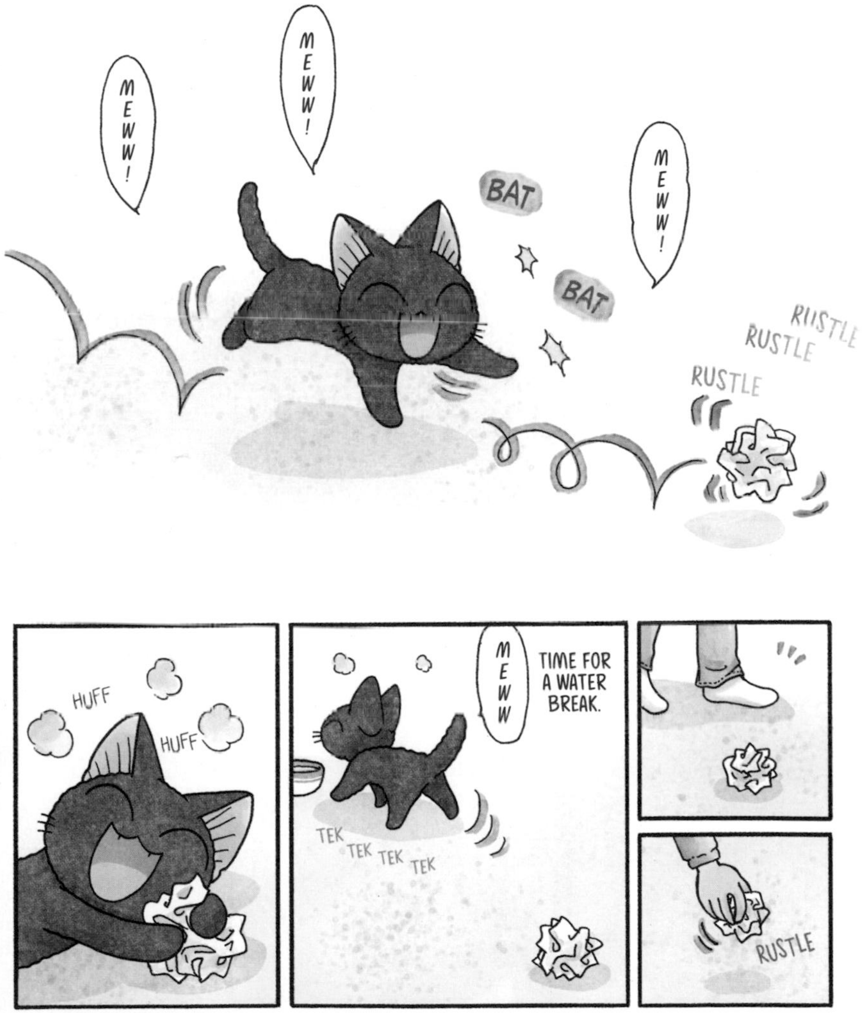
MEWW!
MEWW!
BAT
BAT
MEWW!
RUSTLE
RUSTLE
RUSTLE
HUFF
HUFF
MEWW
TIME FOR A WATER BREAK.
TEK TEK TEK TEK
RUSTLE

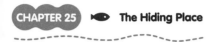

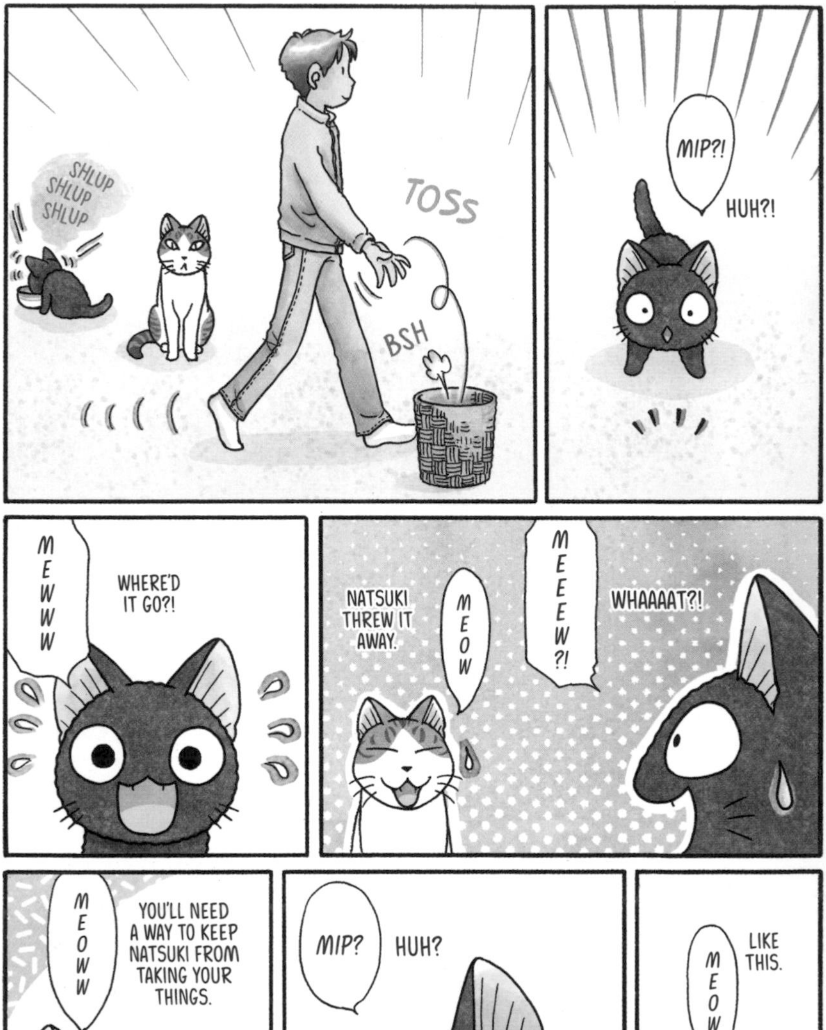
SHLUP
SHLUP
SHLUP
TOSS
BSH
MIP?!
HUH?!
MEWWW
WHERE'D IT GO?!
NATSUKI THREW IT AWAY.
MEOW
MEEEW?!
WHAAAAT?!
MEOWW
YOU'LL NEED A WAY TO KEEP NATSUKI FROM TAKING YOUR THINGS.
MIP?
HUH?
MEOW
LIKE THIS.
STEP
STEP

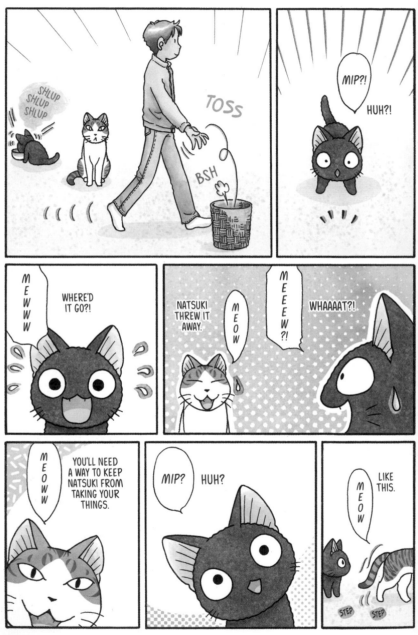

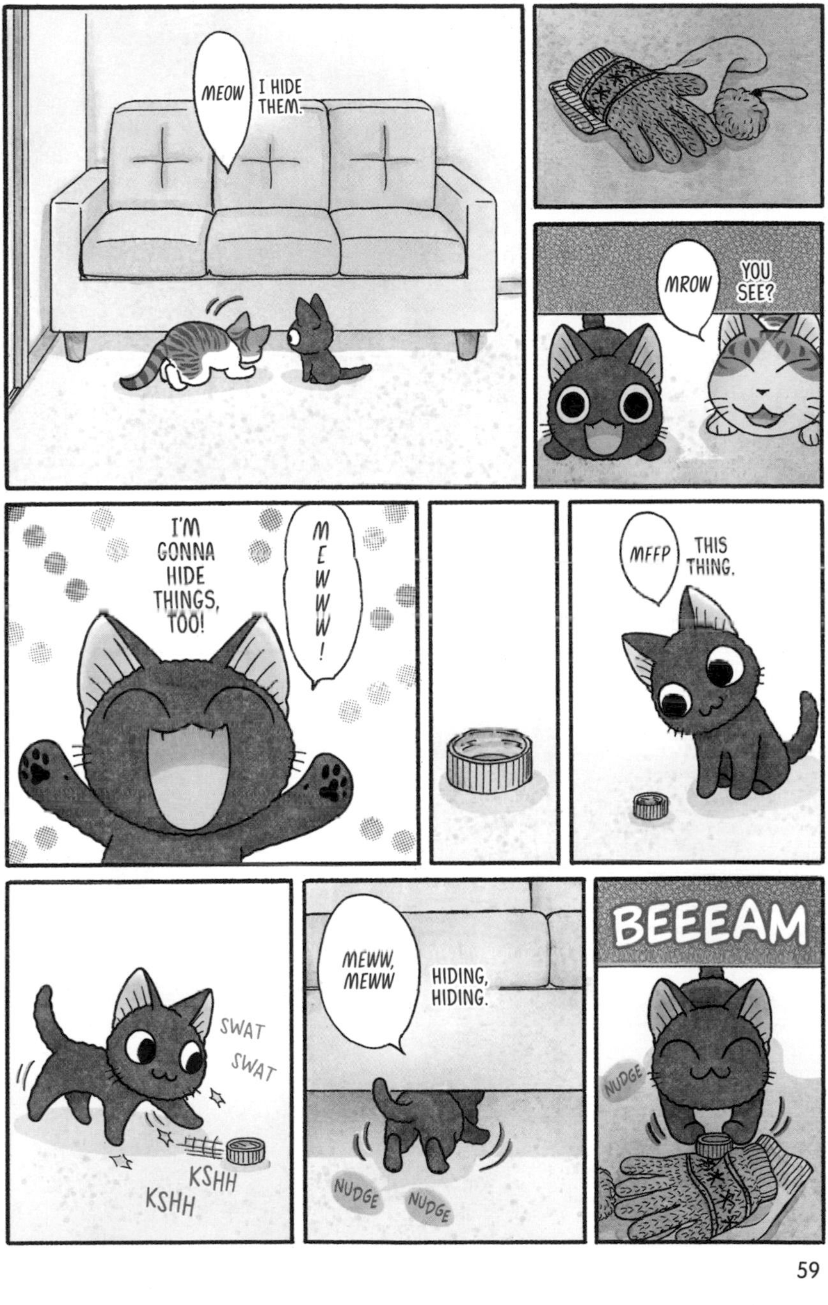
MEOW
I HIDE THEM.
MROW
YOU SEE?
I'M GONNA HIDE THINGS, TOO!
MEWWW!
MFFP
THIS THING.
SWAT
SWAT
KSHH
KSHH
MEWW, MEWW
HIDING, HIDING.
NUDGE
NUDGE
BEEEAM
NUDGE

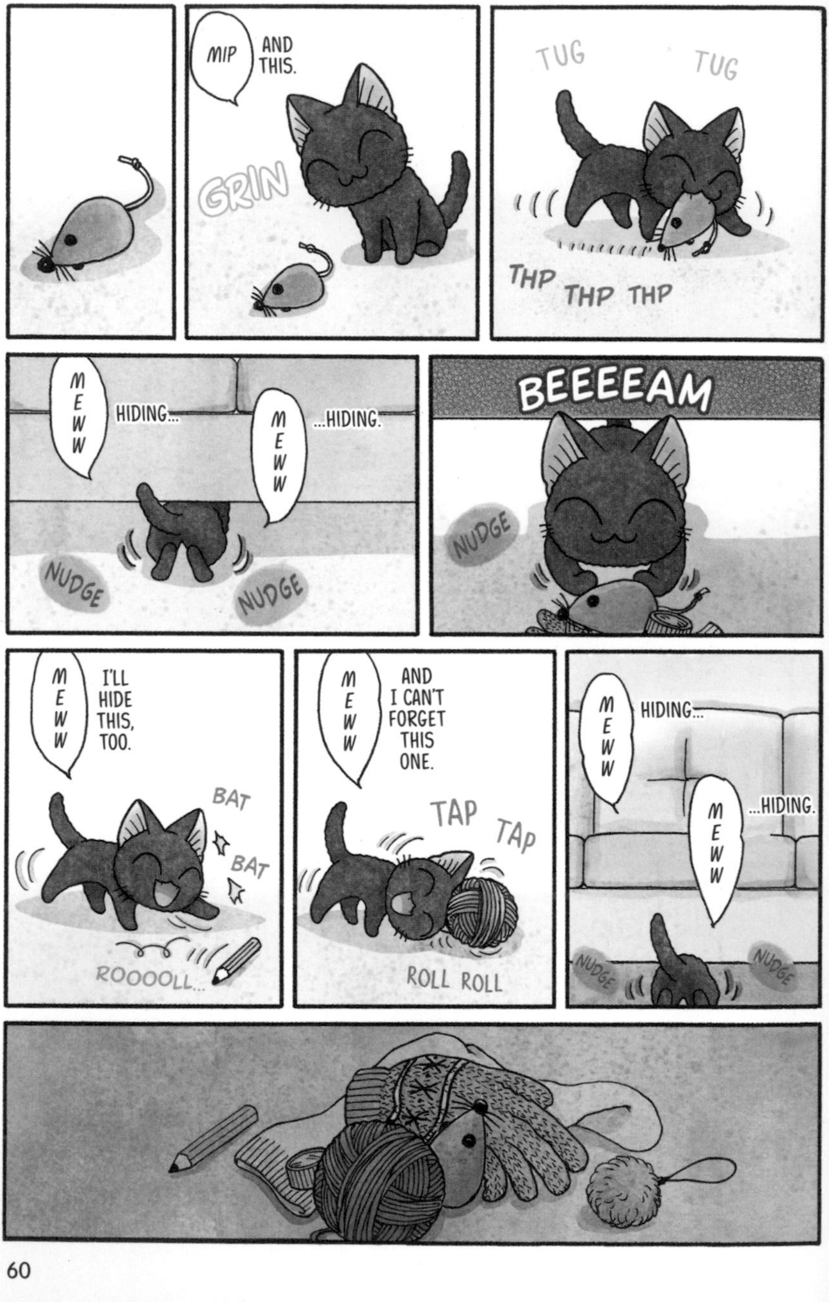
MIP
AND THIS.
GRIN
TUG
TUG
THP THP THP
MEWW
HIDING...
MEWW
...HIDING.
NUDGE
NUDGE
BEEEEAM
NUDGE
MEWW
I'LL HIDE THIS, TOO.
BAT
BAT
ROOOOLL...
MEWW
AND I CAN'T FORGET THIS ONE.
TAP
TAP
ROLL ROLL
MEWW
HIDING...
MEWW
...HIDING.
NUDGE
NUDGE

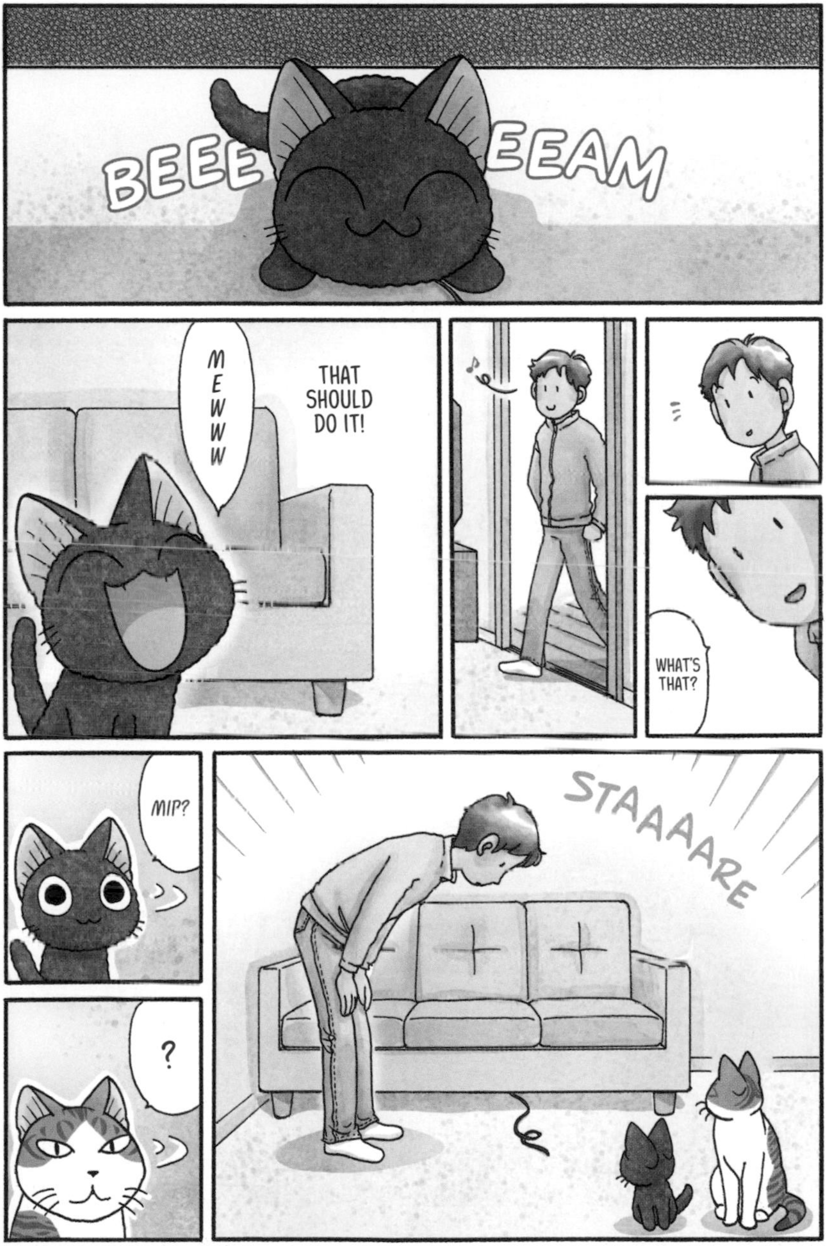
BEEEEEAM
MEWWW
THAT SHOULD DO IT!
WHAT'S THAT?
MIP?
?
STAAAARE

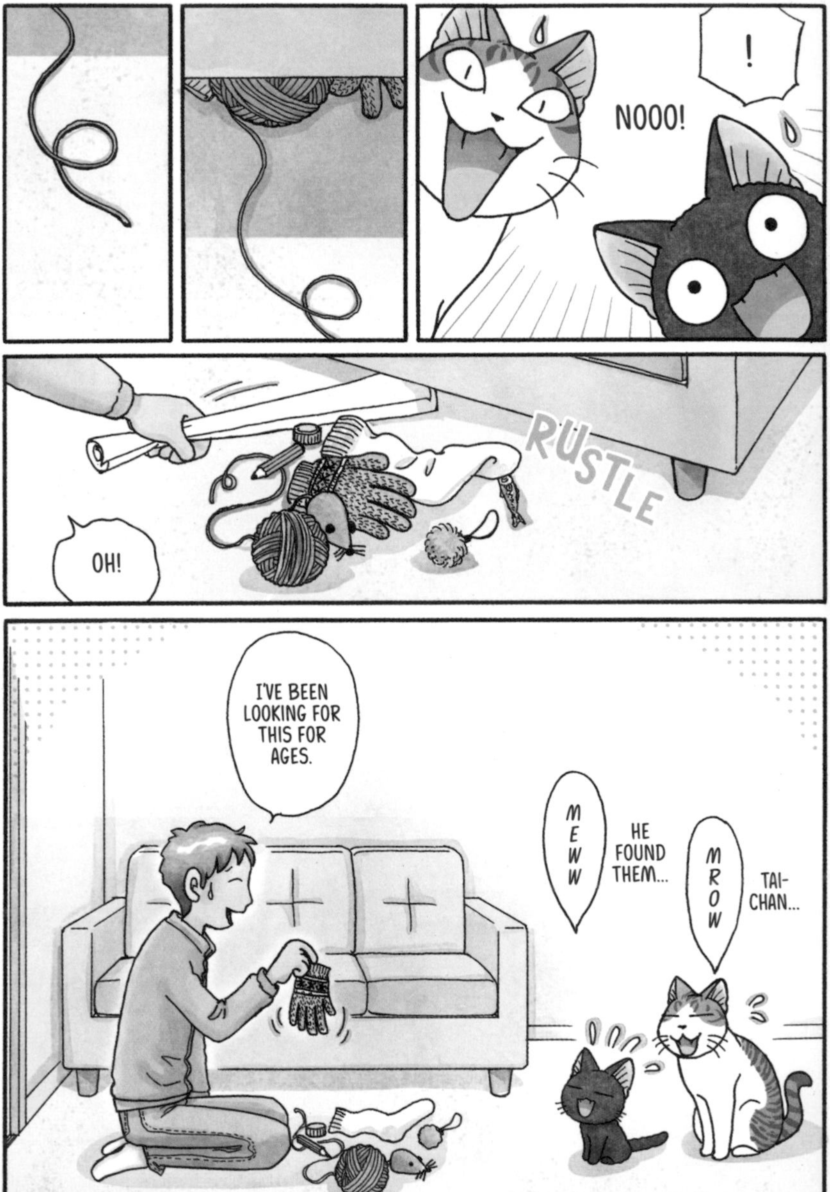
!
NOOO!
RUSTLE
OH!
I'VE BEEN LOOKING FOR THIS FOR AGES.
MEWW
HE FOUND THEM...
MROW
TAI-CHAN...

CHAPTER 26 Kitty's First Snowfall

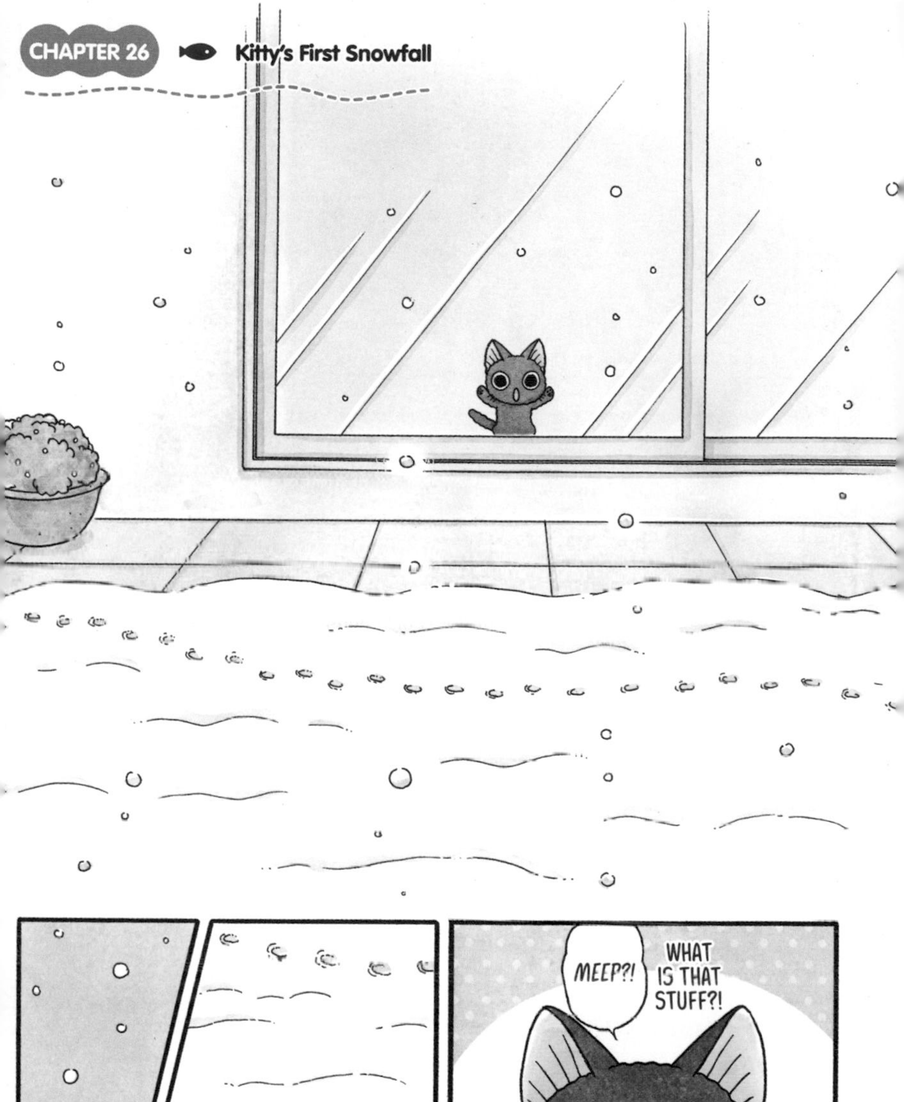
MEEP?!
WHAT IS THAT STUFF?!

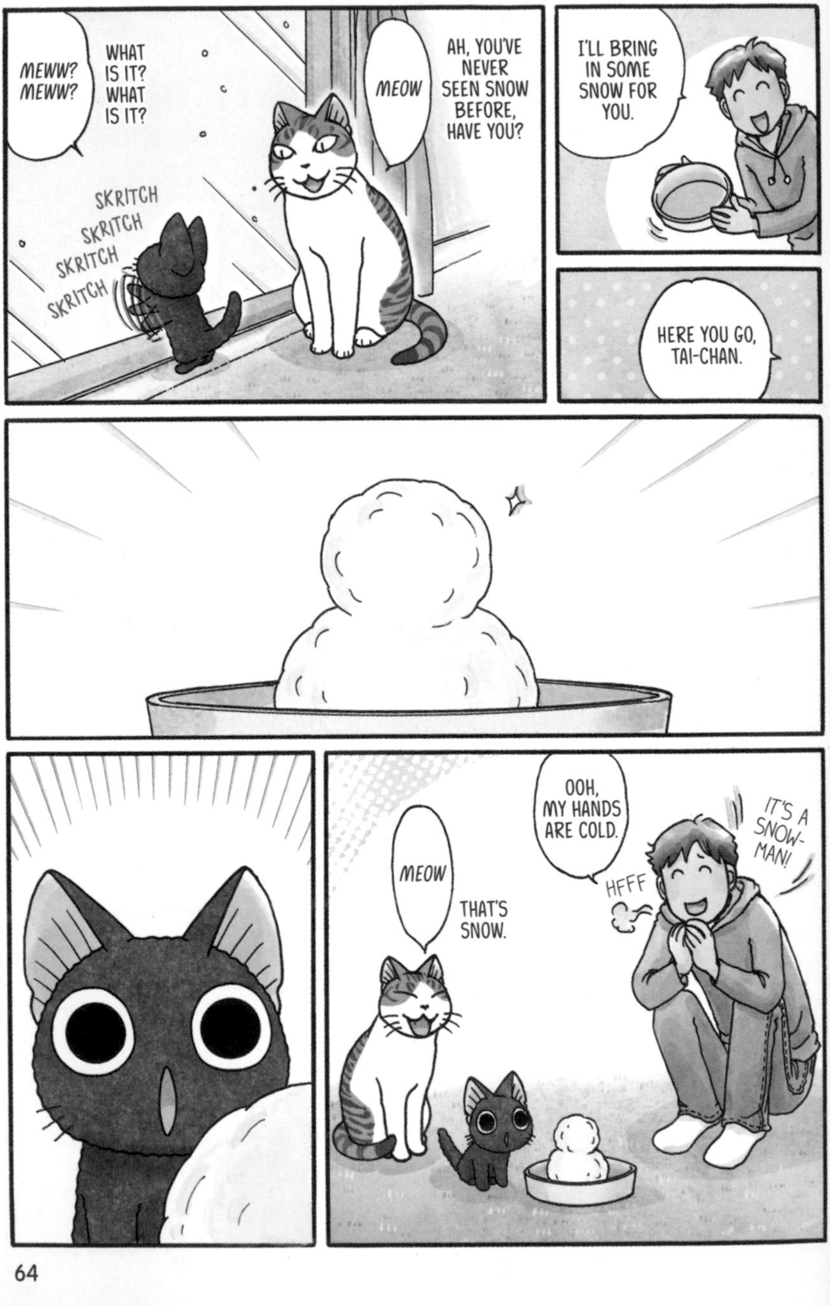
MEWW? MEWW?
WHAT IS IT? WHAT IS IT?
SKRITCH SKRITCH SKRITCH SKRITCH
MEOW
AH, YOU'VE NEVER SEEN SNOW BEFORE, HAVE YOU?
I'LL BRING IN SOME SNOW FOR YOU.
HERE YOU GO, TAI-CHAN.
OOH, MY HANDS ARE COLD.
IT'S A SNOW-MAN!
HFFF
MEOW
THAT'S SNOW.

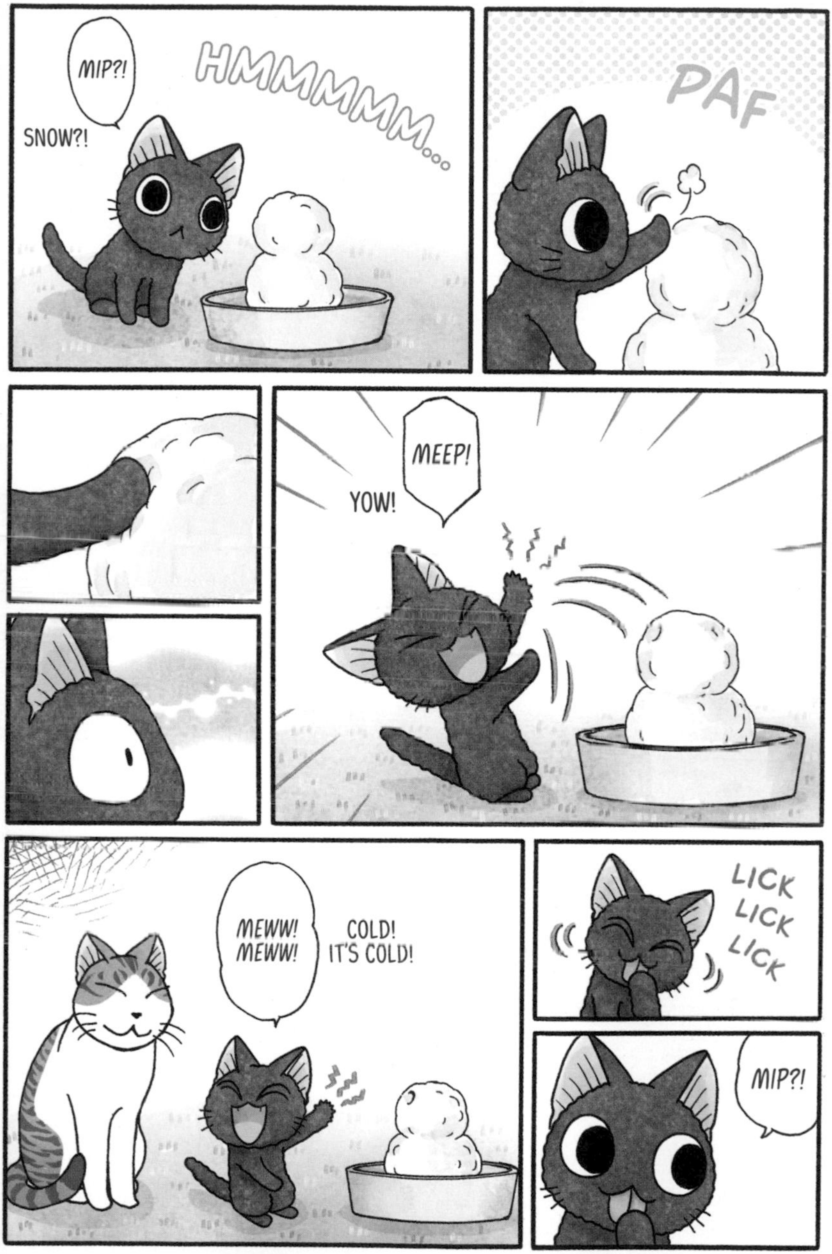
MIP?!
SNOW?!
HMMMMMM...
PAF
MEEP!
YOW!
MEWW! MEWW!
COLD! IT'S COLD!
LICK LICK LICK
MIP?!

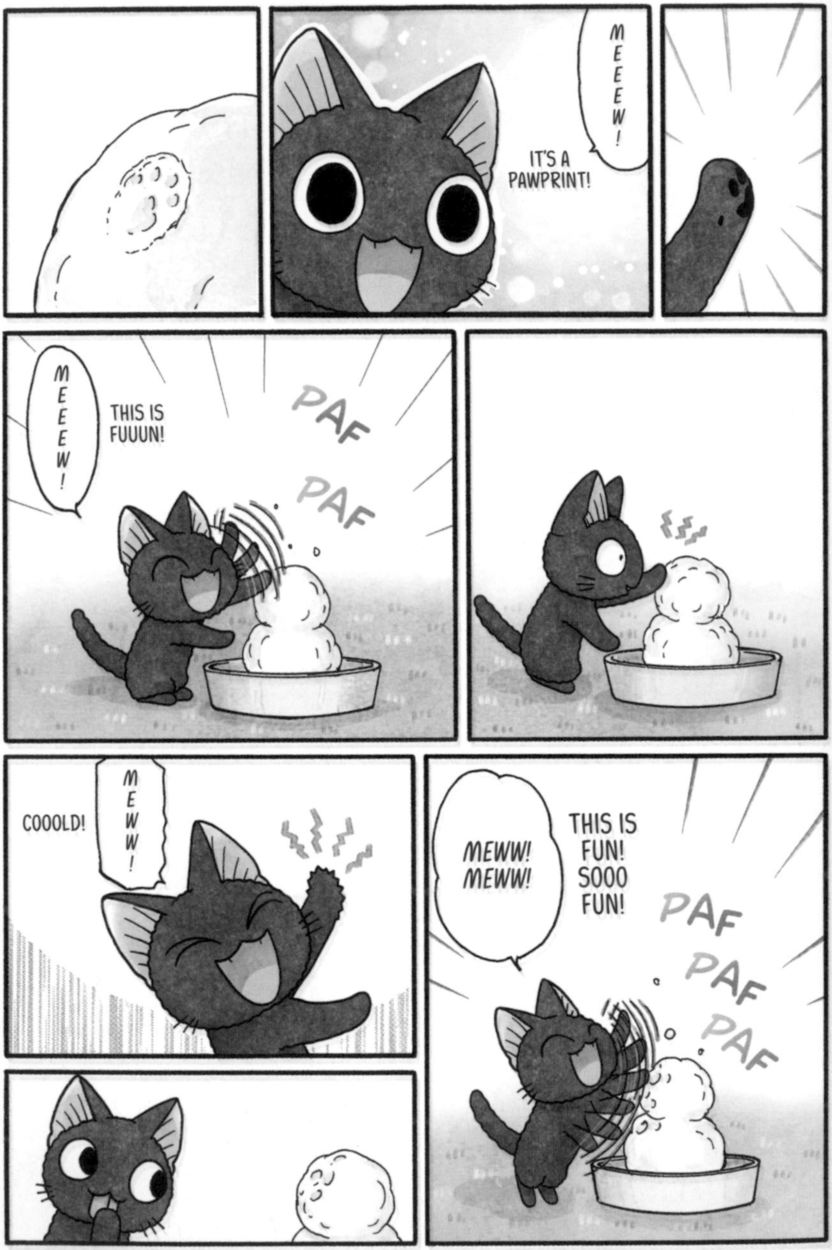
MEEEEW!
IT'S A PAWPRINT!
MEEEEW!
THIS IS FUUUN!
PAF
PAF
MEWW!
COOOLD!
MEWW! MEWW!
THIS IS FUN! SOOO FUN!
PAF
PAF
PAF

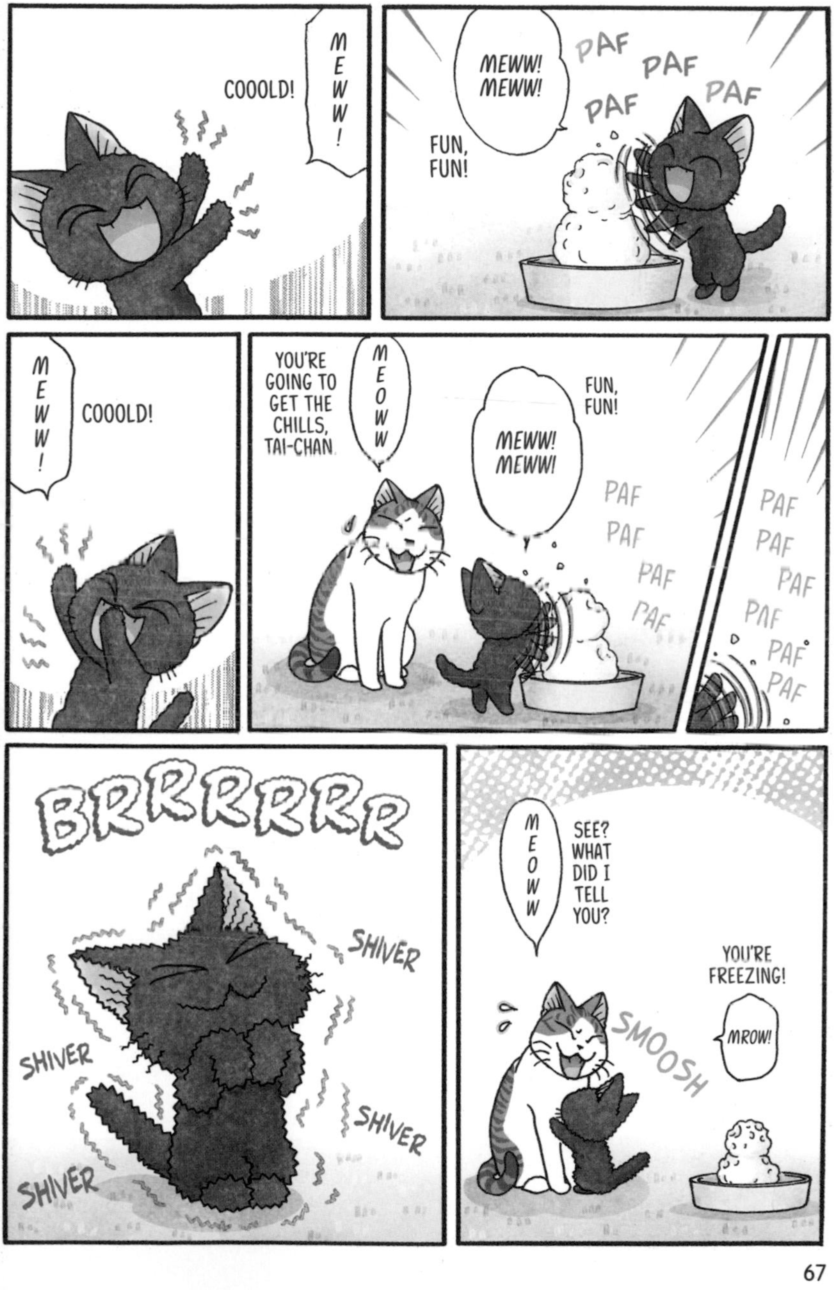
MEWW!
COOOLD!
MEWW! MEWW!
FUN, FUN!
PAF PAF PAF PAF
MEWW!
COOOLD!
YOU'RE GOING TO GET THE CHILLS, TAI-CHAN.
MEOWW
FUN, FUN!
MEWW! MEWW!
PAF PAF PAF PAF
PAF PAF PAF PAF PAF PAF
BRRRRRR
SHIVER
SHIVER
SHIVER
SHIVER
MEOWW
SEE? WHAT DID I TELL YOU?
YOU'RE FREEZING!
MROW!
SMOOSH

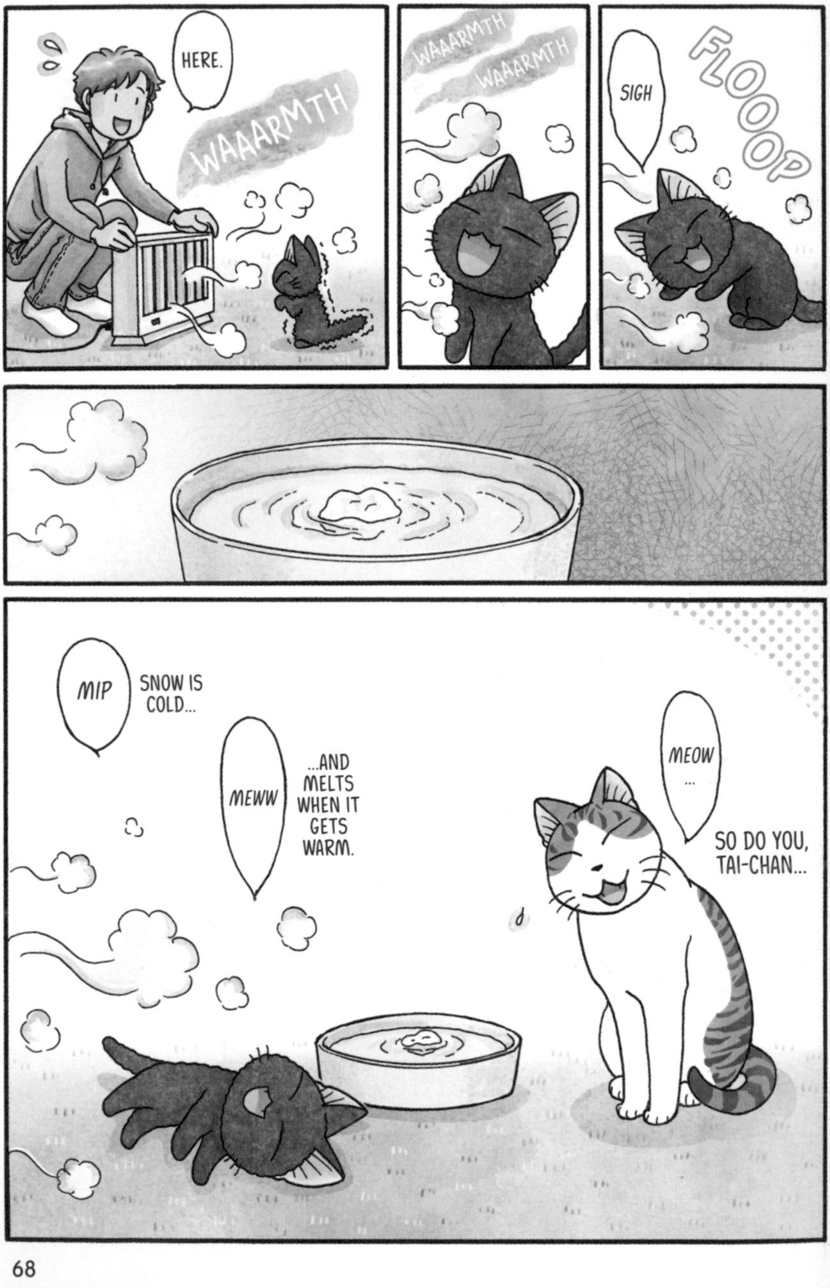
HERE.
WAAARMTH
WAAARMTH
WAAARMTH
SIGH
FLOOP
MIP
SNOW IS COLD...
MEWW
...AND MELTS WHEN IT GETS WARM.
MEOW ...
SO DO YOU, TAI-CHAN...

CHAPTER 27 Only Those Two Know

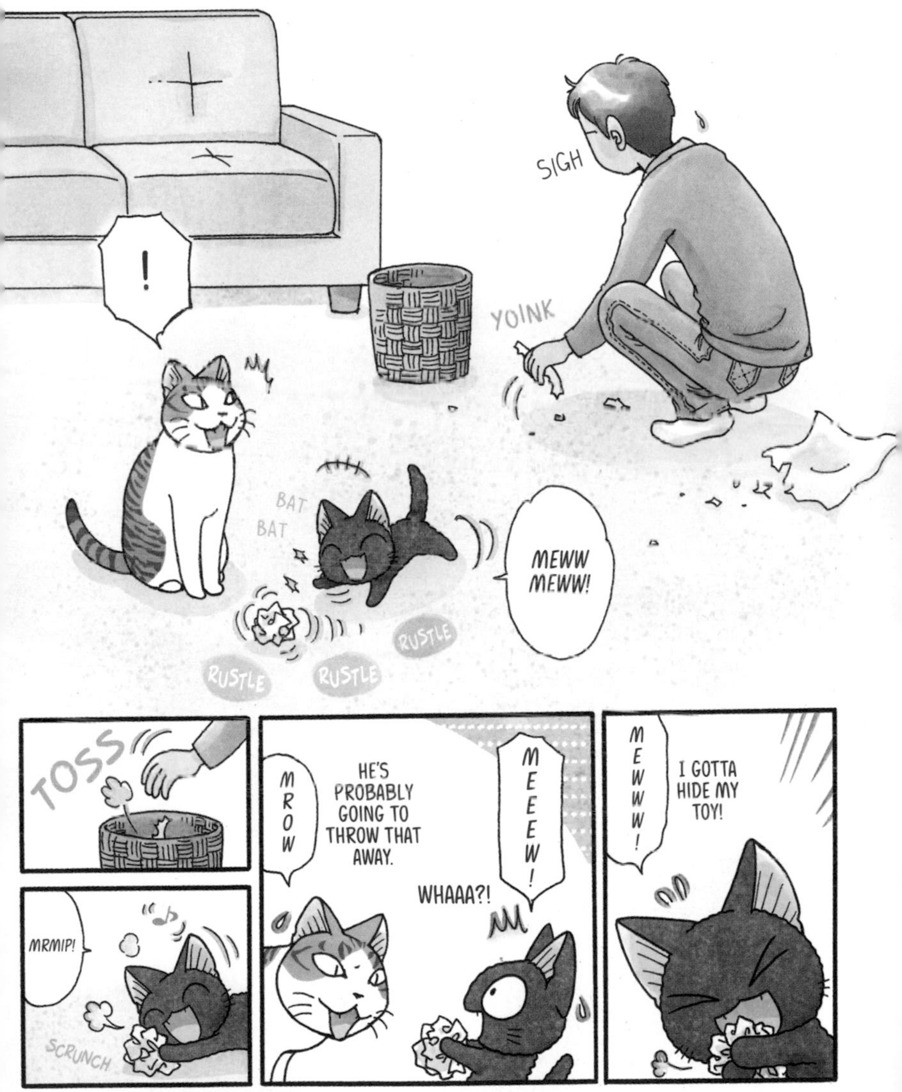
!
SIGH
YOINK
BAT
BAT
MEWW MEWW!
RUSTLE
RUSTLE
RUSTLE
TOSS
MRMIP!
SCRUNCH
MROW
HE'S PROBABLY GOING TO THROW THAT AWAY.
MEEEEW!
WHAAA?!
MEWWW!
I GOTTA HIDE MY TOY!

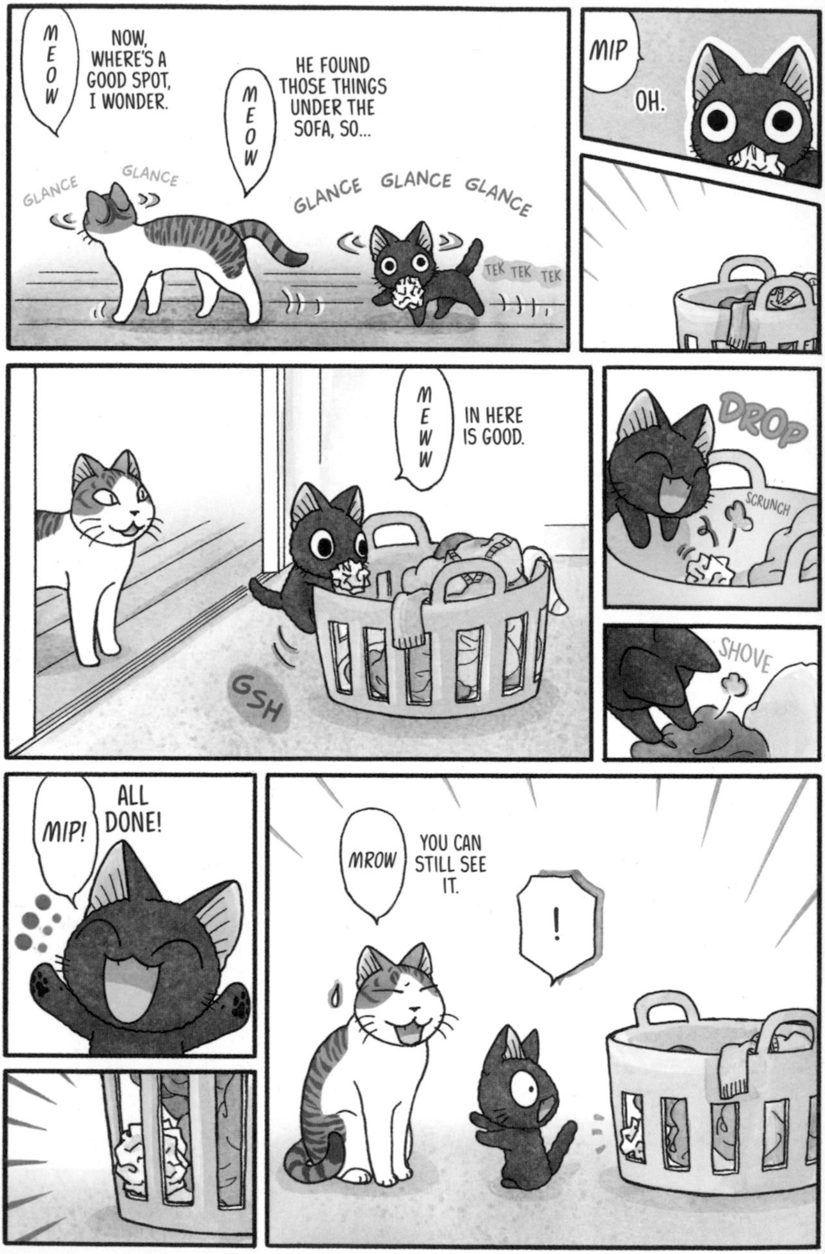
MEOW
NOW, WHERE'S A GOOD SPOT, I WONDER.
MEOW
HE FOUND THOSE THINGS UNDER THE SOFA, SO...
GLANCE
GLANCE
GLANCE GLANCE GLANCE
TEK TEK TEK
MIP
OH.
MEWW
IN HERE IS GOOD.
GSH
DROP
SCRUNCH
SHOVE
MIP!
ALL DONE!
MROW
YOU CAN STILL SEE IT.
!

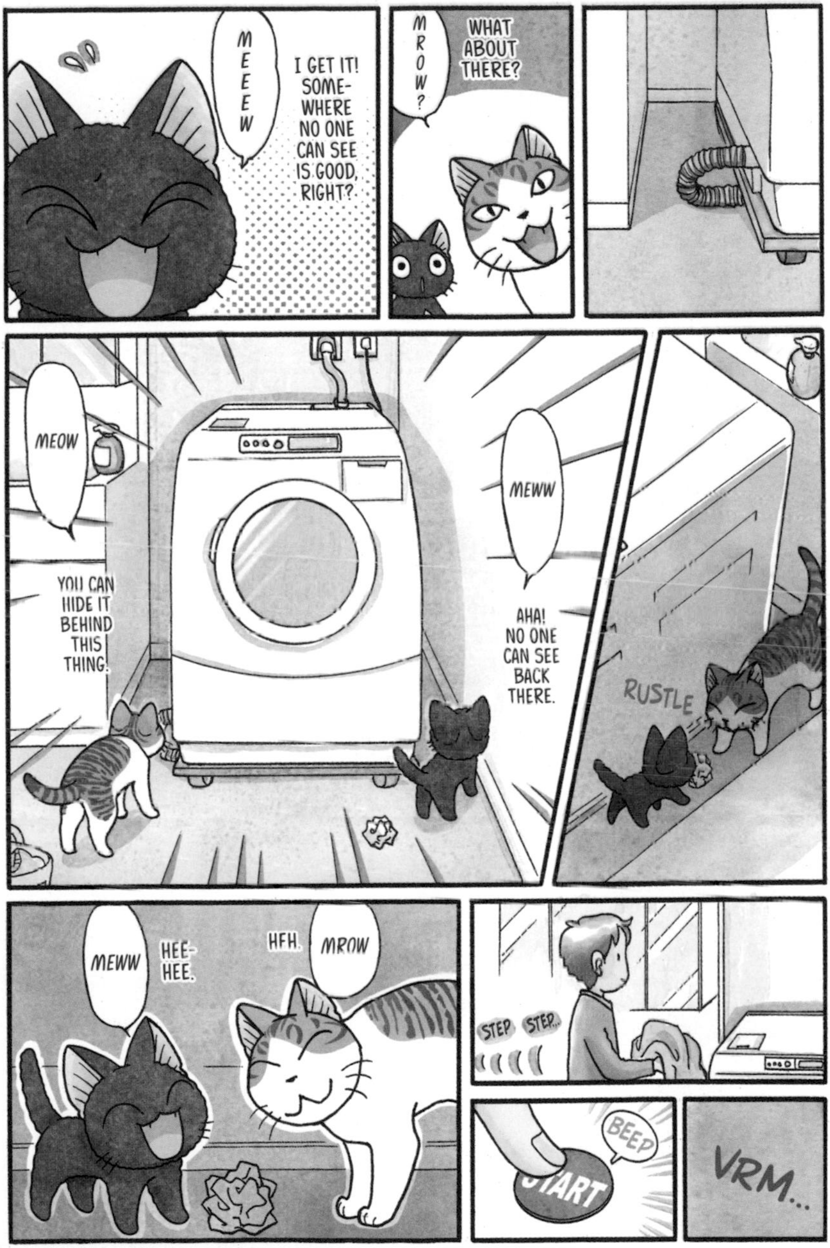
MEEEW
I GET IT! SOME-WHERE NO ONE CAN SEE IS GOOD, RIGHT?
MROW?
WHAT ABOUT THERE?
MEOW
YOU CAN HIDE IT BEHIND THIS THING!
MEWW
AHA! NO ONE CAN SEE BACK THERE.
RUSTLE
MEWW
HEE-HEE.
HEH.
MROW
STEP STEP...
START
BEEP
VRM...

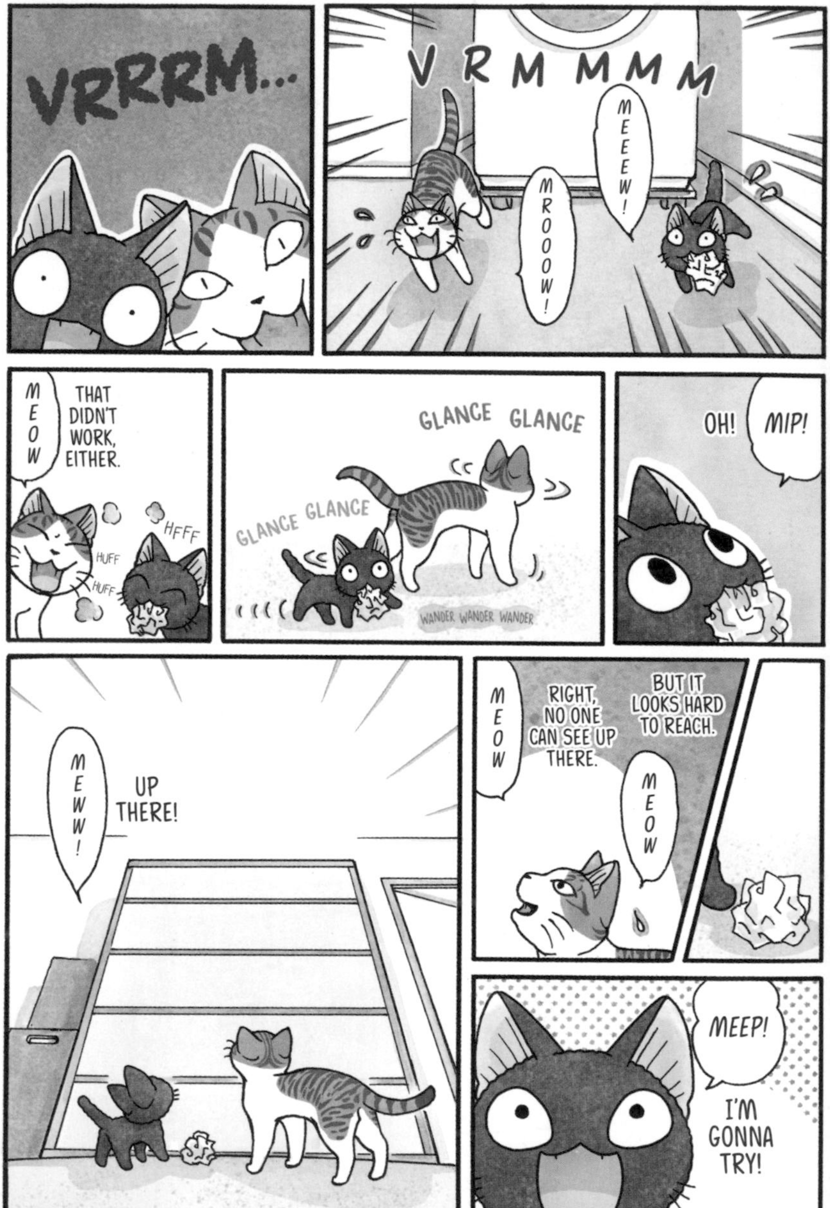
VRRRM...
V R M M M M
MEEEW!
MROOOOW!
MEOW
THAT DIDN'T WORK, EITHER.
HFFF
HUFF
HUFF
GLANCE GLANCE
GLANCE GLANCE
WANDER WANDER WANDER
OH!
MIP!
MEWW!
UP THERE!
MEOW
RIGHT, NO ONE CAN SEE UP THERE.
BUT IT LOOKS HARD TO REACH.
MEOW
MEEP!
I'M GONNA TRY!

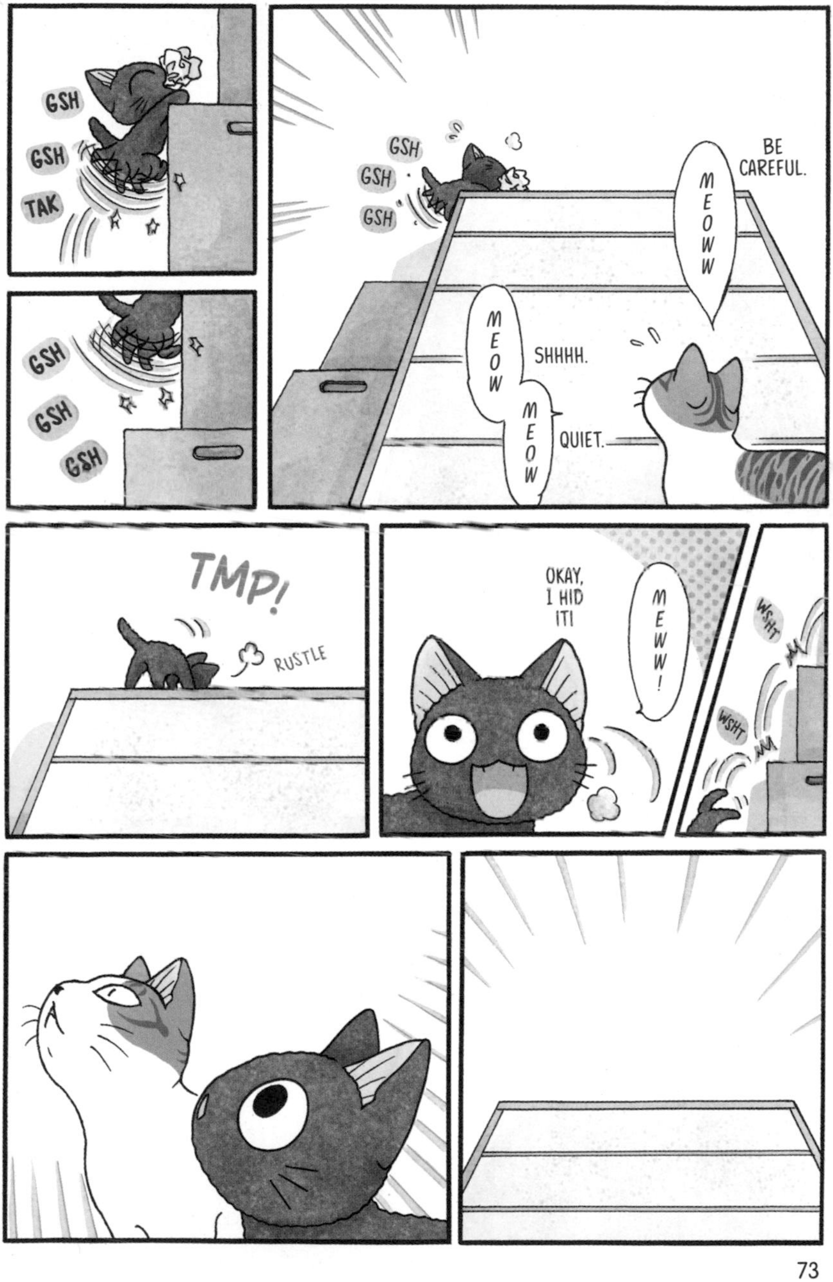
GSH
GSH
TAK
GSH
GSH
GSH
GSH
GSH
GSH
MEOWW
BE CAREFUL.
MEOW
SHHHH.
MEOW
QUIET.
TMP!
RUSTLE
MEWW!
OKAY, I HID IT!
WSHT
WSHT

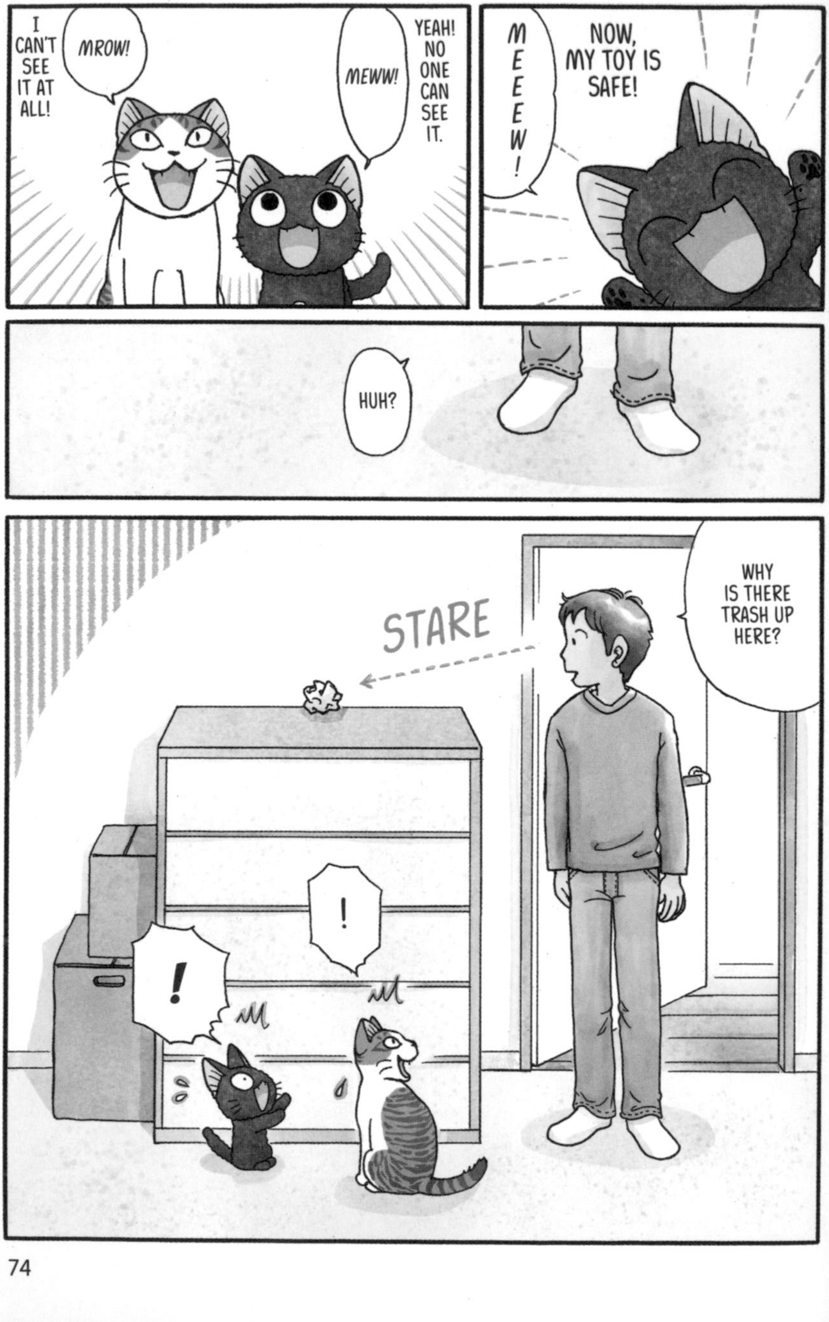
I CAN'T SEE IT AT ALL!
MROW!
MEWW!
YEAH! NO ONE CAN SEE IT.
MEEEW!
NOW, MY TOY IS SAFE!
HUH?
STARE
WHY IS THERE TRASH UP HERE?
!
!

CHAPTER 28 When Natsuki Isn't Home...

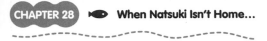

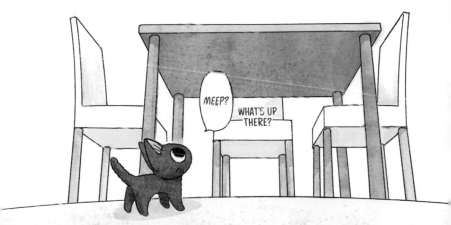

MEEP?
WHAT'S UP THERE?
!
WSHT
WSHT
MEOWW
WE'RE NOT SUPPOSED TO CLIMB ON THAT, TAI-CHAN.

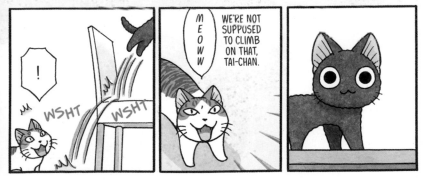

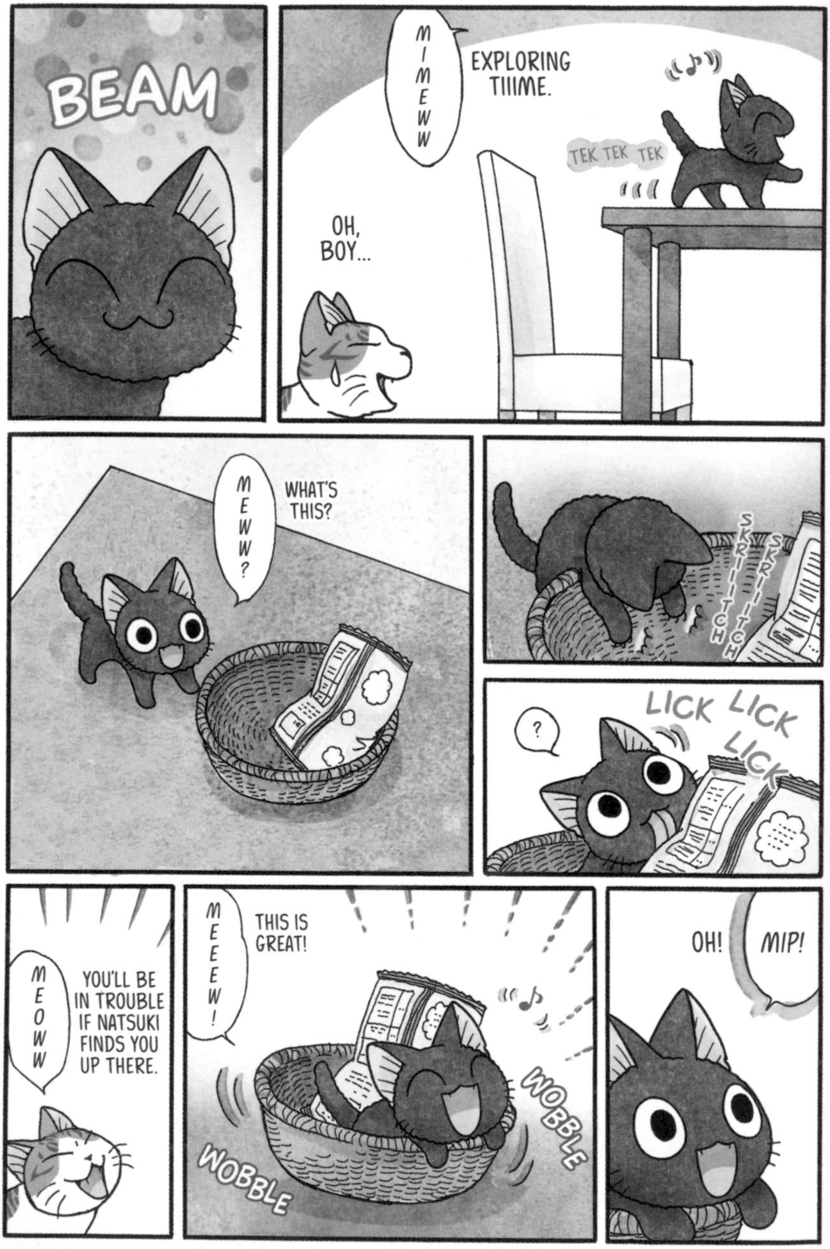
BEAM
MIMEWW
EXPLORING TIIIME.
TEK TEK TEK
OH, BOY...
MEWW?
WHAT'S THIS?
SKRIIITCH
SKRIIITCH
?
LICK LICK
LICK
MEOWW
YOU'LL BE IN TROUBLE IF NATSUKI FINDS YOU UP THERE.
MEEEEW!
THIS IS GREAT!
WOBBLE
WOBBLE
OH!
MIP!

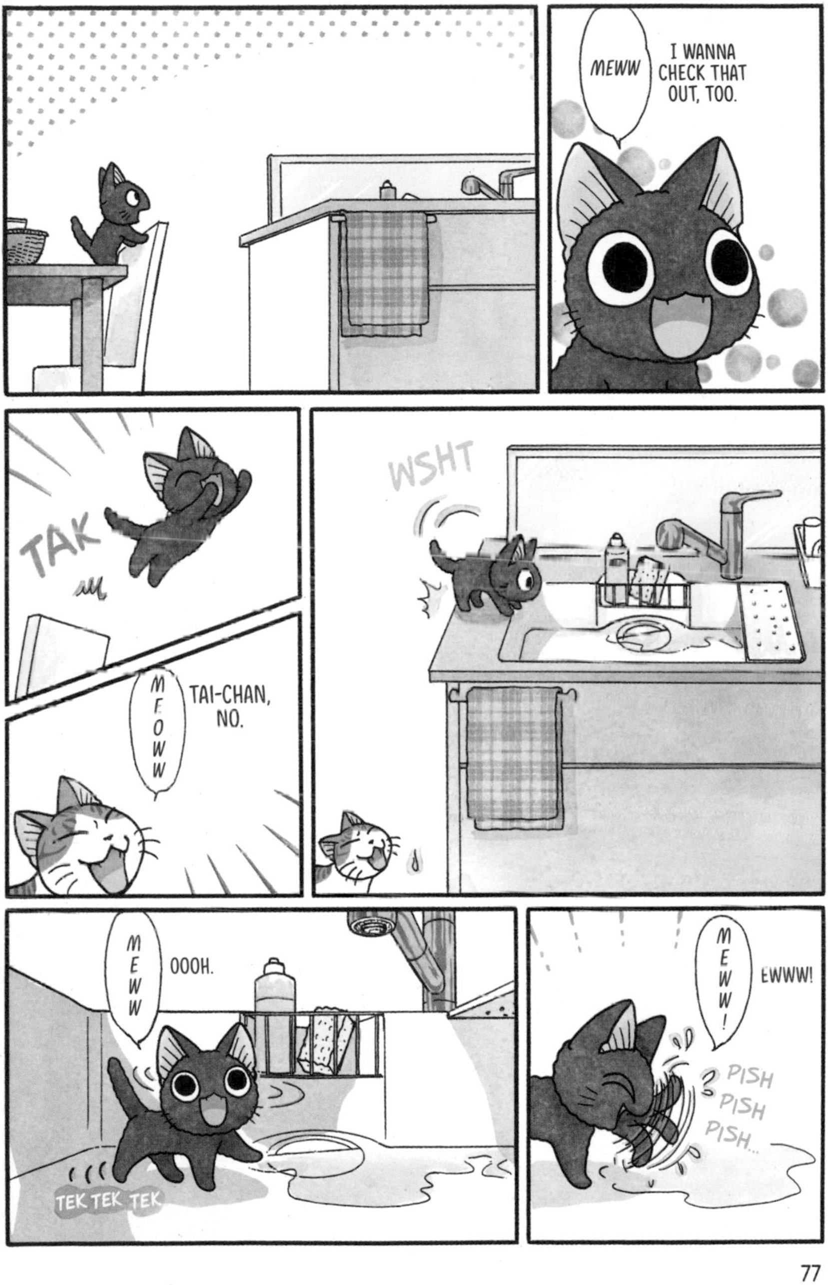
MEWW
I WANNA CHECK THAT OUT, TOO.
TAK
WSHT
MEOWW
TAI-CHAN, NO.
MEWW
OOOH.
TEK TEK TEK
MEWW!
EWWW!
PISH
PISH
PISH...

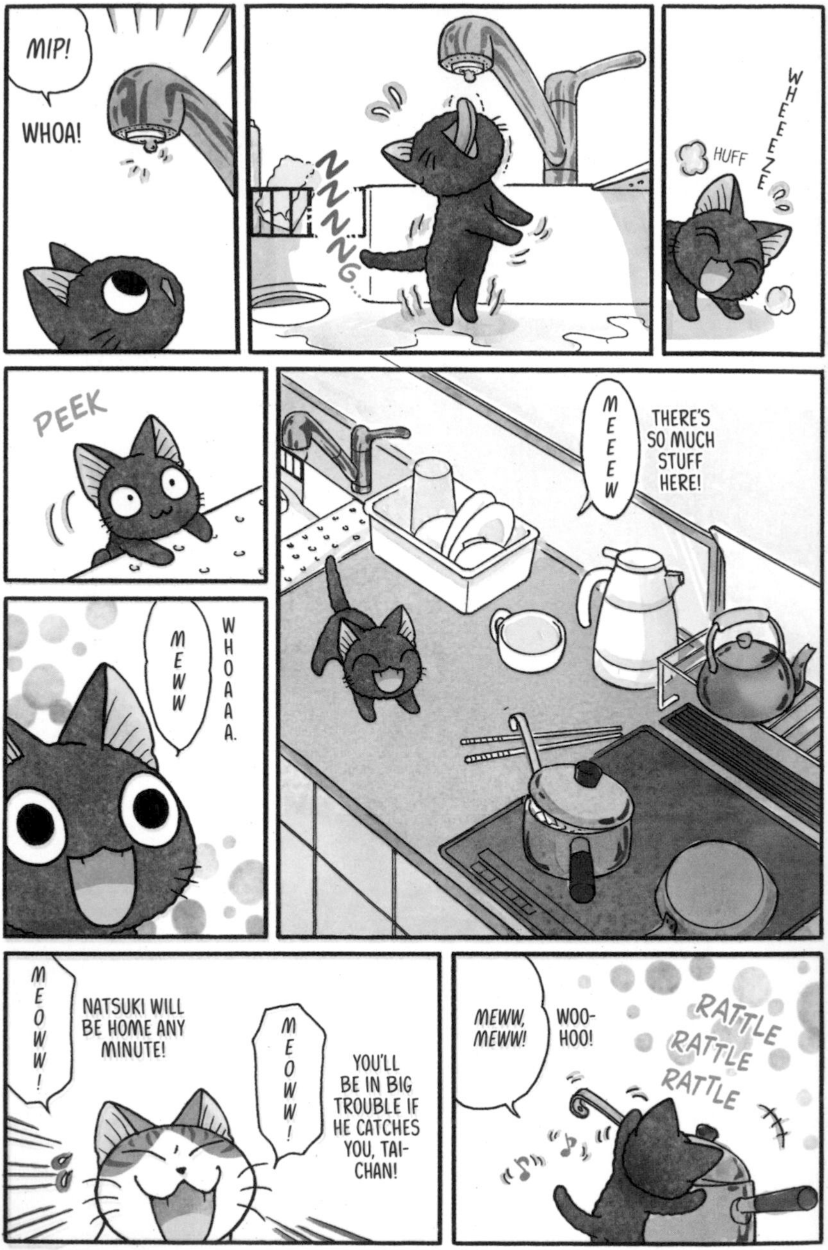
MIP!
WHOA!
ZZZZNG
HUFF
WHEEEEZE
PEEK
MEWW
WHOAAAA.
MEEEEW
THERE'S SO MUCH STUFF HERE!
MEOWW!
NATSUKI WILL BE HOME ANY MINUTE!
MEOWW!
YOU'LL BE IN BIG TROUBLE IF HE CATCHES YOU, TAI-CHAN!
MEWW, MEWW!
WOO-HOO!
RATTLE RATTLE RATTLE

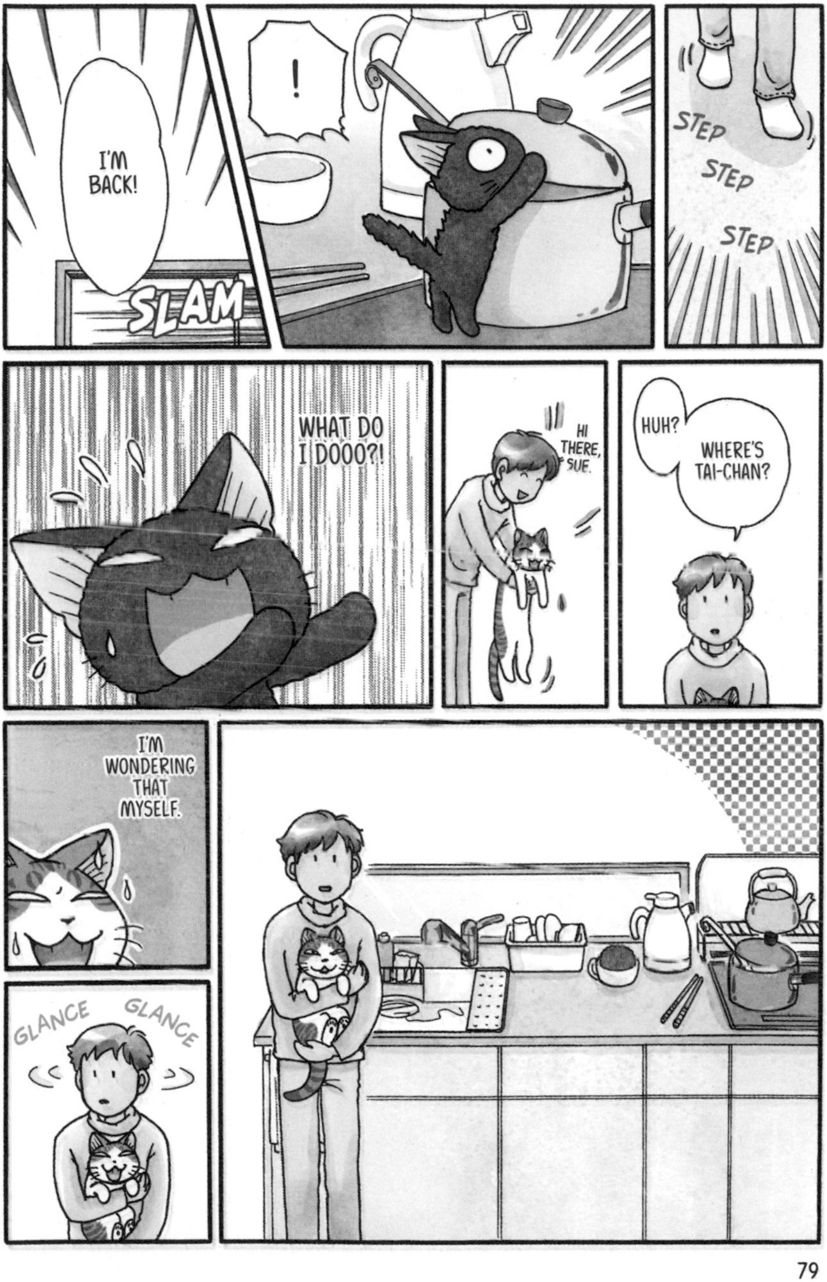
I'M BACK!
SLAM
!
STEP
STEP
STEP
WHAT DO I DOOO?!
HI THERE, SUE.
HUH?
WHERE'S TAI-CHAN?
I'M WONDERING THAT MYSELF.
GLANCE
GLANCE

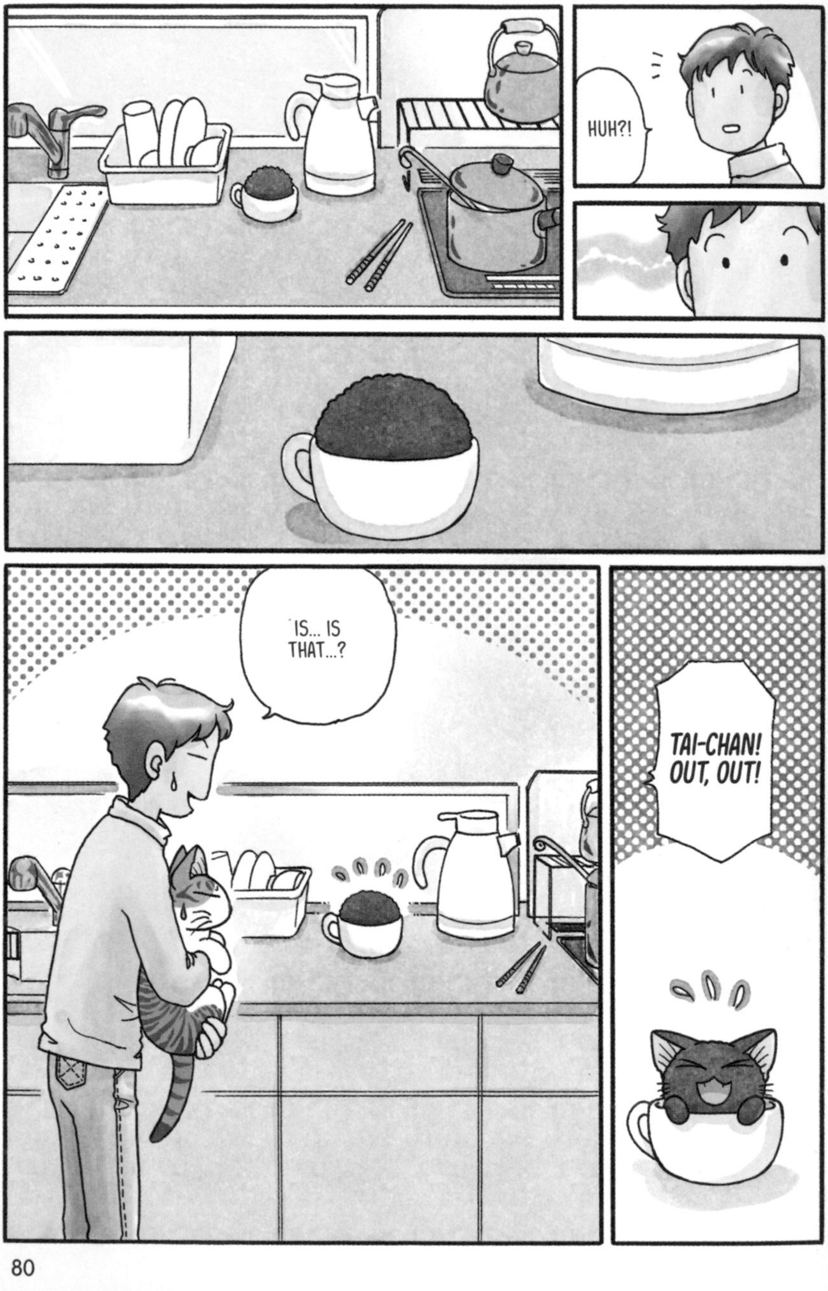
HUH?!
IS... IS THAT...?
TAI-CHAN! OUT, OUT!

Sue & Tai-chan

CHAPTER 29 Whose Lap Is It?

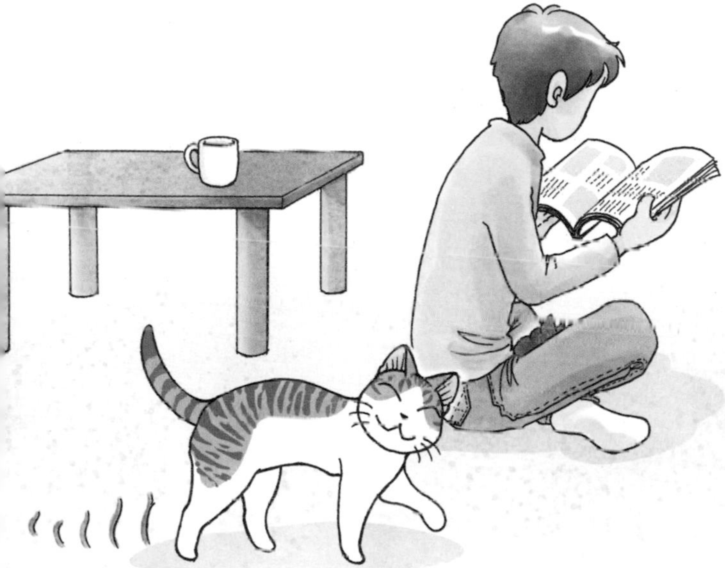

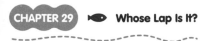

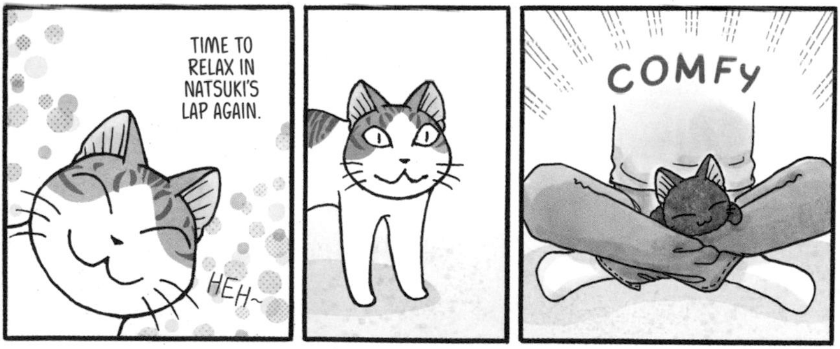
TIME TO RELAX IN NATSUKI'S LAP AGAIN.
HEH~
COMFY

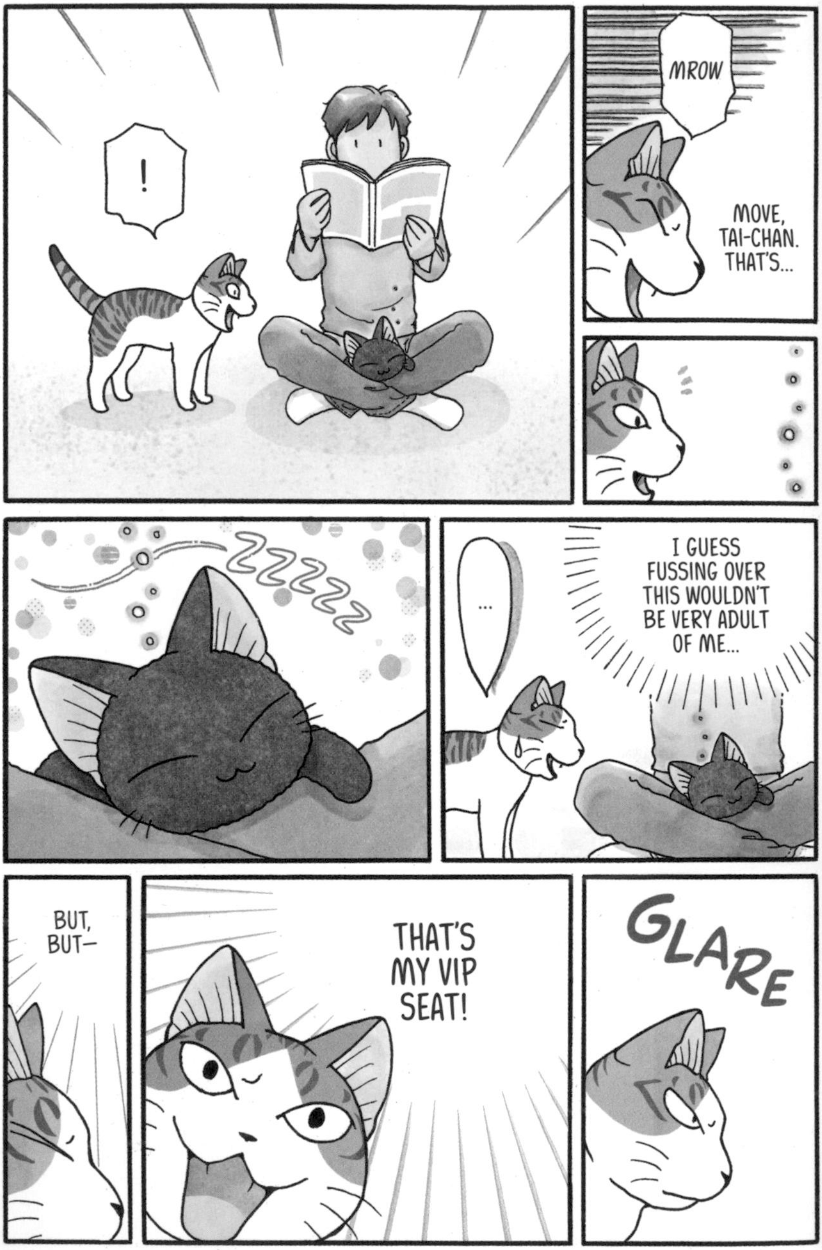
!
MROW
MOVE, TAI-CHAN. THAT'S...
ZZZZZZ
...
I GUESS FUSSING OVER THIS WOULDN'T BE VERY ADULT OF ME...
BUT, BUT—
THAT'S MY VIP SEAT!
GLARE

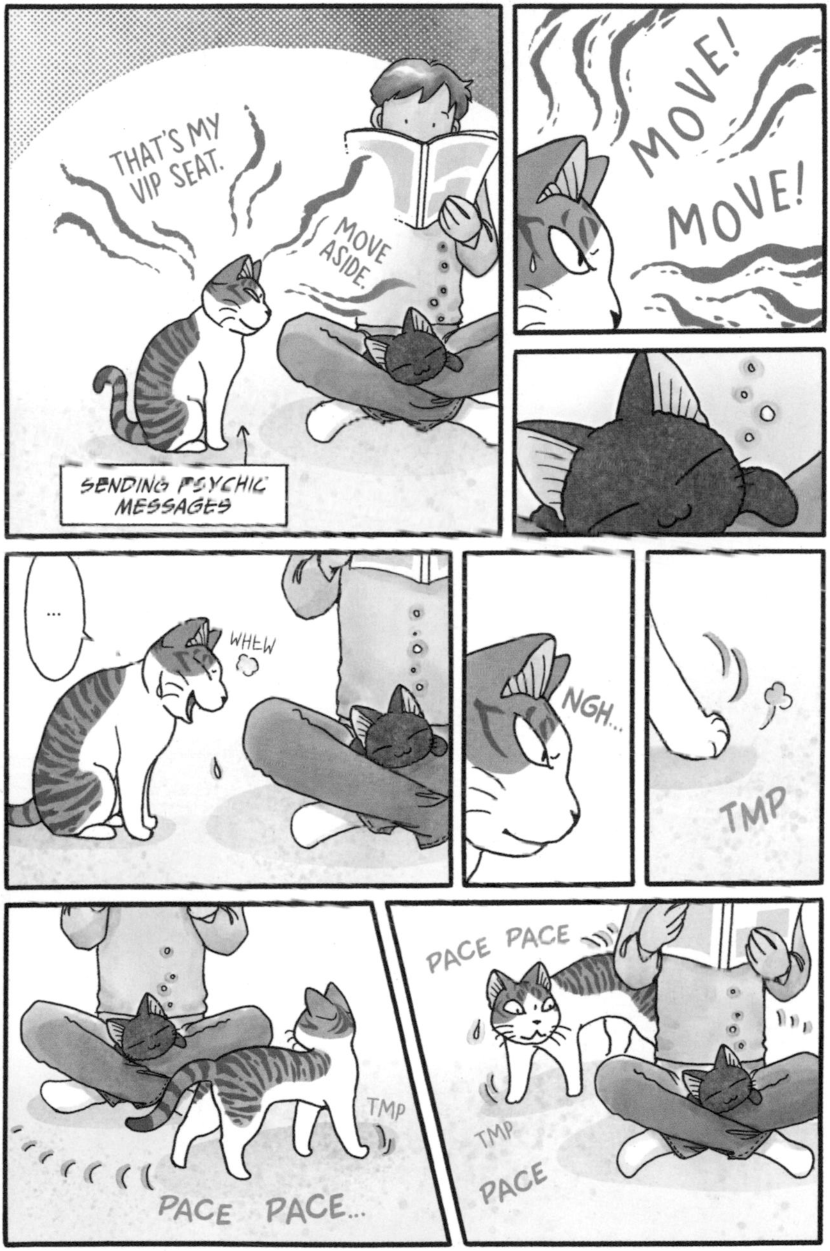
THAT'S MY VIP SEAT.
MOVE ASIDE.
SENDING PSYCHIC MESSAGES
MOVE!
MOVE!
...
WHEW
NGH...
TMP
TMP
PACE PACE...
PACE PACE
TMP
PACE

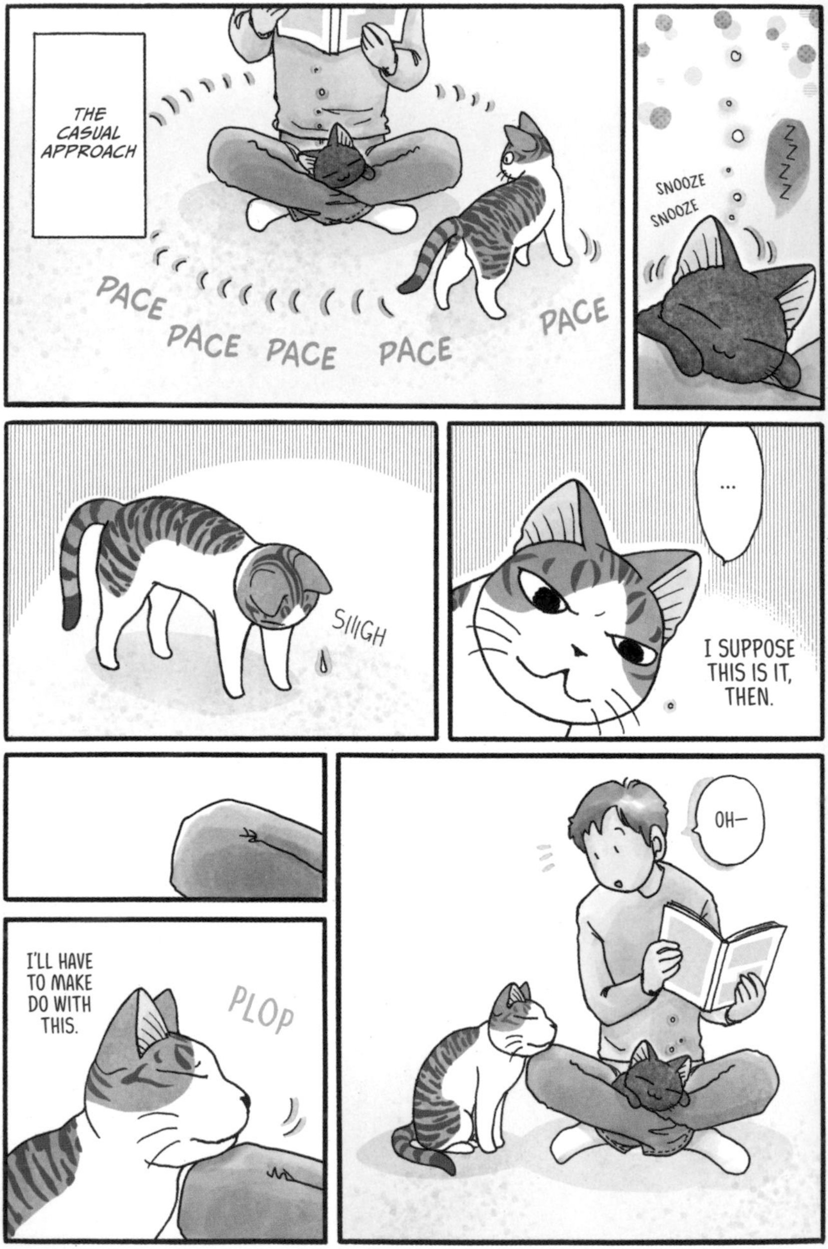
THE CASUAL APPROACH
PACE
PACE
PACE
PACE
PACE
SNOOZE
SNOOZE
ZZZZ
SIIIGH
...
I SUPPOSE THIS IS IT, THEN.
I'LL HAVE TO MAKE DO WITH THIS.
PLOP
OH—

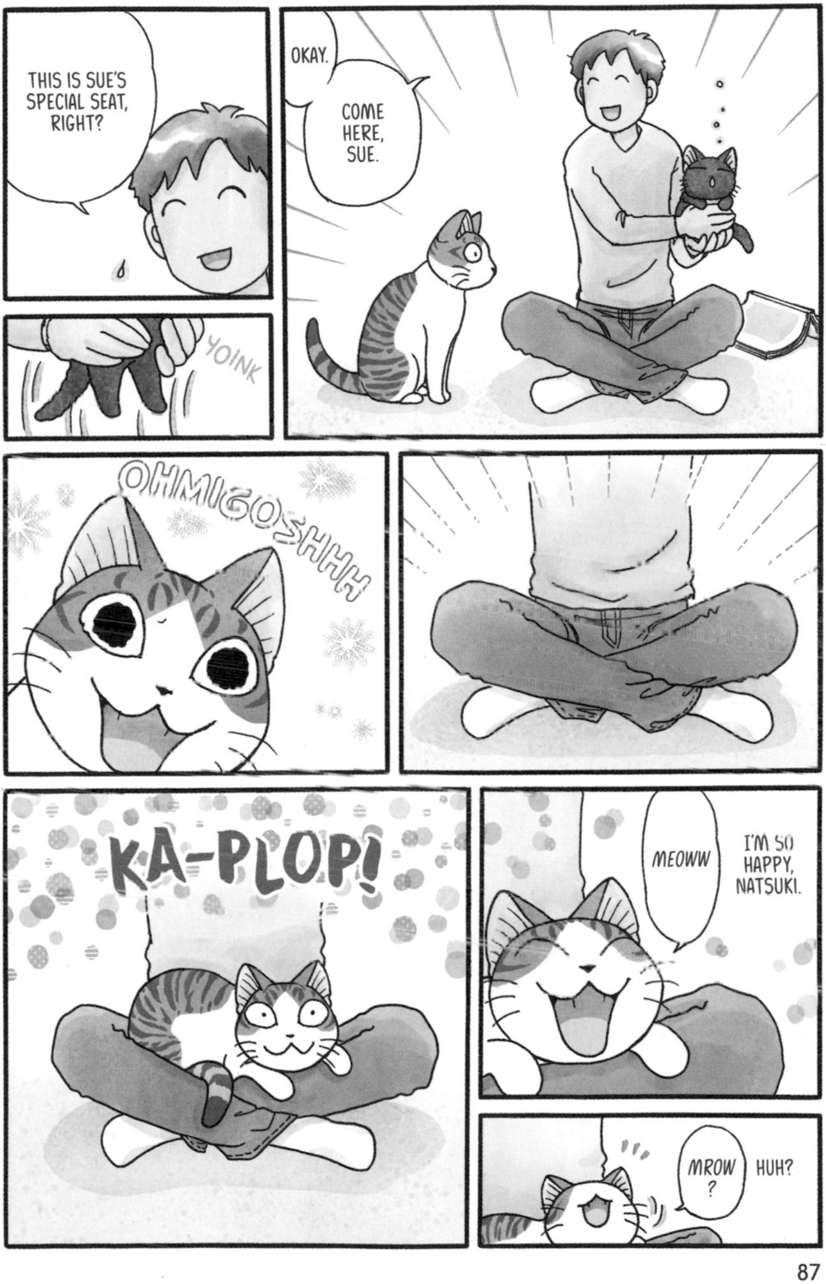

THIS IS SUE'S SPECIAL SEAT, RIGHT?
YOINK
OKAY.
COME HERE, SUE.
OHMIGOSHHH
KA-PLOP!
MEOWW
I'M SO HAPPY, NATSUKI.
MROW ?
HUH?

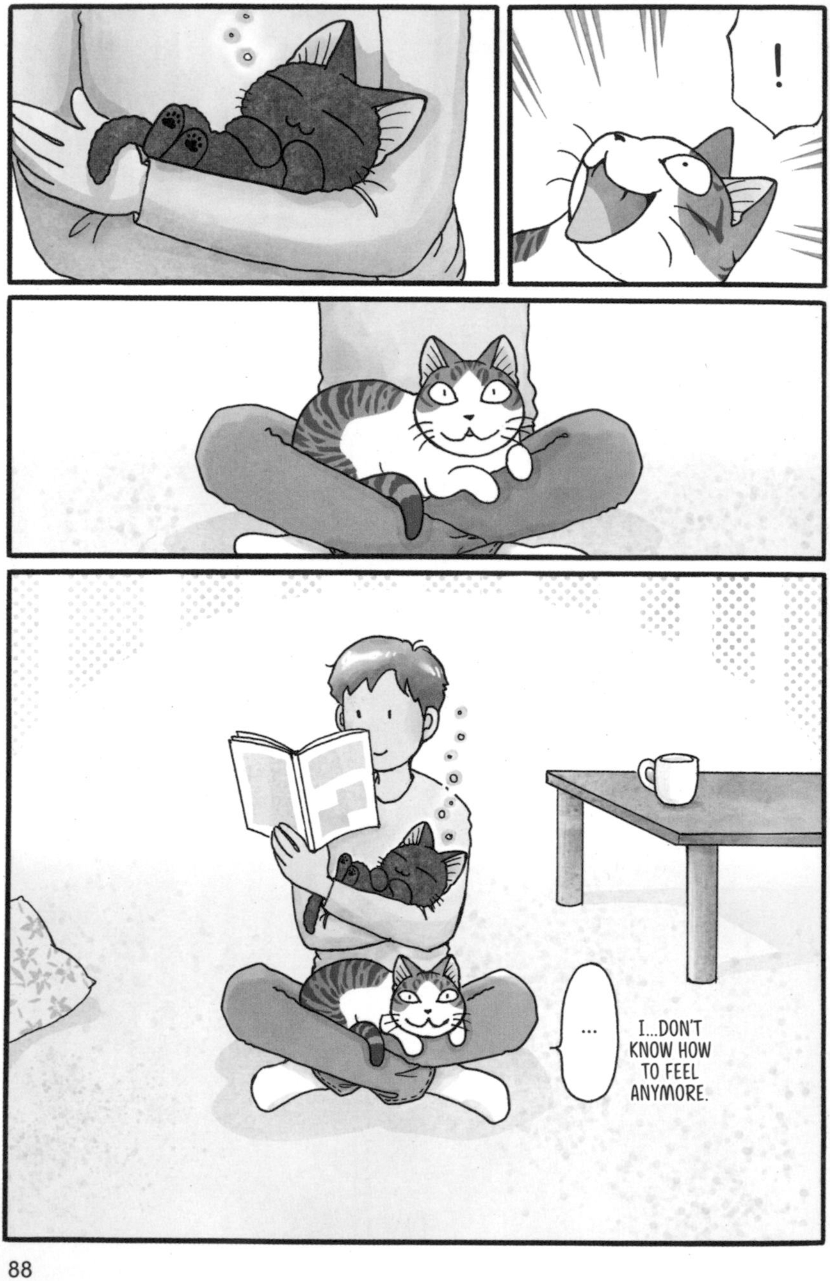
!
...
I...DON'T KNOW HOW TO FEEL ANYMORE.

CHAPTER 30 Which One Is Which?!

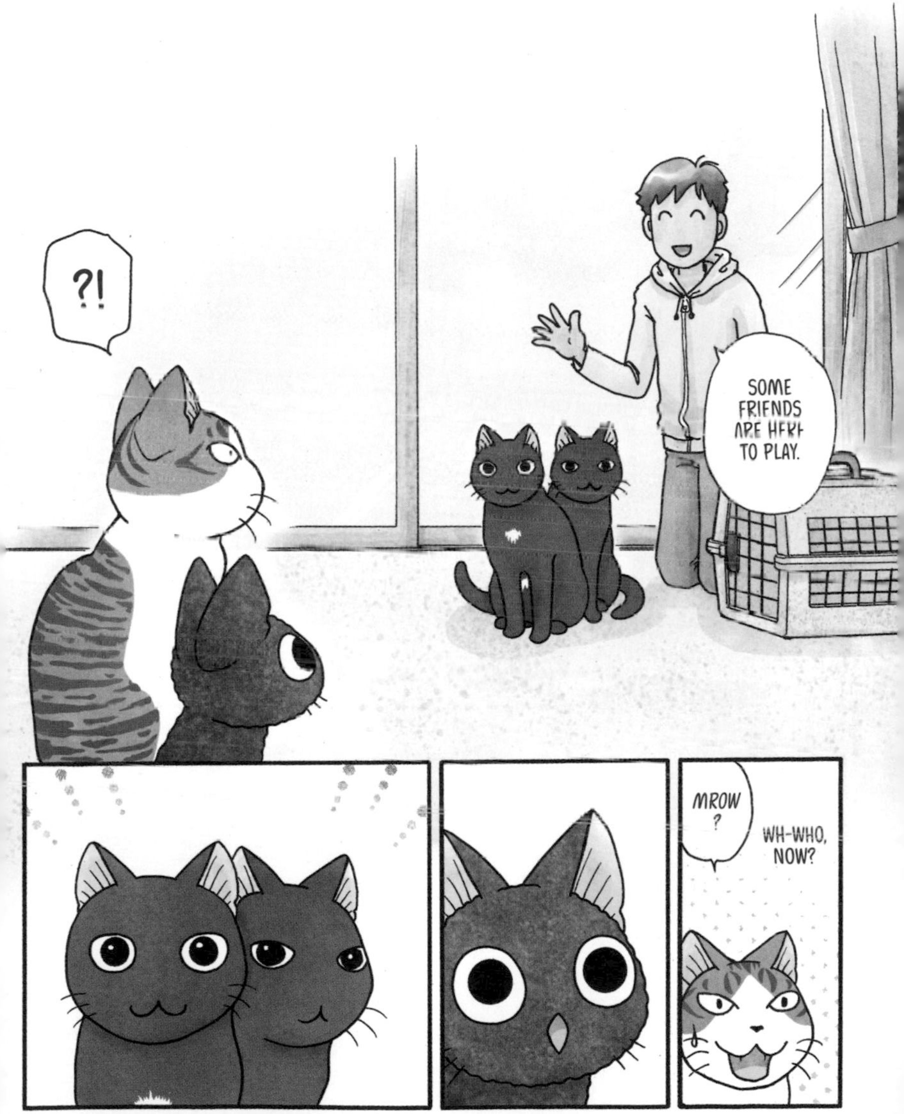
?!
SOME FRIENDS ARE HERE TO PLAY.
MROW?
WH-WHO, NOW?

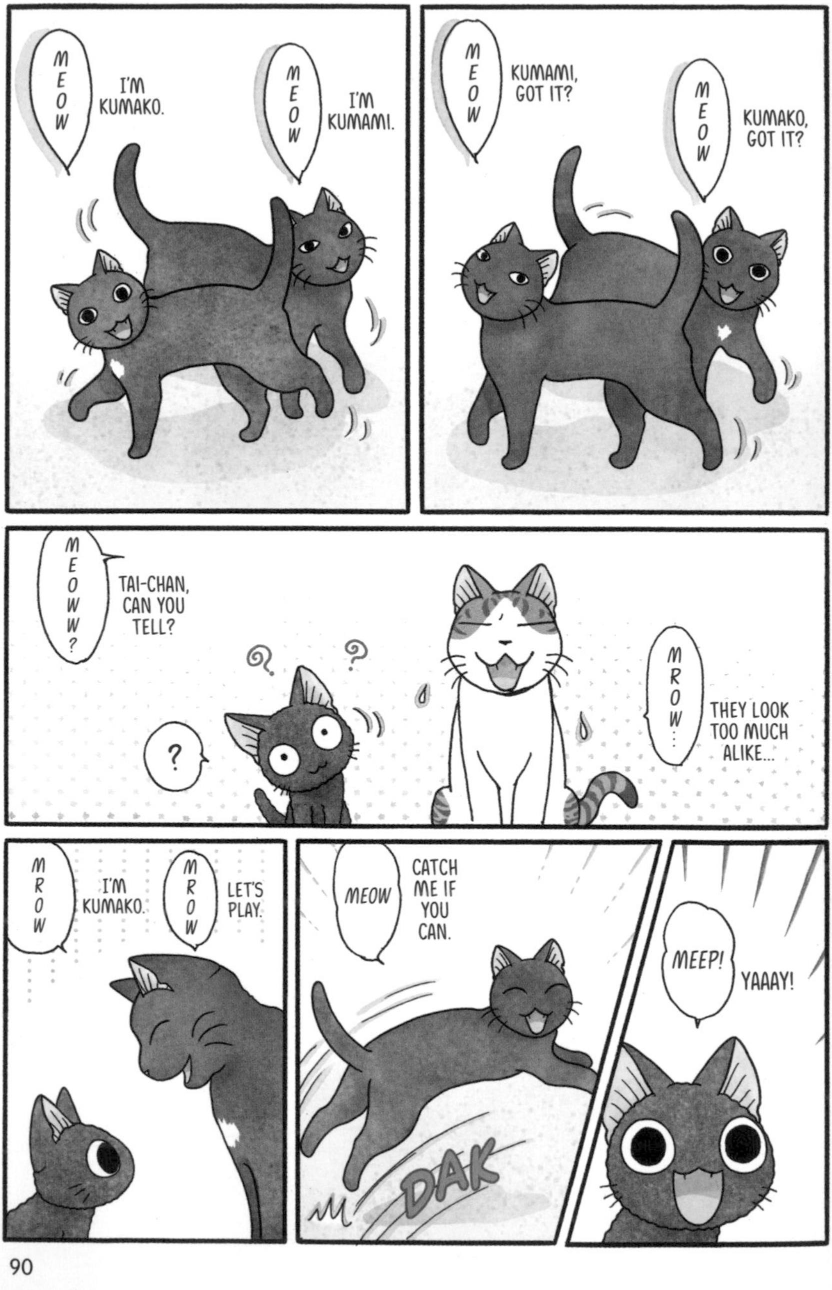
MEOW
I'M KUMAKO.
MEOW
I'M KUMAMI.
MEOW
KUMAMI, GOT IT?
MEOW
KUMAKO, GOT IT?
MEOWW?
TAI-CHAN, CAN YOU TELL?
?
MROW...
THEY LOOK TOO MUCH ALIKE...
MROW
I'M KUMAKO.
MROW
LET'S PLAY.
MEOW
CATCH ME IF YOU CAN.
DAK
MEEP!
YAAAY!

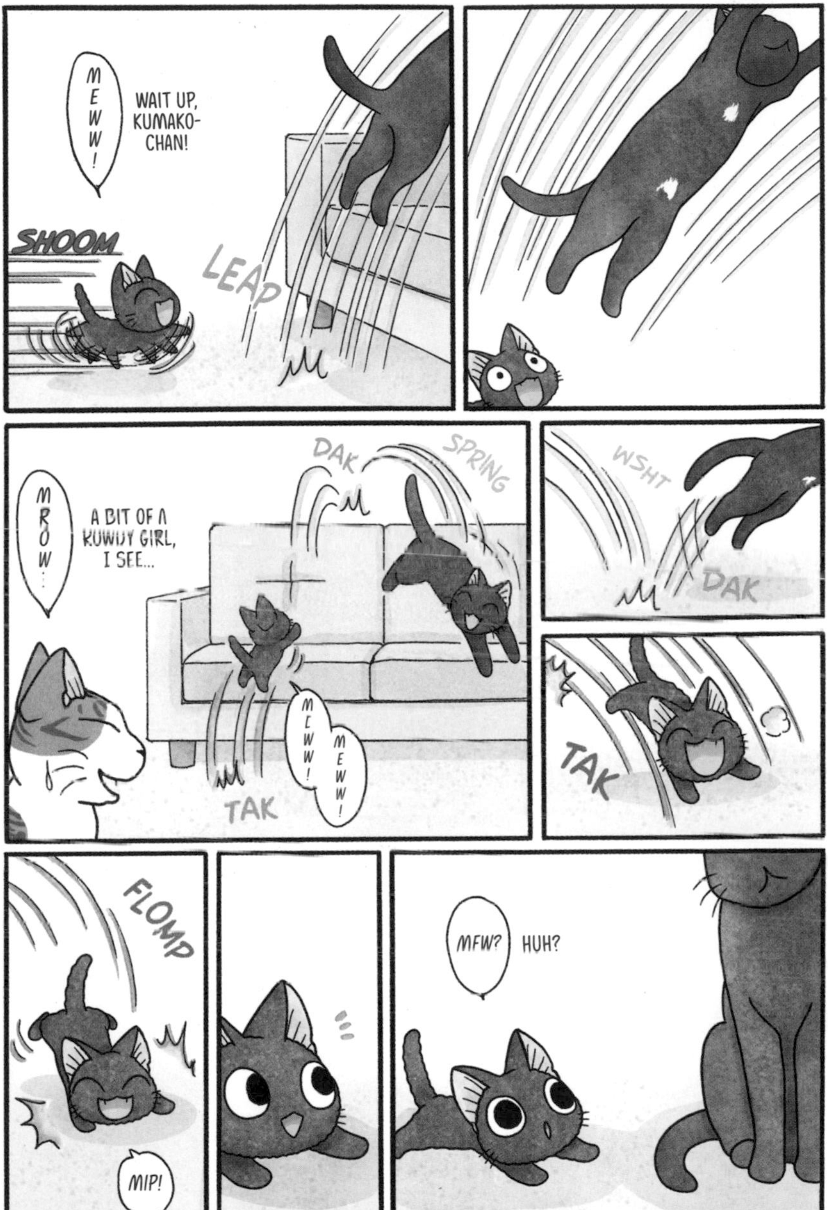
MEWW!
WAIT UP, KUMAKO-CHAN!
SHOOM
LEAP
DAK
SPRING
MROW...
A BIT OF A ROWDY GIRL, I SEE...
MEWW!
MEWW!
TAK
WSHT
DAK
TAK
FLOMP
MIP!
MFW?
HUH?

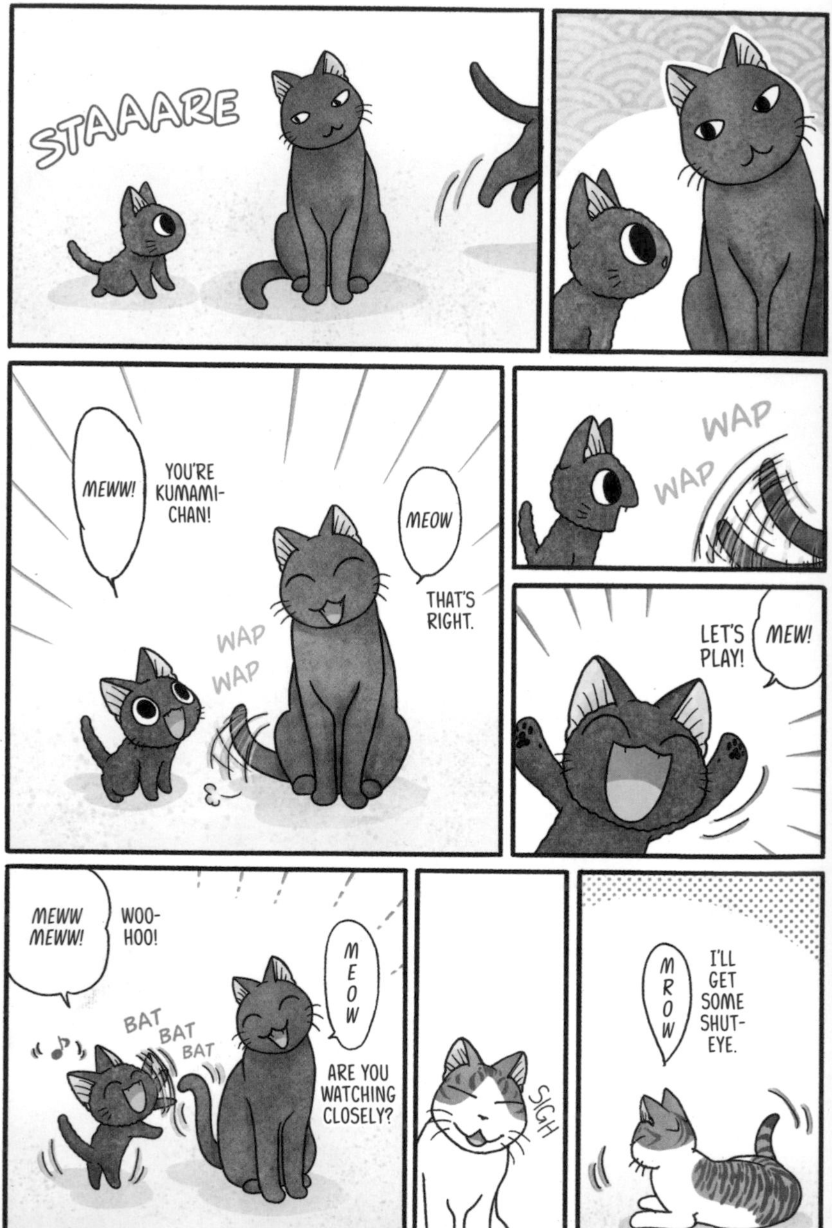
STAAARE
MEWW!
YOU'RE KUMAMI-CHAN!
MEOW
THAT'S RIGHT.
WAP WAP
WAP WAP
LET'S PLAY!
MEW!
MEWW MEWW!
WOO-HOO!
BAT BAT BAT
MEOW
ARE YOU WATCHING CLOSELY?
SIGH
MROW
I'LL GET SOME SHUT-EYE.

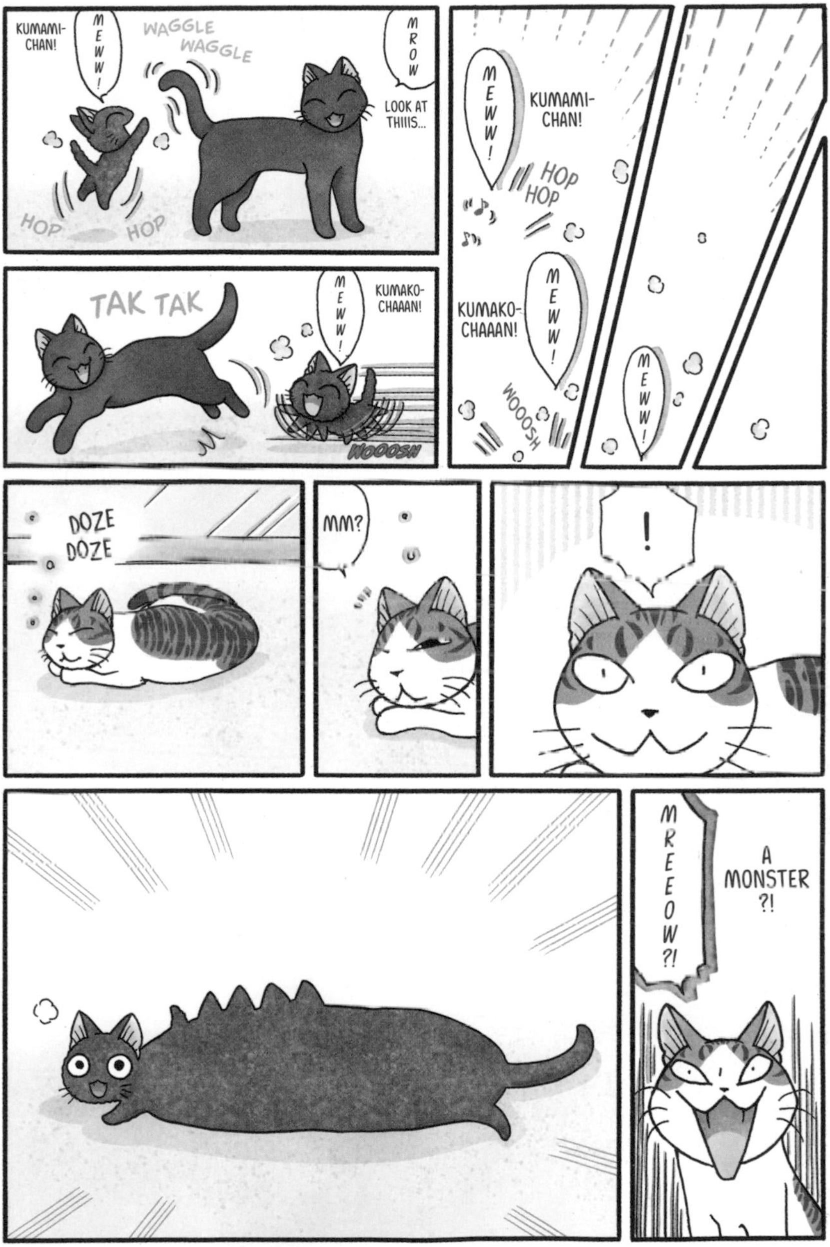
KUMAMI-CHAN!
MEWW!
WAGGLE WAGGLE
MROW
LOOK AT THIIIS...
HOP HOP
TAK TAK
MEWW!
KUMAKO-CHAAAN!
WOOOSH
MEWW!
KUMAMI-CHAN!
HOP HOP
MEWW!
KUMAKO-CHAAAN!
WOOOSH
MEWW!
DOZE DOZE
MM?
!
MREEEOW?!
A MONSTER?!

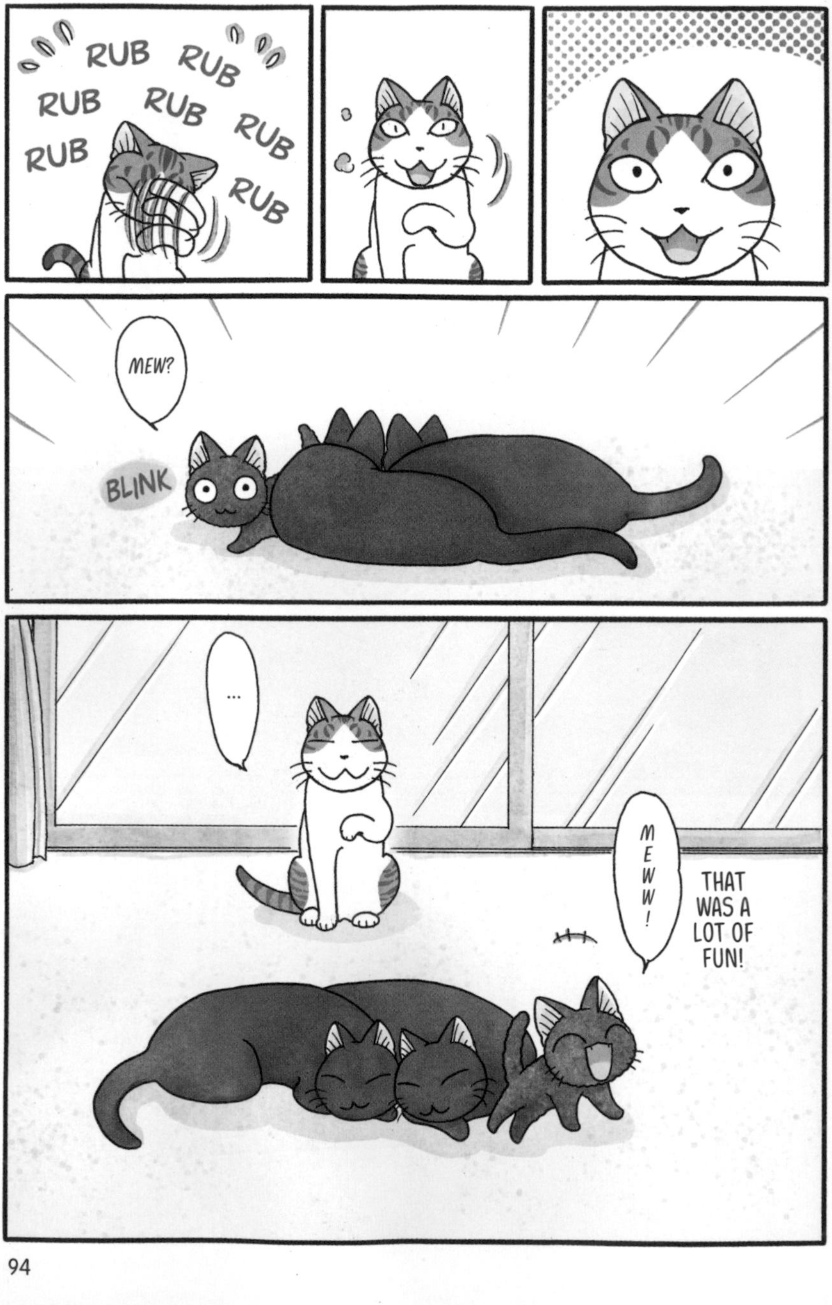
RUB RUB
RUB RUB RUB
RUB RUB
MEW?
BLINK
...
MEWW!
THAT WAS A LOT OF FUN!

CHAPTER 31 Wake Him Up!

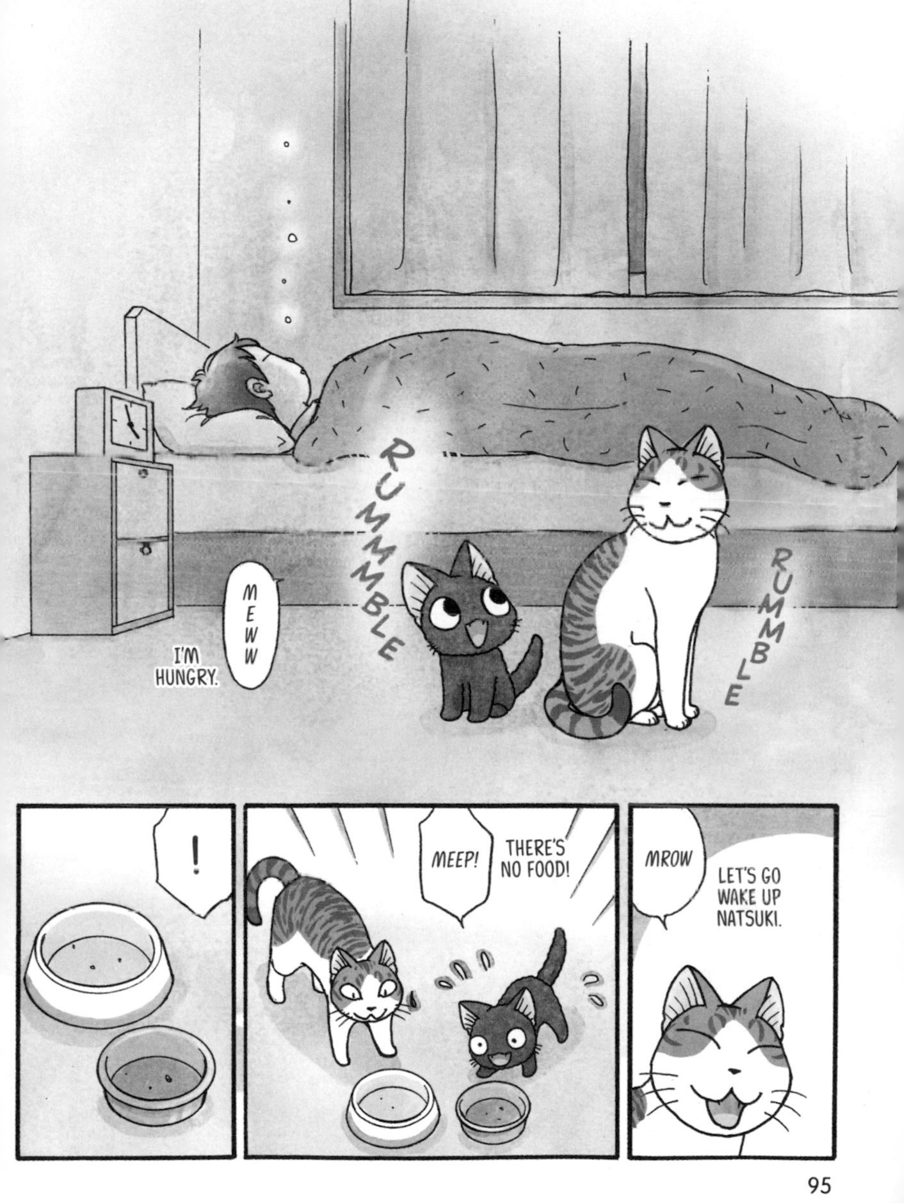
MEWW
I'M HUNGRY.
RUMMMBLE
RUMMBLE
!
MEEP!
THERE'S NO FOOD!
MROW
LET'S GO WAKE UP NATSUKI.

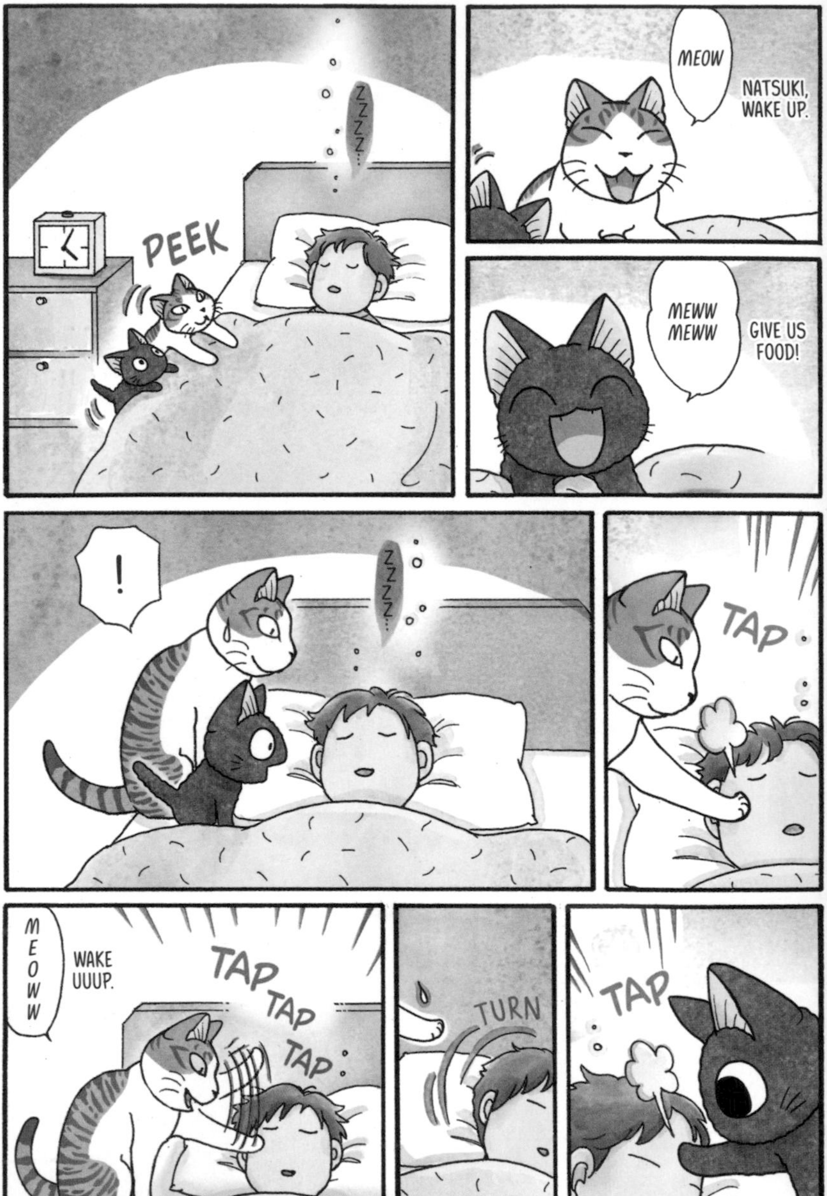
Z Z Z Z...
PEEK
MEOW
NATSUKI, WAKE UP.
MEWW MEWW
GIVE US FOOD!
!
Z Z Z Z...
TAP
MEOWW
WAKE UUUP.
TAP TAP TAP
TURN
TAP

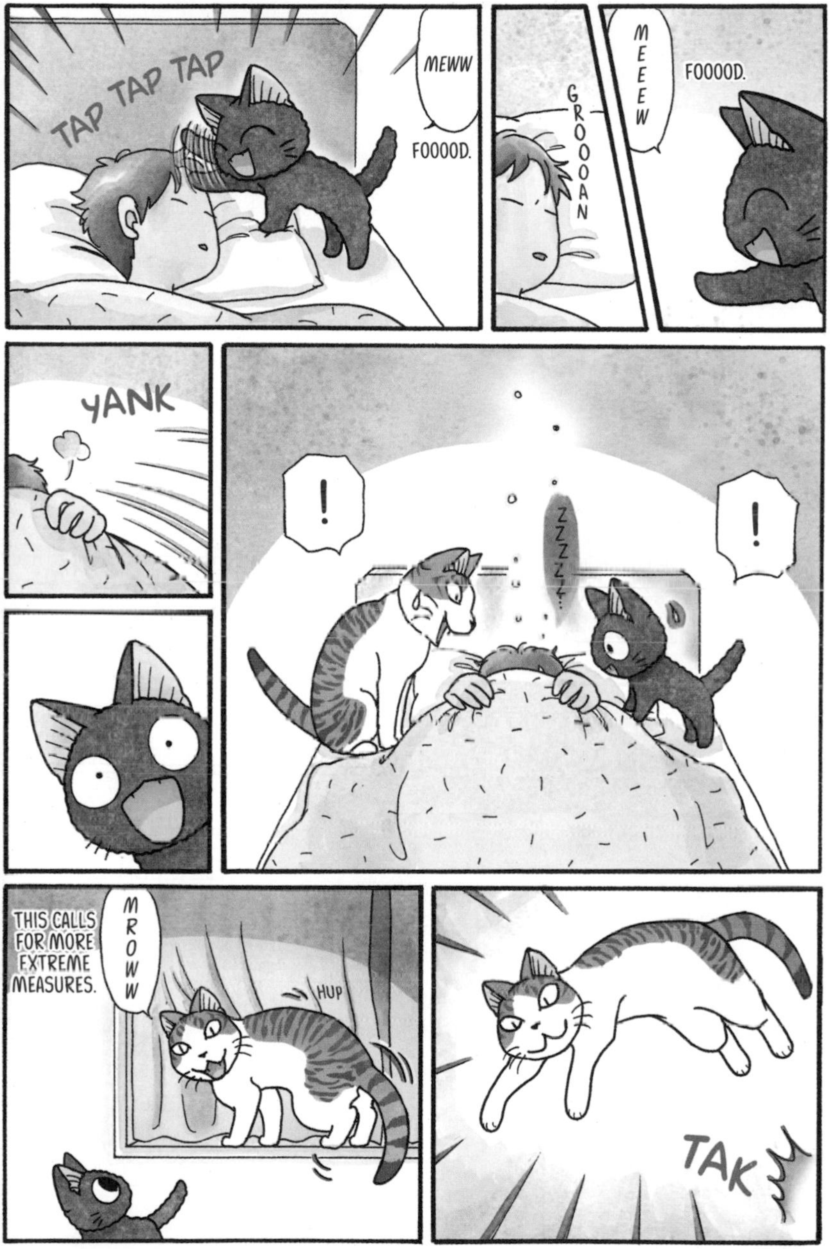
TAP TAP TAP
MEWW
FOOOOD.
GROOOAN
MEEEW
FOOOOD.
YANK
!
ZZZZZ...
!
THIS CALLS FOR MORE EXTREME MEASURES.
MROWW
HUP
TAK

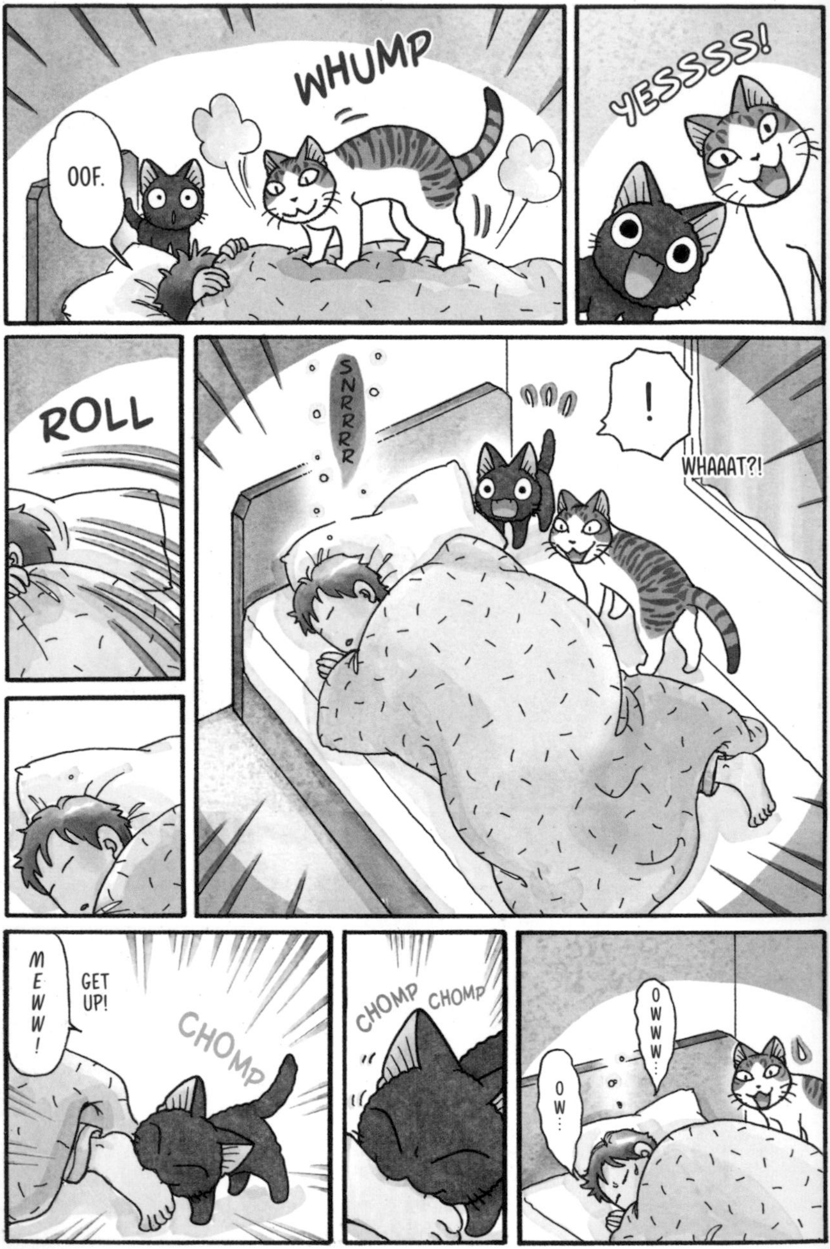
OOF.
WHUMP
YESSSSS!
ROLL
SNRRRR
!
WHAAAT?!
MEWW!
GET UP!
CHOMP
CHOMP CHOMP
OWWW...
OW...

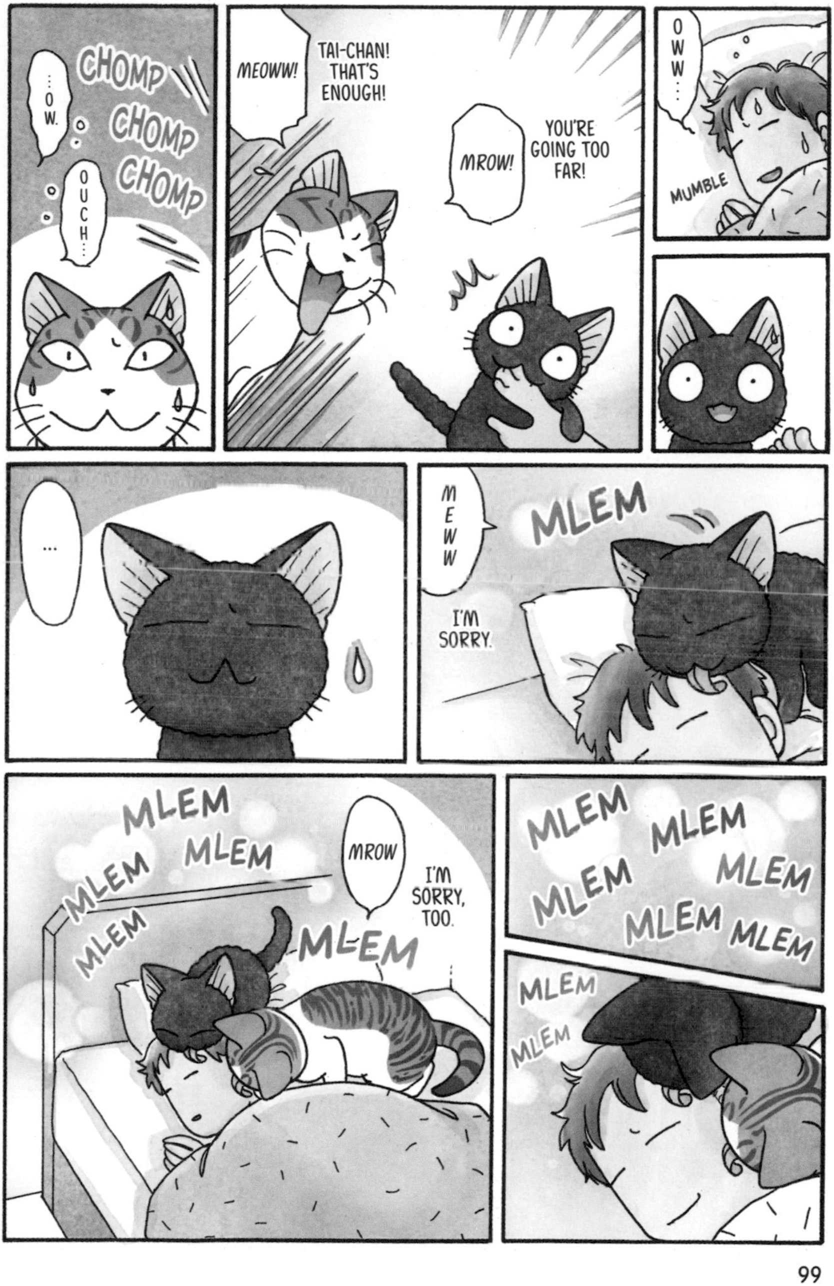
...OW.
OUCH...
CHOMP
CHOMP
CHOMP
MEOWW!
TAI-CHAN! THAT'S ENOUGH!
MROW!
YOU'RE GOING TOO FAR!
OWW...
MUMBLE
...
MEWW
I'M SORRY.
MLEM
MLEM
MLEM
MLEM
MLEM
MROW
I'M SORRY, TOO.
MLEM
MLEM
MLEM
MLEM
MLEM
MLEM
MLEM
MLEM
MLEM
MLEM

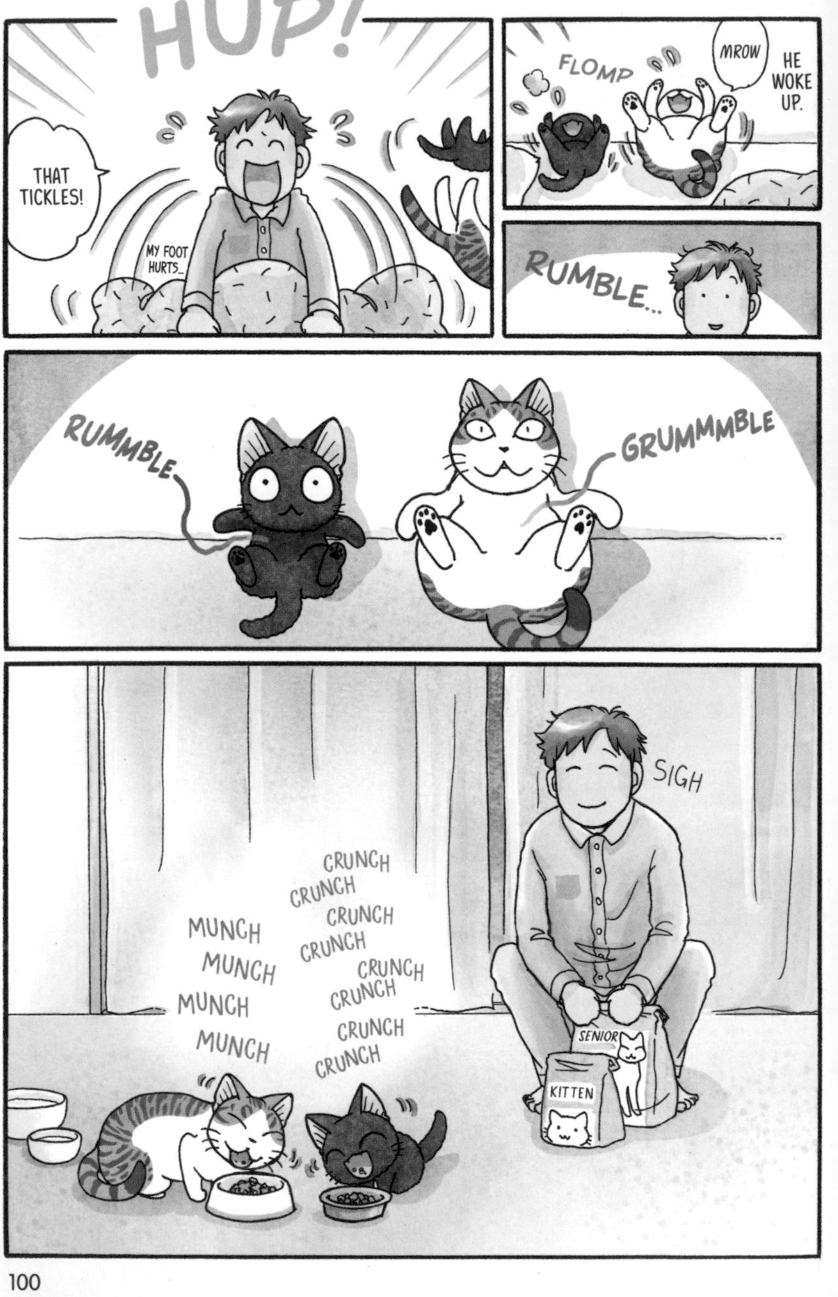
HUP!
THAT TICKLES!
MY FOOT HURTS...
FLOMP
MROW
HE WOKE UP.
RUMBLE...
RUMMBLE
GRUMMMBLE
SIGH
CRUNCH
CRUNCH
CRUNCH
CRUNCH
CRUNCH
CRUNCH
CRUNCH
CRUNCH
MUNCH
MUNCH
MUNCH
MUNCH
SENIOR
KITTEN

Sue & Tai-chan

CHAPTER 32 A *Tai* Windsock?!

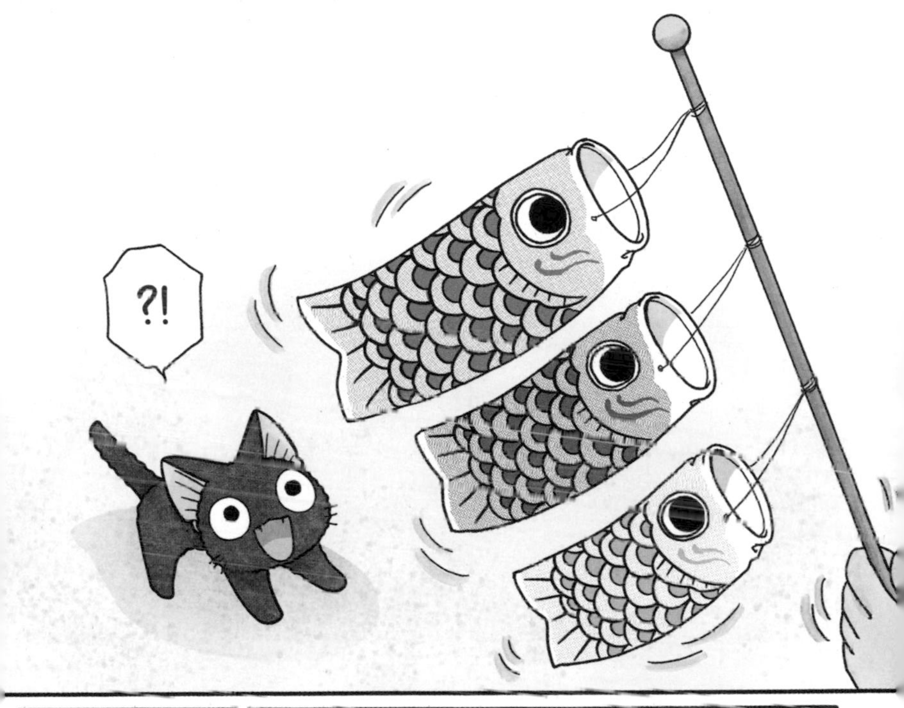

?!

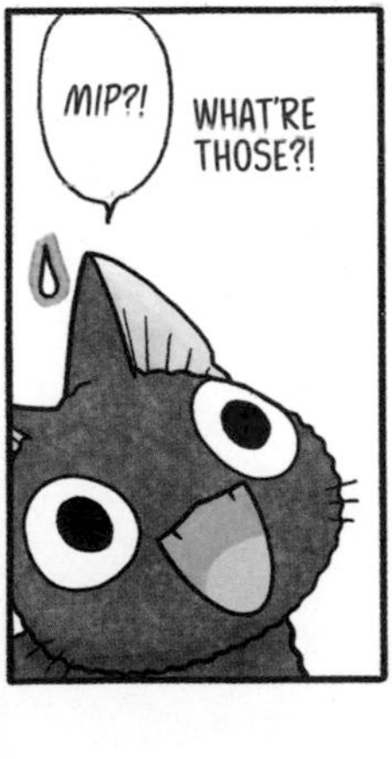

MIP?!
WHAT'RE THOSE?!

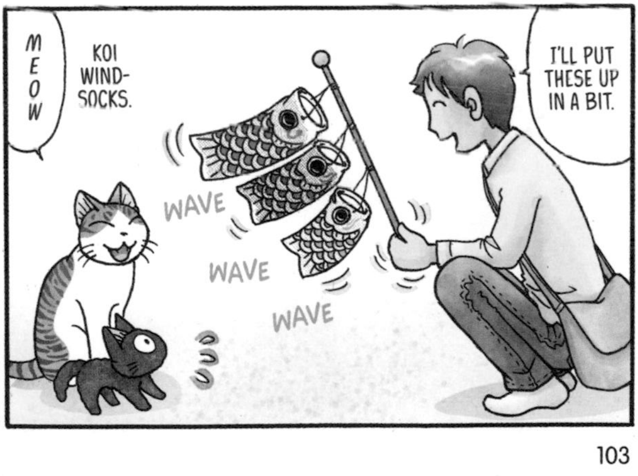

MEOW
KOI WIND-SOCKS.
I'LL PUT THESE UP IN A BIT.
WAVE
WAVE
WAVE

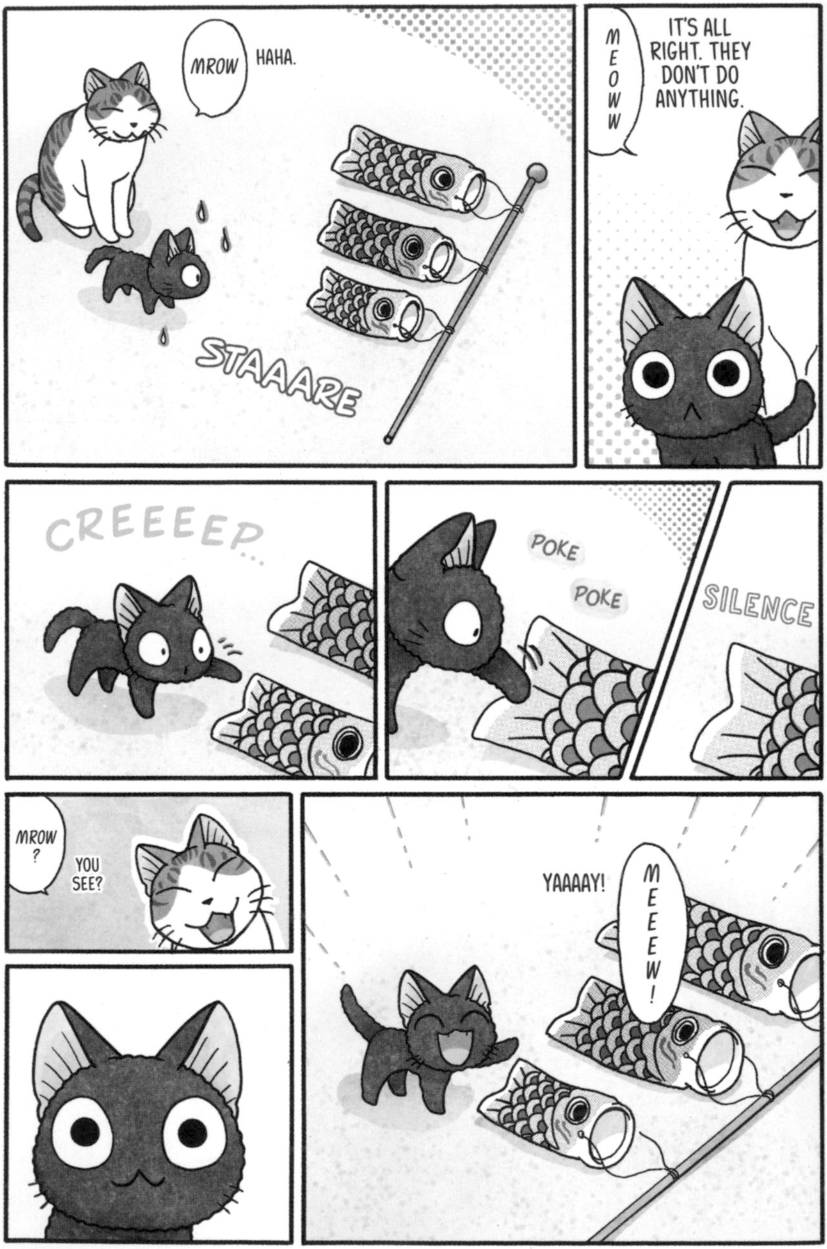
MROW
HAHA.
STAAARE
MEOWW
IT'S ALL RIGHT. THEY DON'T DO ANYTHING.
CREEEEP...
POKE
POKE
SILENCE
MROW?
YOU SEE?
YAAAAY!
MEEEW!

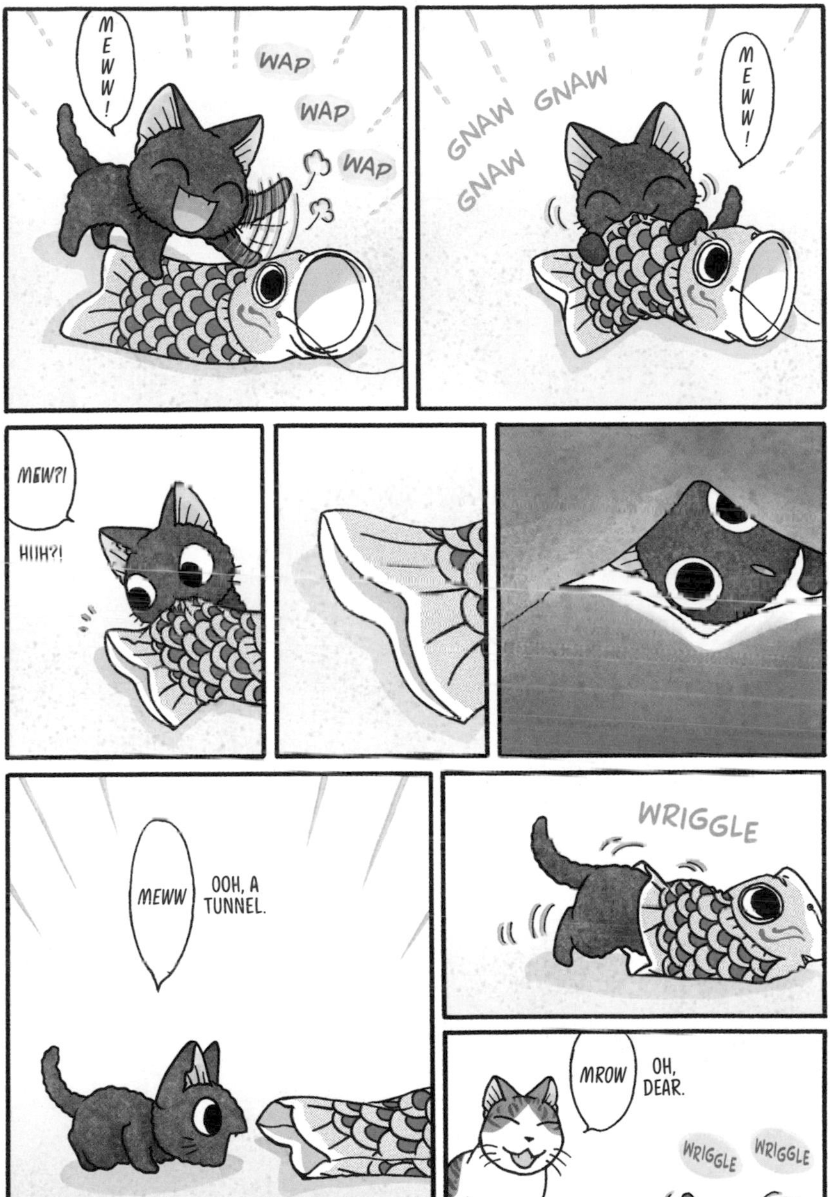
MEWW!
WAP
WAP
WAP
GNAW GNAW
GNAW
MEWW!
MEW?!
HUH?!
MEWW
OOH, A TUNNEL.
WRIGGLE
MROW
OH, DEAR.
WRIGGLE
WRIGGLE

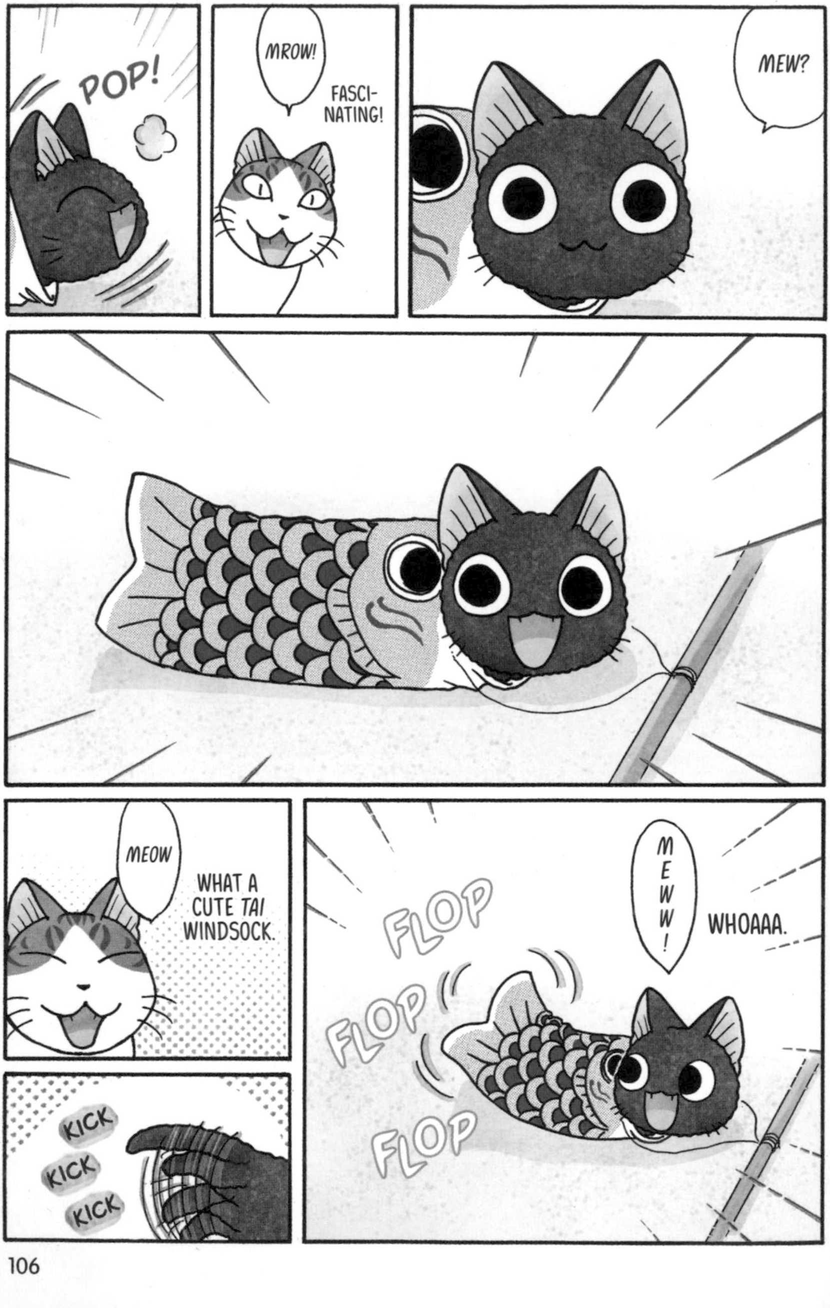
POP!
MROW!
FASCI-
NATING!
MEW?
MEOW
WHAT A
CUTE *TAI*
WINDSOCK.
KICK
KICK
KICK
FLOP
FLOP
FLOP
MEWW!
WHOAAA.

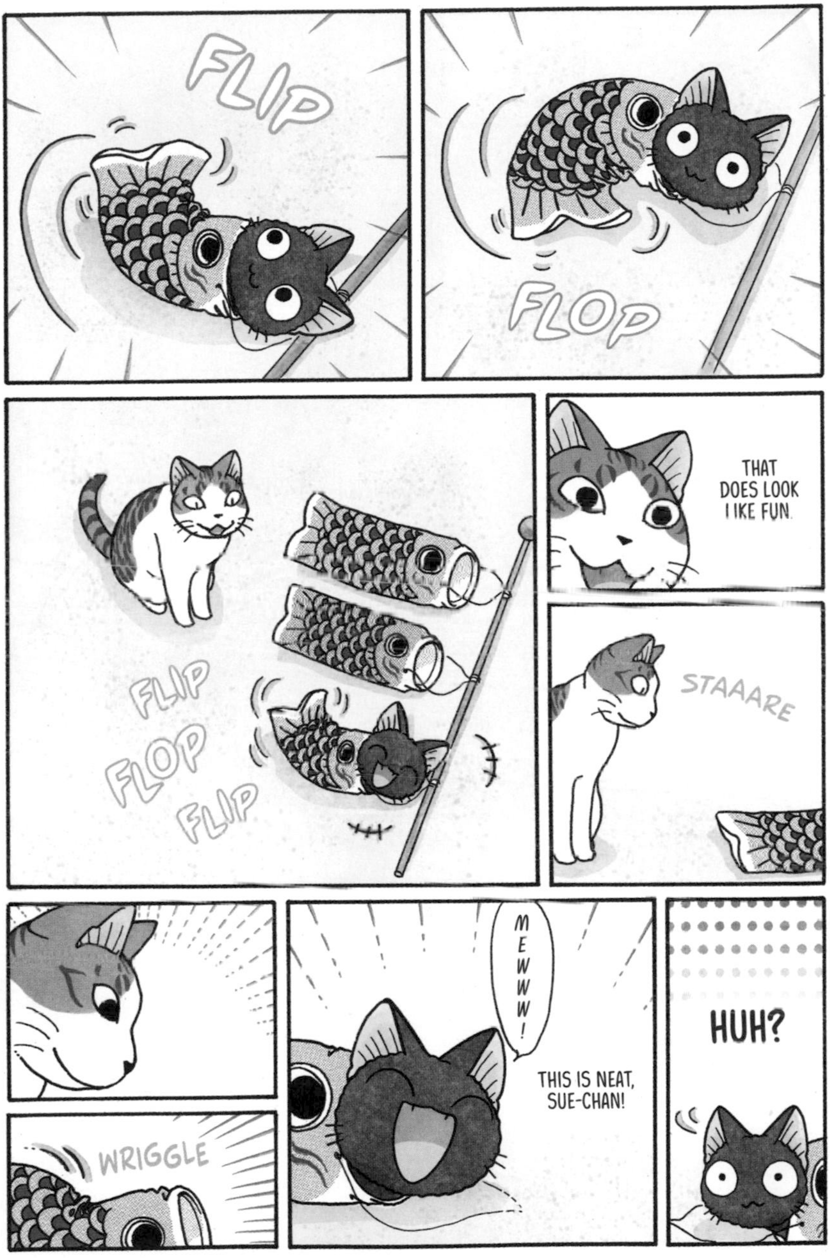
FLIP
FLOP
FLIP
FLOP
FLIP
THAT DOES LOOK LIKE FUN.
STAAARE
WRIGGLE
MEWWW!
THIS IS NEAT, SUE-CHAN!
HUH?

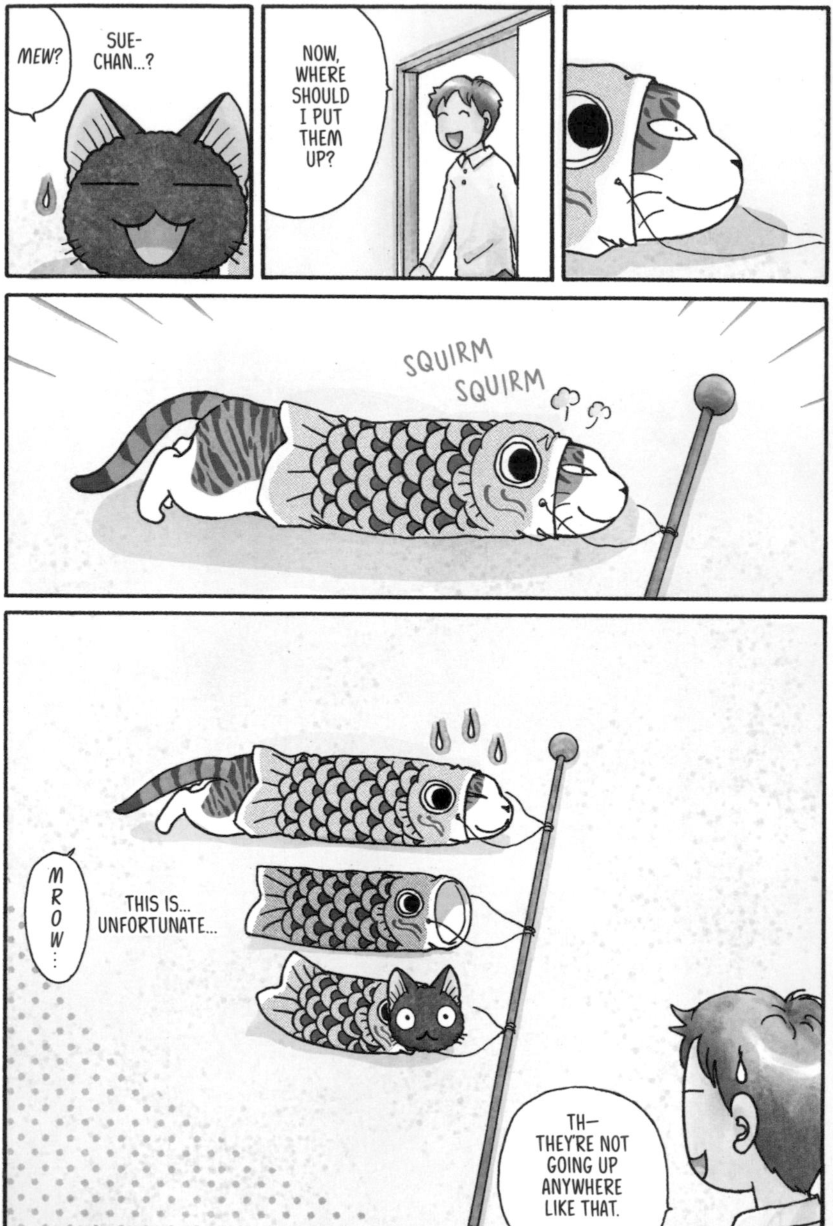
MEW?
SUE-CHAN...?
NOW, WHERE SHOULD I PUT THEM UP?
SQUIRM SQUIRM
MROW...
THIS IS... UNFORTUNATE...
TH— THEY'RE NOT GOING UP ANYWHERE LIKE THAT.

CHAPTER 33 Hide-and-SCARE

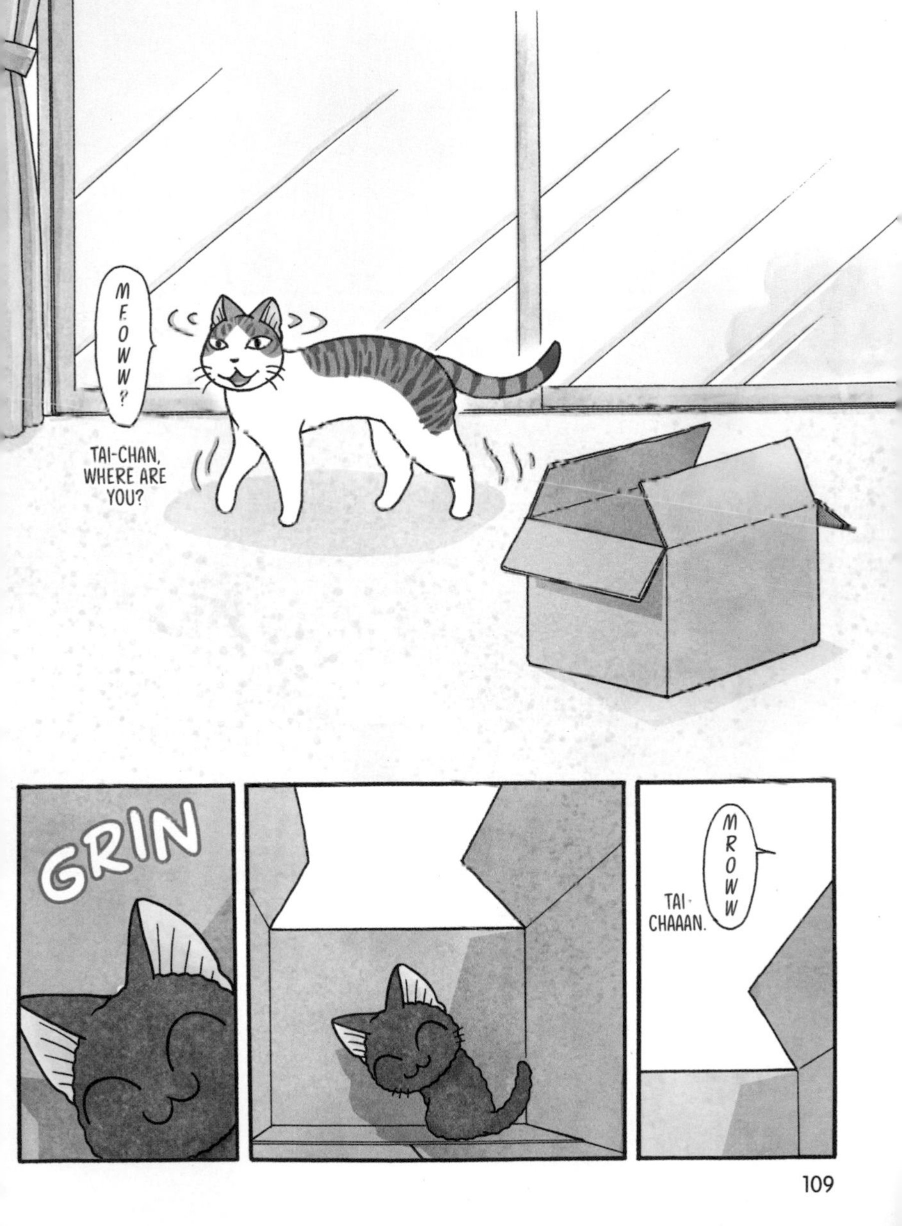
MEOWW?
TAI-CHAN, WHERE ARE YOU?
GRIN
MROWW
TAI-CHAAAN.

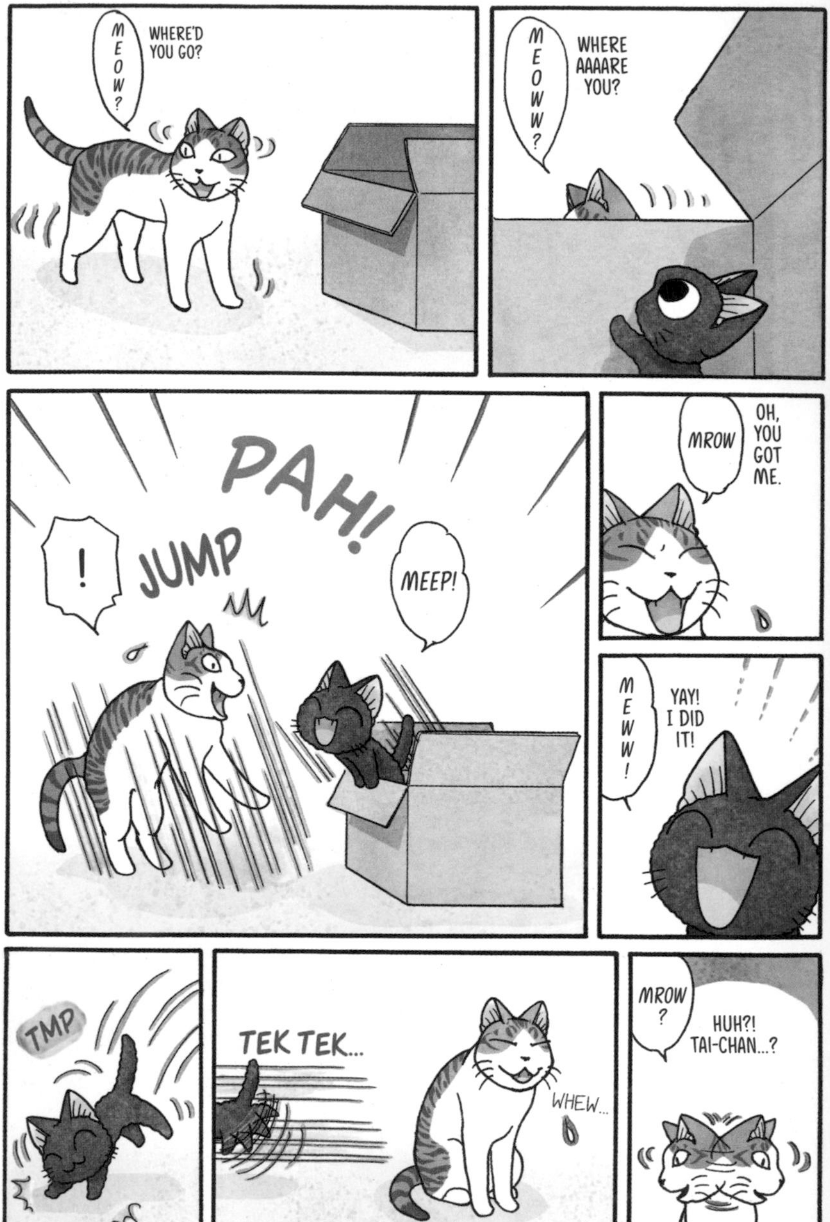
MEOW?
WHERE'D YOU GO?
MEOWW?
WHERE AAAARE YOU?
!
JUMP
PAH!
MEEP!
MROW
OH, YOU GOT ME.
MEWW!
YAY! I DID IT!
TMP
TEK TEK...
WHEW...
MROW?
HUH?! TAI-CHAN...?

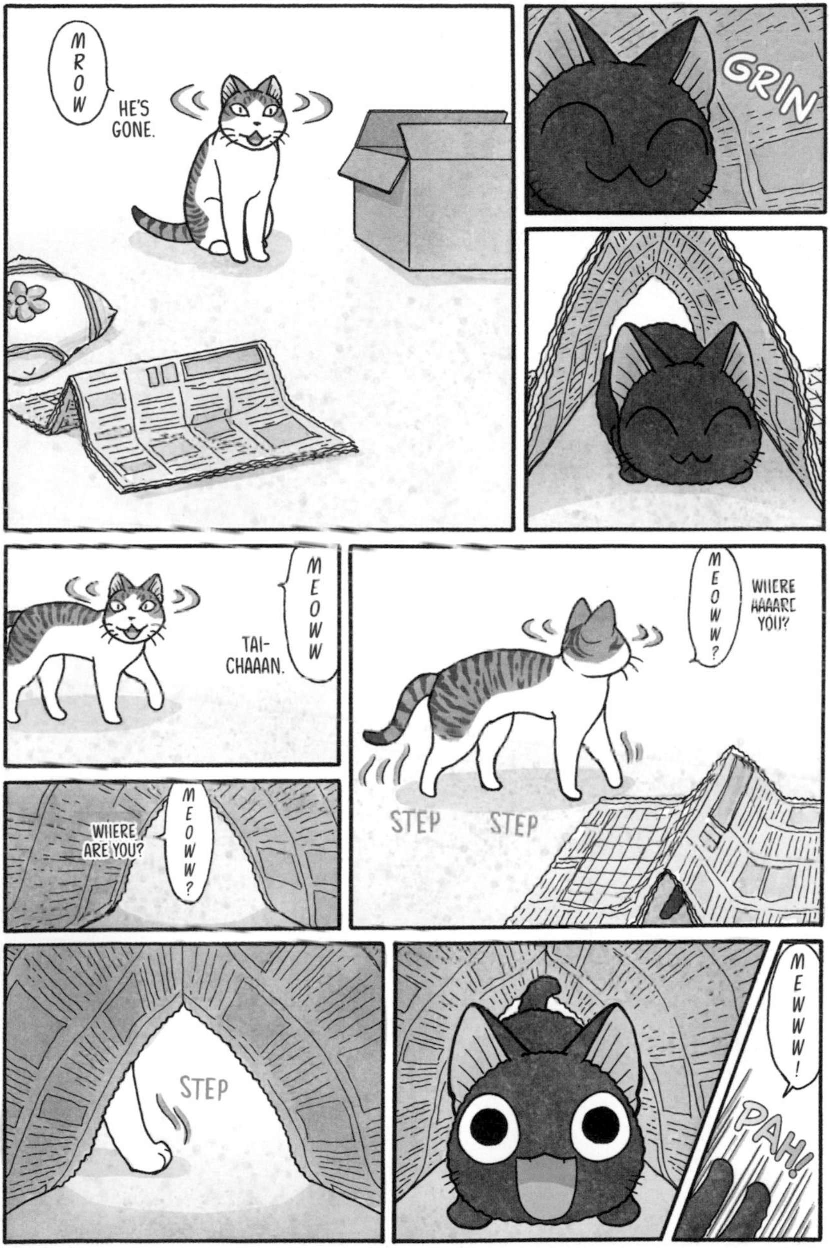
MROW
HE'S GONE.
GRIN
MEOWW
TAI-CHAAAN.
MEOWW?
WHERE ARE YOU?
MEOWW?
WHERE AAAARE YOU?
STEP STEP
STEP
MEWWW!
PAH!

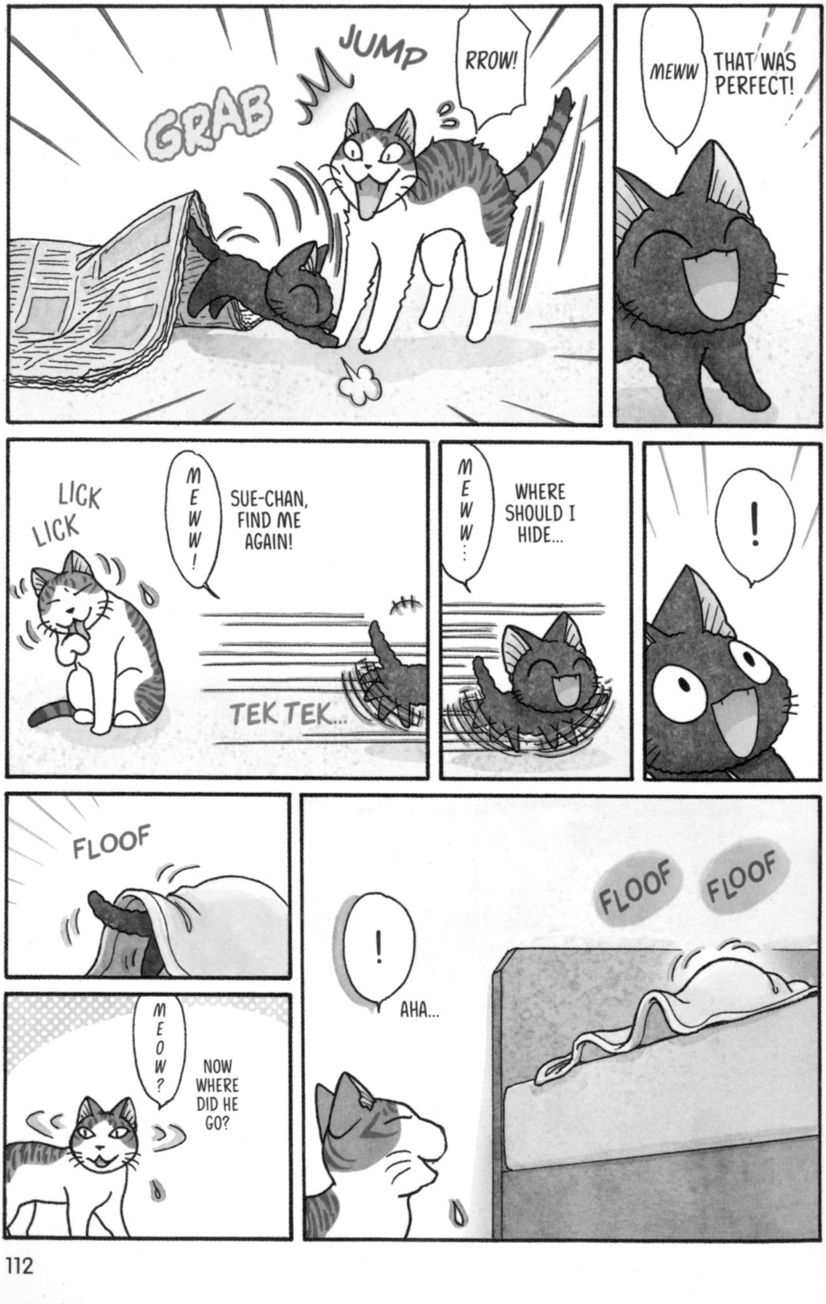
GRAB
JUMP
RROW!
MEWW
THAT WAS PERFECT!
LICK
LICK
MEWW!
SUE-CHAN, FIND ME AGAIN!
TEK TEK...
MEWW...
WHERE SHOULD I HIDE...
!
FLOOF
MEOW?
NOW WHERE DID HE GO?
!
AHA...
FLOOF
FLOOF

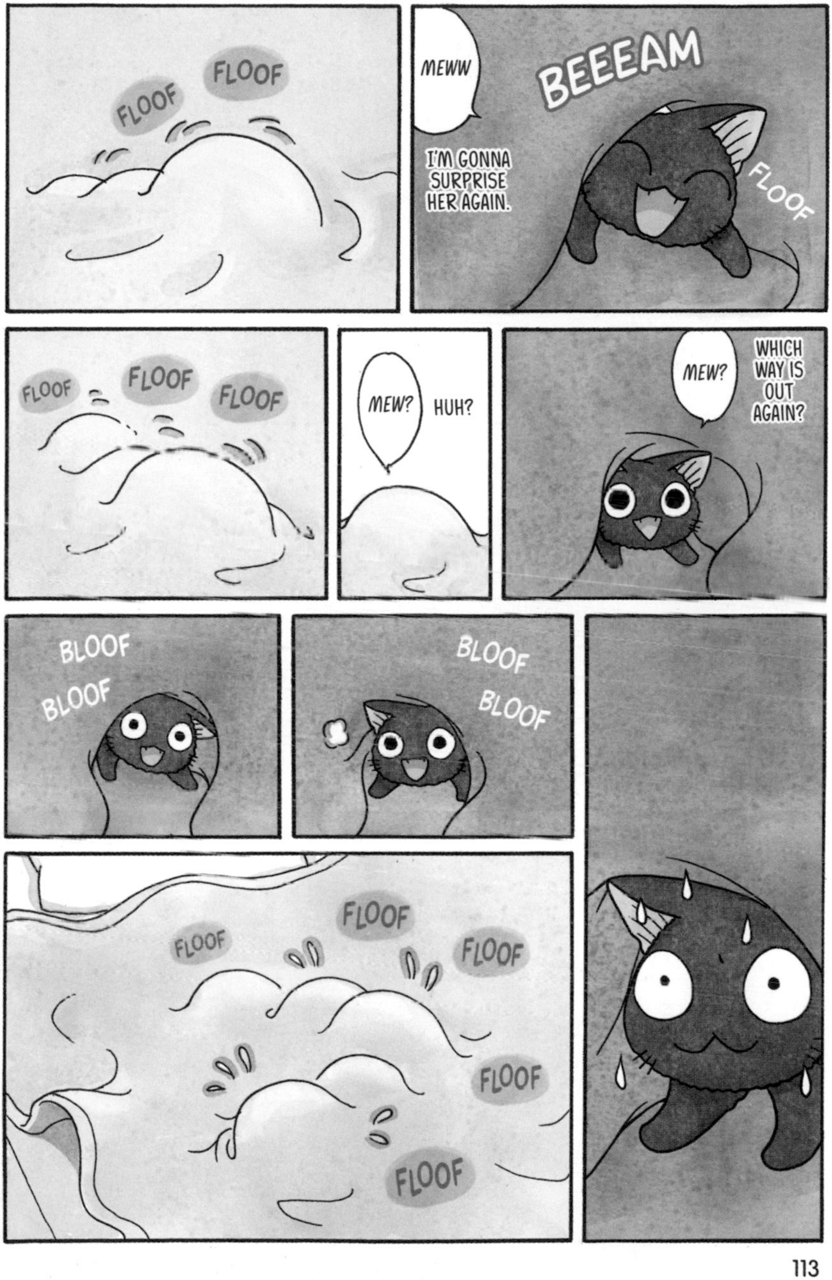
FLOOF
FLOOF
MEWW
I'M GONNA SURPRISE HER AGAIN.
BEEEAM
FLOOF
FLOOF
FLOOF
FLOOF
MEW?
HUH?
MEW?
WHICH WAY IS OUT AGAIN?
BLOOF
BLOOF
BLOOF
BLOOF
FLOOF
FLOOF
FLOOF
FLOOF
FLOOF

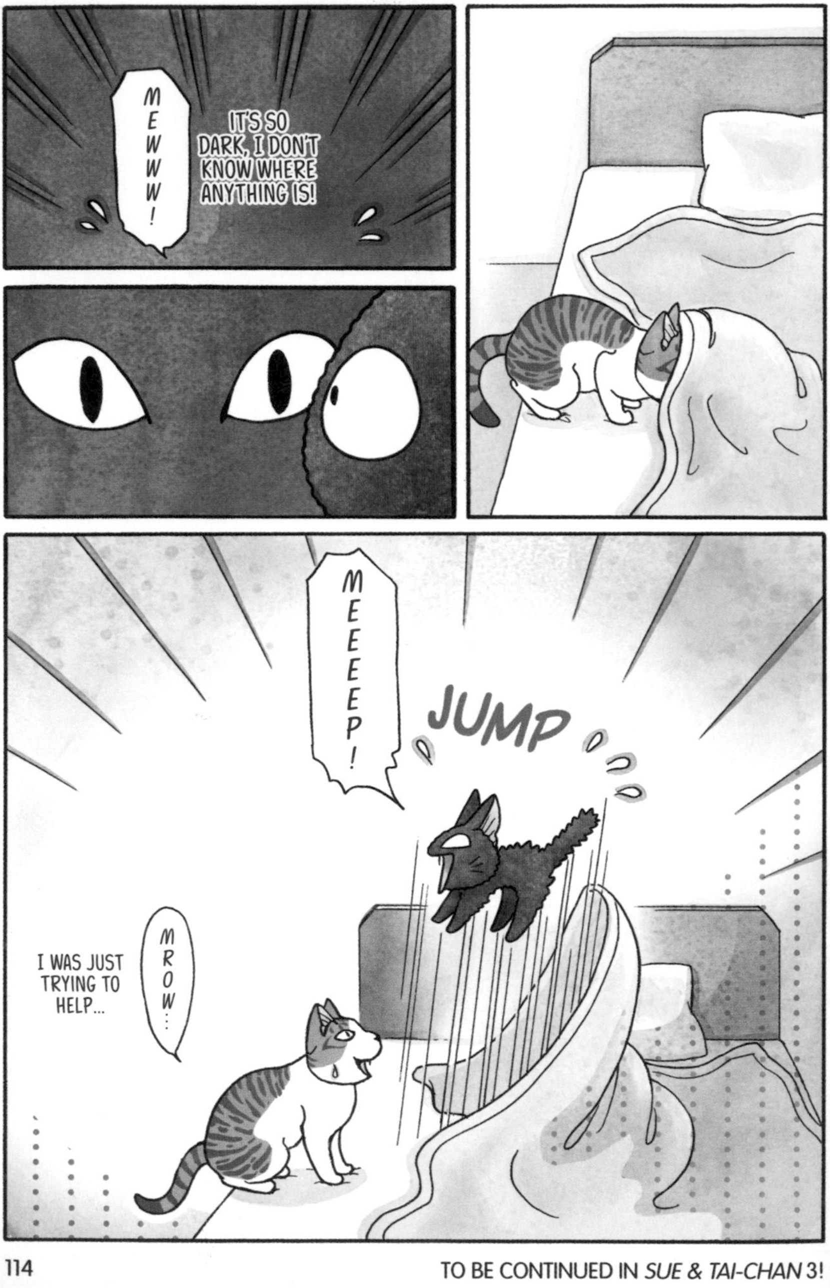
MEWWW!
IT'S SO DARK, I DON'T KNOW WHERE ANYTHING IS!
MEEEEEP!
JUMP
MROW...
I WAS JUST TRYING TO HELP...

TO BE CONTINUED IN *SUE & TAI-CHAN* 3!

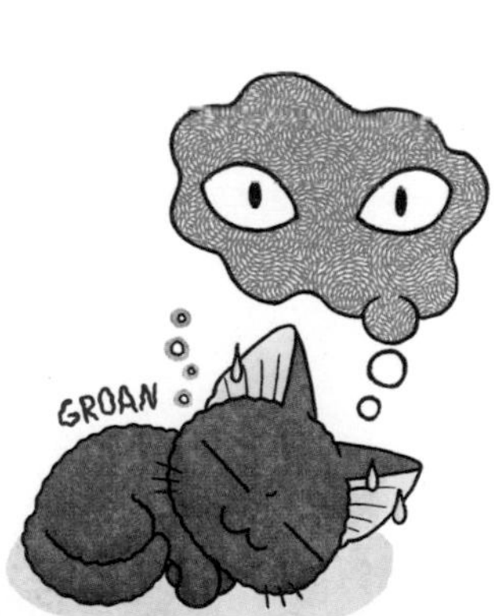
GROAN

WHAT'S THAT?

FLOP

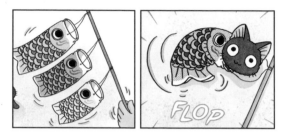

In Japan, koi windsocks are decorations traditionally used for celebrating **Children's Day**.

It is believed that koi, or carp, are very strong and full of life. They symbolize the hope that children (or kittens) will grow up strong and healthy.

Honorifics Review

THIS IS MIKEKO-SAN, FROM THE HOUSE BEHIND OURS.
MROW
MIKEKO-SAN...
MEWW

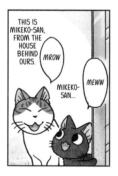

-chan is a cutesy honorific for showing affection, like saying "Little Tai."

-san is a polite honorific for showing respect, like "Mr.", "Ms.", or "Mx."

Not using an honorific means you must be *very* close to someone!

Sue & Tai-chan

This Book is the Cat's Meow

Celebrating the conclusion of Konami Kanata's international megahit *Chi's Sweet Home*, **The Complete Chi** is a new edition that honors some of the best Japan has ever offered in the field of cat comics. A multiple *New York Times* Best Seller and two-time winner of the *Manga.Ask.com* Awards for Best Children's Manga, Konami Kanata's tale of a lost kitten has been acclaimed by readers worldwide as an excellent example of a comic that has truly been accepted by readers of all ages.

Presented in a brand new larger omnibus format each edition compiles three volumes of kitty cartoon tales, including two bonus cat comics from Konami Kanata's **FukuFuku** franchise, making **The Complete Chi's Sweet Home** a must have for every cat lover out there.

"*Chi's Sweet Home* made me smile throughout... It's utterly endearing. This is the first manga I've read in several years where I'm looking forward to the [next] volume."

—Chris Beveridge, *Mania.com*

"Konami Kanata does some pretty things with watercolor, and paces each of the little vignettes chronicling Chi's new life to highlight just the right moments for maximum effect... This is truly a visual treat." **—***Comics and More*

All Parts 1 - 4
Available Now!

The Complete Chi's Sweet Home

Konami Kanata

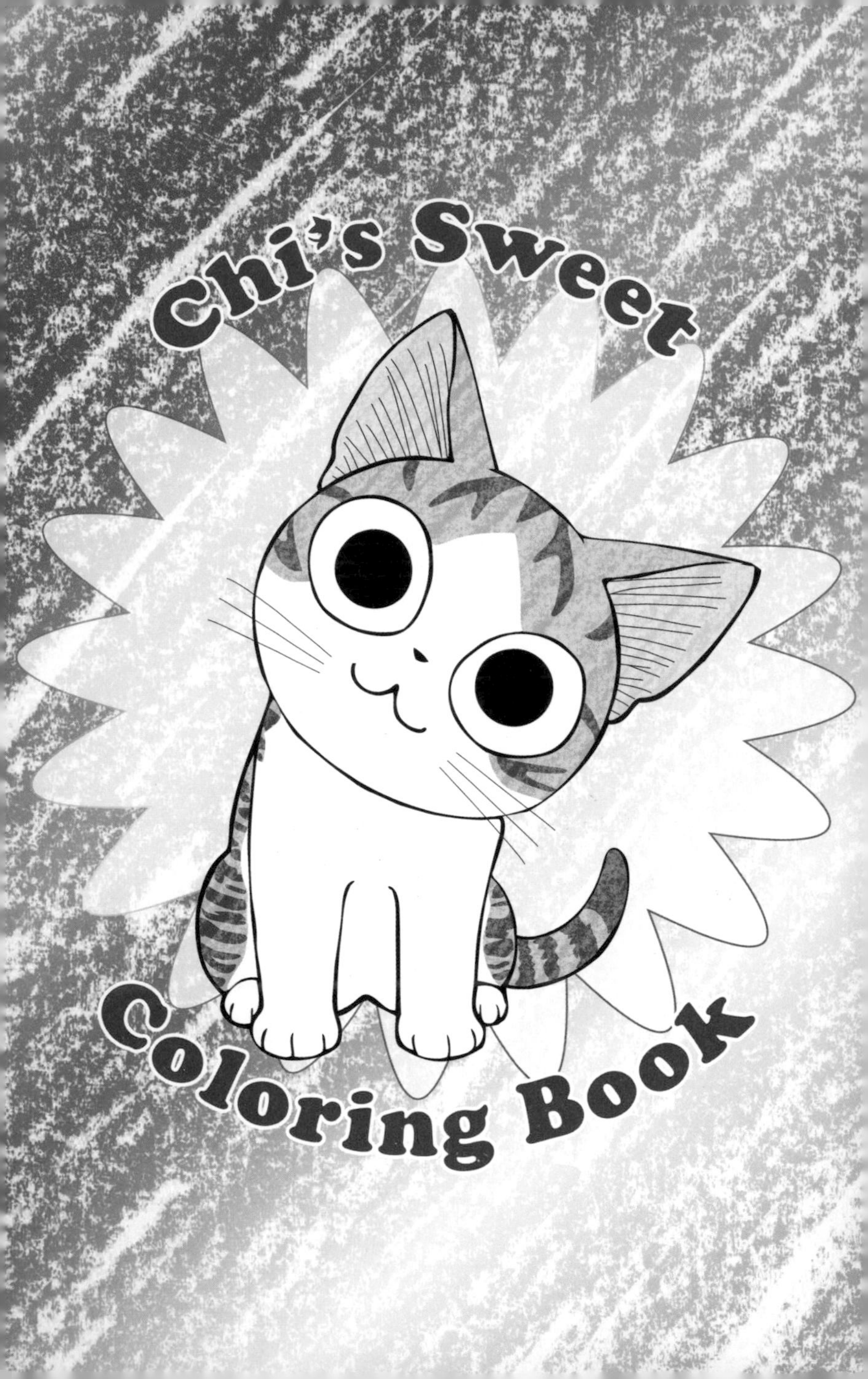
Chi's Sweet
Coloring Book

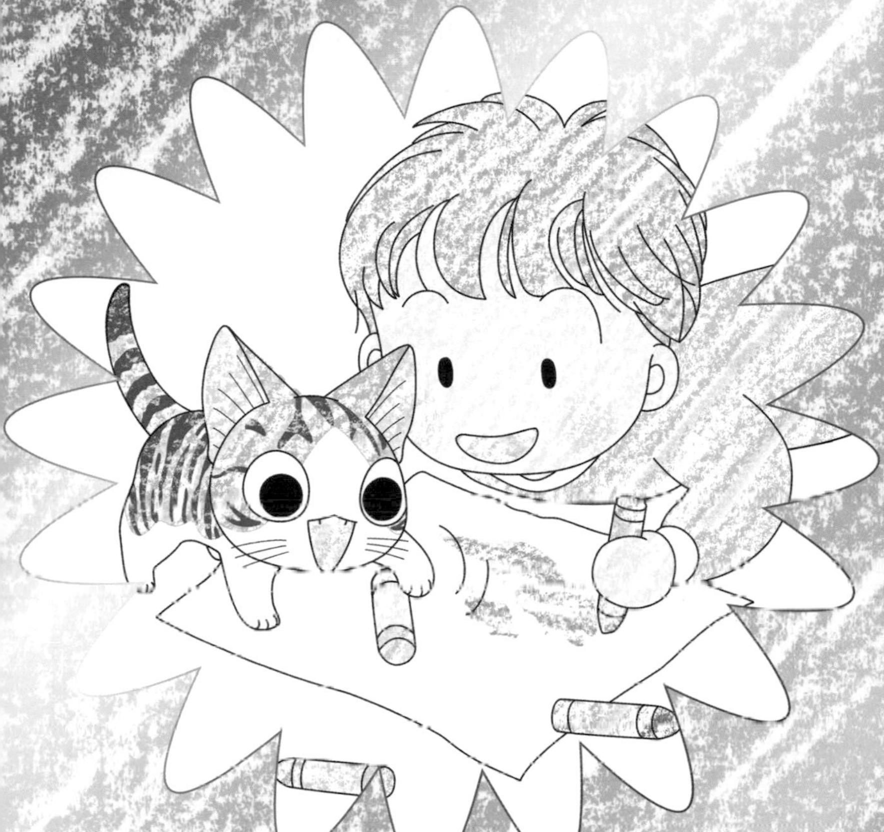

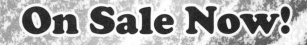

Created by Konami Kanata
Adapted by Kinoko Natsume

Chi is back! Manga's most famous cat
returns with a brand new series!
Chi's Sweet Adventures collects dozens
of new full-color kitty tales made
for readers of all ages!

Volumes 1-4
On Sale Now!

Chi's

Sweet Adventures

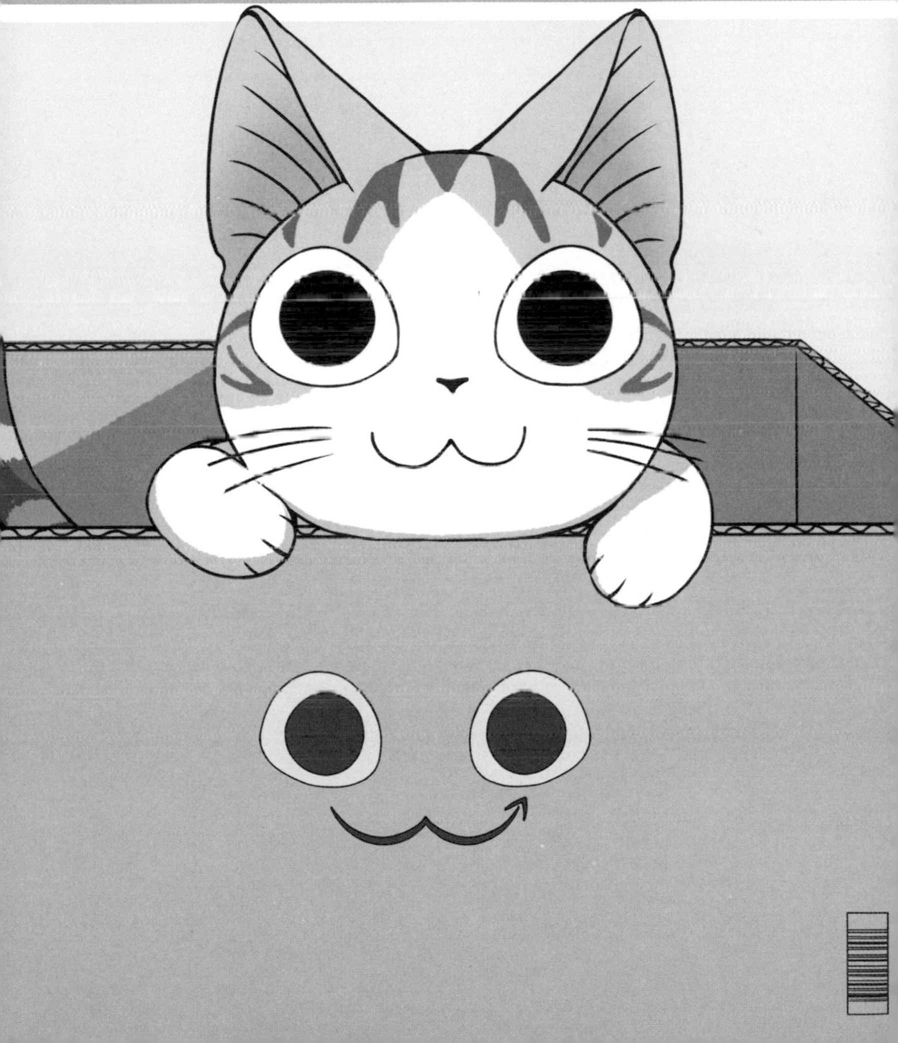

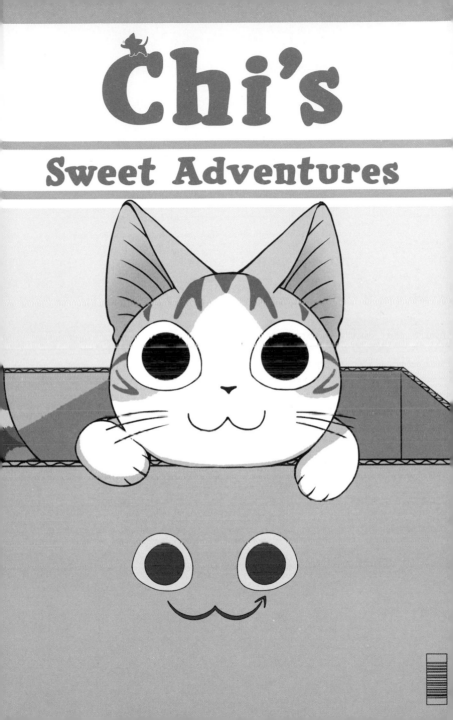

#My Sue & Tai-chan Photo Contest

WINNERS

There was a photo contest in Japan to
celebrate the release of *Sue & Tai-chan* volume 1!
So many kitty entries came pouring in! ♪
Let's meet the pair of black cats who took the grand prize,
and the five other kitties receiving honorable mentions.

A rowdy girl with white spots on her chest and tummy.

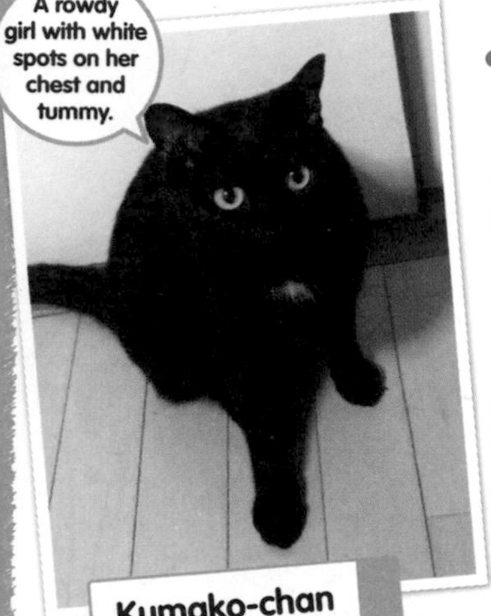

Kumako-chan

Kumako-chan & Kumami-chan

A black cat who plays it cool but really likes you.

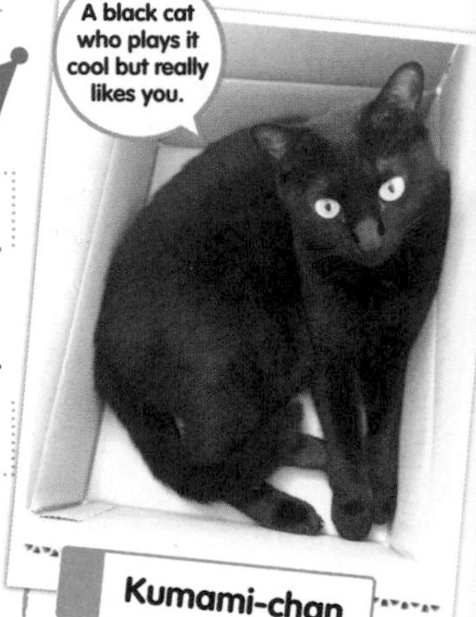

Kumami-chan

Kumako-chan and Kumami-chan made their guest appearance in Chapter 30 — Which One Is Which?!♪

At first it seems like you're seeing double, but look again, and their different personalities come through, as they leap around the pages of *Sue & Tai-chan*♥

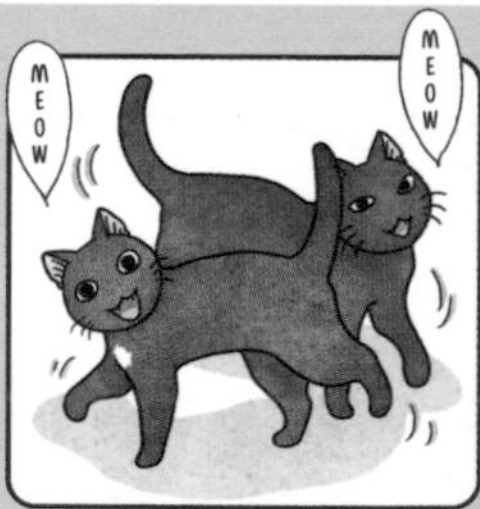
MEOW
MEOW

Honorable Mentions

Gureko-chan
Mugi-chan
Yuri-chan
Rum-chan
Lady-chan
(in no particular order!)

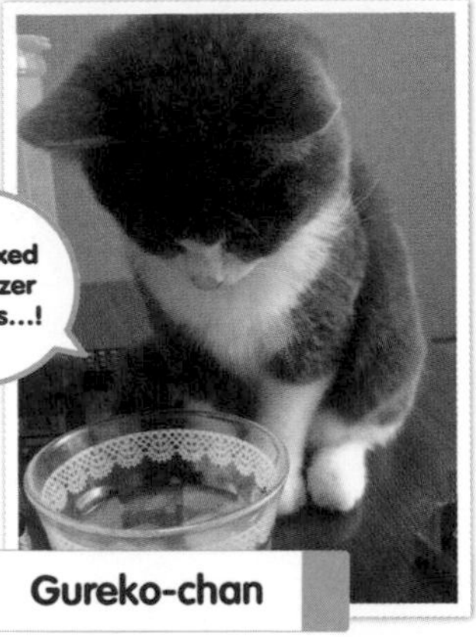
Perplexed by seltzer bubbles...!
Gureko-chan

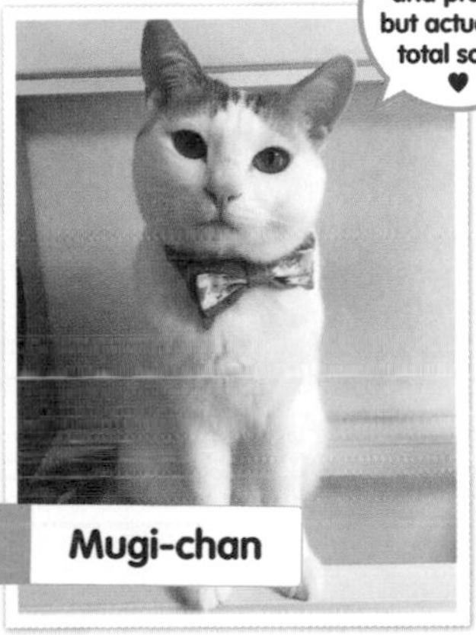
Looks prim and proper, but actually a total softie ♥
Mugi-chan

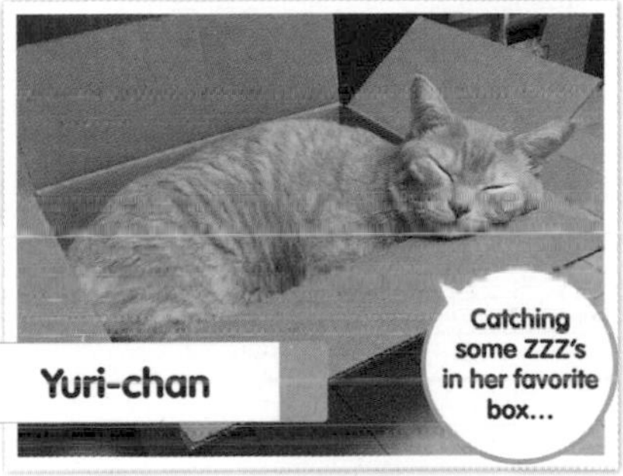
Yuri-chan
Catching some ZZZ's in her favorite box...

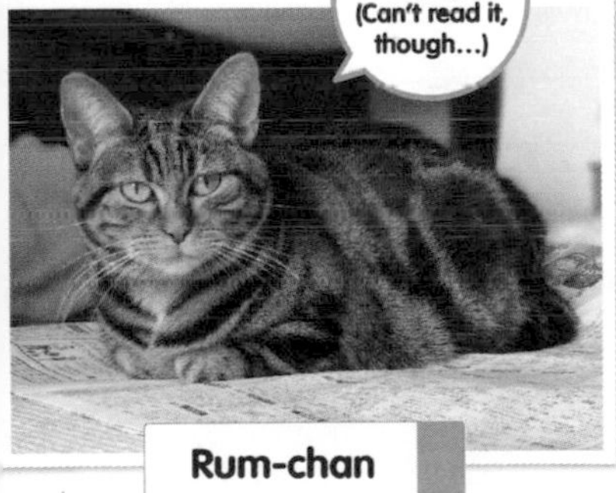
Loves the newspaper! (Can't read it, though...)
Rum-chan

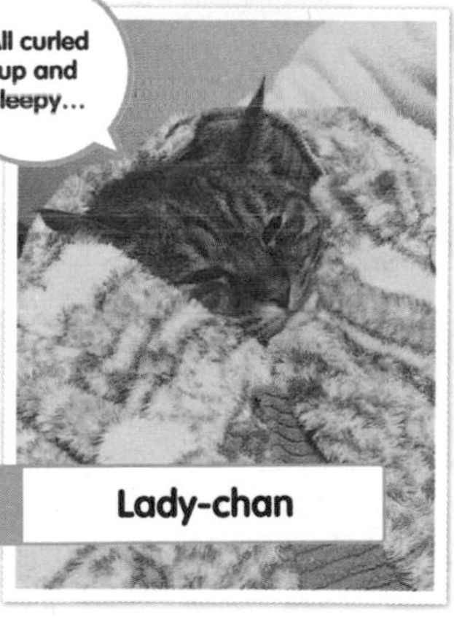
All curled up and sleepy...
Lady-chan

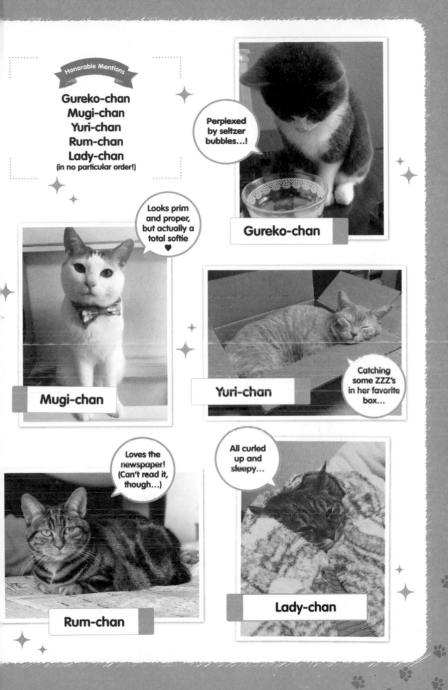

Next Volume

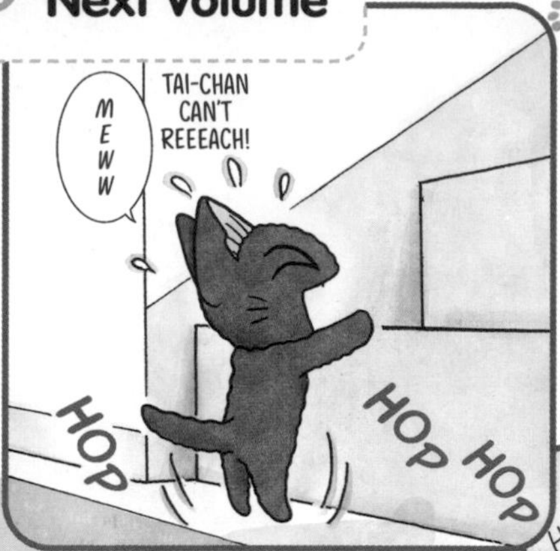
MEWW
TAI-CHAN CAN'T REEEACH!
HOP
HOP HOP

It's not easy for a senior cat to keep up with a kitten...

...but SUE and TAI-CHAN are getting along great!!

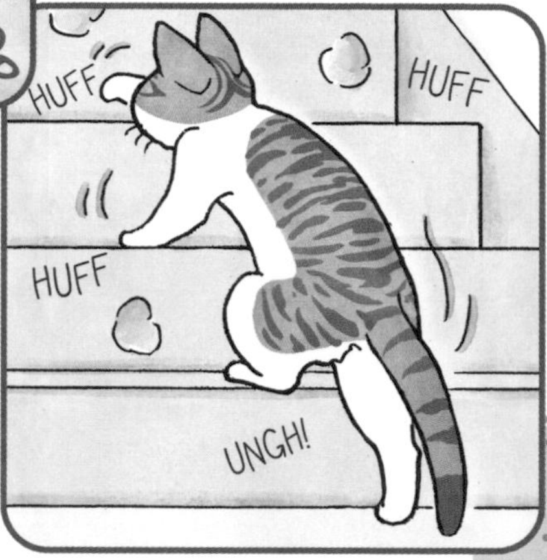
HUFF
HUFF
HUFF
UNGH!

Whatever it is—

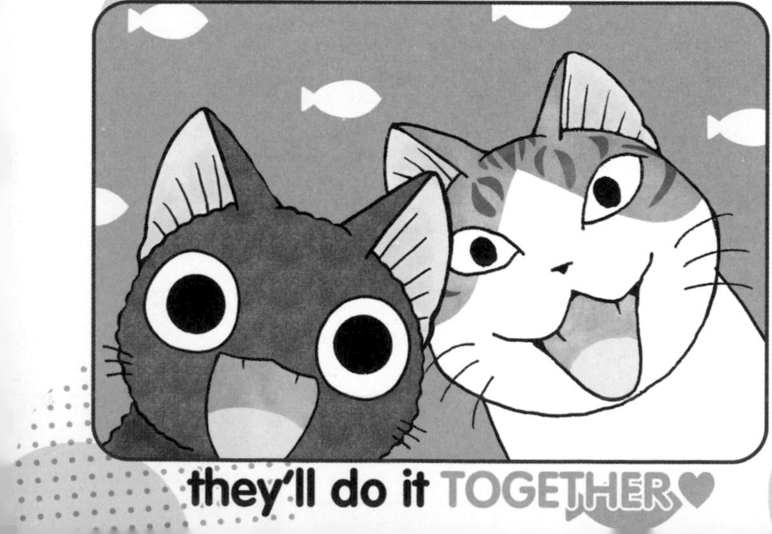

they'll do it TOGETHER♥

Breathing as one ♥ An incredible sync rate!

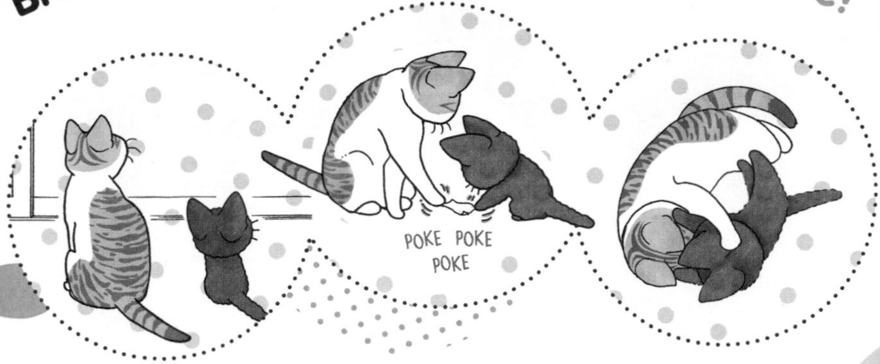
POKE POKE
POKE

Who would SPLIT UP a pair like this?!

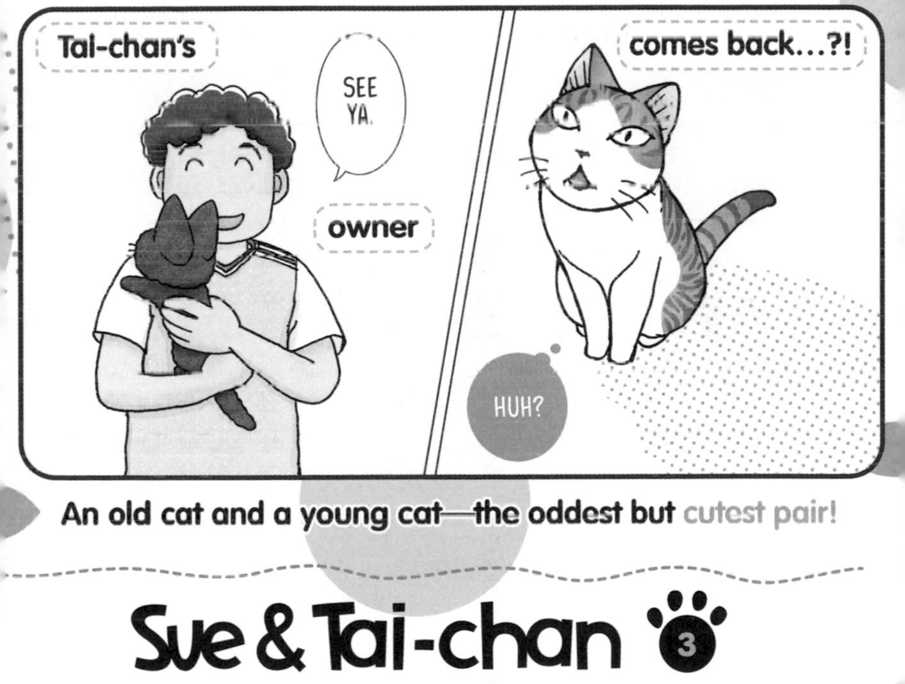
Tai-chan's
SEE YA.
owner
comes back...?!
HUH?

An old cat and a young cat—the oddest but cutest pair!

Sue & Tai-chan 3

A Kodansha Comics Trade Paperback Original
Sue & Tai-chan 2 copyright © 2018 Konami Kanata
English translation copyright © 2020 Konami Kanata

Published in the United States by Kodansha Comics, an imprint of Kodansha USA Publishing, LLC, New York.

Publication rights for this English edition arranged through Kodansha Ltd., Tokyo.

First published in Japan in 2018 by Kodansha Ltd., Tokyo.

ISBN 978-1-64651-070-2

Original cover design by Kohei Nawata Design Office

Printed in China.

www.kodanshacomics.com

9 8 7 6 5 4 3 2 1
Translation: Melissa Tanaka
Lettering: Phil Christie
Editing: Vanessa Tenazas
Kodansha Comics edition cover design by Phil Balsman

Publisher: Kiichiro Sugawara
Vice president of marketing & publicity: Naho Yamada

Director of publishing services: Ben Applegate
Associate director of operations: Stephen Pakula
Publishing services managing editor: Noelle Webster
Assistant production manager: Emi Lotto, Angela Zurlo
Logo and character art ©Kodansha USA Publishing, LLC